MEMORIALS

OF HIS TIME

Classics of British Historical Literature

JOHN CLIVE, EDITOR

Henry Cockburn

—

Memorials
of His Time

EDITED AND WITH AN INTRODUCTION BY
KARL F. C. MILLER

The University of Chicago Press
CHICAGO AND LONDON

DA
816
C6
.A2
1974

The University of Chicago Press, Chicago 60637
The University of Chicago Press, Ltd., London
© 1974 by The University of Chicago
All rights reserved. Published 1974
Printed in the United States of America
International Standard Book Number: 0-226-11164-4
Library of Congress Catalog Card Number: 74-5737

Contents

Series Editor's Preface

This series of reprints has one major purpose: to put into the hands of students and other interested readers outstanding—and sometimes neglected—works dealing with British history which have either gone out of print or are obtainable only at a forbiddingly high price.

The phrase Classics of British Historical Literature requires some explanation, in view of the fact that the two companion series published by the University of Chicago Press are entitled Classic European Historians and Classic American Historians. Why, then, introduce the word *literature* into the title of this series?

One reason is obvious. History, if it is to live beyond its own generation, must be memorably written. The greatest British historians—Clarendon, Gibbon, Hume, Carlyle, Macaulay—survive today, not merely because they contributed to the cumulative historical knowledge about their subjects, but because they were masters of style and literary artists as well. And even historians of the second rank, if they deserve to survive, are able to do so only because they can still be read with pleasure. To emphasize this truth at the present time, when much eminently solid and worthy academic history suffers from being almost totally unreadable, seems worth doing.

The other reason for including the word *literature* in the title of the series has to do with its scope. To read history is to learn about the past. But if, in trying to learn about the British past, one were to restrict oneself to the reading of formal works of

vii

history, one would miss a great deal. Often a historical novel, a sociological inquiry, or an account of events and institutions couched in semifictional form teaches us just as much about the past as does the "history" that calls itself by that name. And, frequently, these "informal" historical works turn out to be less well known than their merit deserves. By calling this series Classics of British Historical Literature it will be possible to include such books without doing violence to the usual nomenclature.

Cockburn's *Memorials* is one of those works hard to fit into a single slot. Part chronicle, part autobiography, part social history, it is still one of the most readable of books not only because it gives a unique picture of Edinburgh during the late eighteenth and early nineteenth centuries, but also because it is written with such verve and vividness. Who, having once read it, will be able to forget the incident of the boy Cockburn making his way along the dark streets of the town at two or three in the morning, mortally afraid he was late for school; or the description of the death of the great scientist Dr. Joseph Black "who died with a bowl of milk on his knee of which his ceasing to live did not spill a drop"?

Karl Miller aptly reminds us in his introduction that the *Memorials* is far more than a work of picturesque social history, that both Cockburn and his subject—Edinburgh on the edge of modernity—contained complexities and ambiguities. Still, only a brilliantly gifted observer could have conjured up a vanished way of life with the consummate skill Cockburn displays in this book. Whether he is dealing with manners and customs, ceremonials, prominent citizens, the arts, the impact of the French Revolution, or the intrigues of local politics, the author of the *Memorials* never loses his masterly touch. Mr. Miller is quite right in linking Cockburn's name with that of the only other man who might have written such a book—Sir Walter Scott.

It would be wrong to suppose that the interest Cockburn's *Memorials* holds for students of history is confined to those primarily concerned with Scotland. Eighteenth-century Edinburgh witnessed one of the great efflorescences of genius and talent in European history. As in fifth-century Athens or Renaissance Florence, civic spirit played a prominent part in that efflorescence. Cockburn lived during the closing stages of the

Scottish Enlightenment, and his depiction of its dying embers should be of great interest to students and practitioners of urban or cultural history, and, in particular, to those fascinated by the phenomenon of "civic humanism." But that is not to imply that this is a book for specialists. On the contrary, it should have great appeal to all those who take delight in the variety of human character and the art of narration and recall.

JOHN CLIVE

Editor's Introduction

I

Henry Cockburn and his contemporary, Walter Scott, are among the best of Scotland's historians. But neither of them is generally acknowledged to have been a historian at all. Cockburn was an annalist and an apologist, who tells of events in which he was himself an actor; but so are many other historians, including Tacitus, with whom his own accounts have some close affinities. Scott was an antiquarian and an artist, and most of his histories are presented as fiction; but these fictions deliver an understanding of the past to which only a historian could have attained. Both men richly deserve the name.

In 1707 Scotland and England were joined. They already shared a monarch; now a single legislative assembly was set up, and a common market. Ever since, the song of a lost sovereignty has been heard at intervals in the North, and it has not been silenced by the requiem sung—to much the same tune—over Britain's entry into the Common Market of Europe. Scotland held onto her Kirk and her courts, but her elected representatives were sent south, where they seldom bothered the series of Scottish managers who ruled the land on behalf of the government in London. Scotland also held onto her arts and learning, and toward the middle of the eighteenth century there ensued the period known as the Scottish Enlightenment, when a true sovereignty of international significance was exercised in Hanoverian Edinburgh. As time went on, Scotsmen became conscious of a quite new commercial prosperity, based on the partnership with England, on the possession of the steam-engine, and on the start of an industrial system; they also became conscious of a sharp rise in the number of Scotsmen. A Scotsman could now be said to lead two lives: he was Scottish and he was a North Briton. Patriots like Scott and Cockburn were keen that Scotland should stay Scottish. Angiophile Whigs like Cockburn were no less keen that Scotland should be improved, should respond publicly and politically to the changes that had taken place in the society, and should share in the civil liberties promised by the British Constitution. While Scotland retained her legal system (with, for example, its Roman or Civilian constituents), she had lost her own legislature. As time went on, the two countries were increasingly bound by the same laws.

Cockburn's *Memorials of His Time*,[1] which is in narrative and retrospective form, ends with the arrival in 1830 of Earl Grey's Whig ministry, which was bent on an extension of the Parliamentary franchise: Cockburn himself would help to draft the Scotch Reform Bill of 1832. His *Journal* takes up the study of his times in the form of diary entries and goes on with it until his last years. Despite this change of procedure, and despite the evidence of a darker mood, and of a measure of disenchantment, in the *Journal*, the two works were intended to constitute, and do constitute, a single account of a lifetime and of an epoch. Yet most readers are barely aware of the second half of this history, for the *Journal* has never been reissued and is hard to obtain. On the basis of the *Memorials'* delightful retrospects, Cockburn is chiefly known as a specialist in nostalgia, a *laudator temporis acti*, a cozy petit-maître embroidering the annals of a parish. This is the Cockburn who was recently made the endearing hero of a brilliant theatrical travesty, *Cocky*, in which an actor performed colorful passages from his works. Cocky—the pawky raconteur, patriot, and local worthy—does in fact contribute to those works. It is Cocky who remarks of a projected monument to the radicals of the 1790s: "Nothing that sticks up without smoking seems to me ever to look ill in Edinburgh."[2] But there is more to Cockburn

---

1. Quotations from the *Memorials* are taken, as is the text which follows, from the edition of 1910. Page references are to the present edition.
2. From his *Examination of the Trials for Sedition which have hitherto occurred in Scotland*, 2 vols. (Edinburgh, 1888), 2:250.

than a repertoire of fetching stories, and the *Memorials* is a far cry from Dean Ramsay's *Reminiscences of Scottish Life and Character*, which it is sometimes thought to resemble.[3]

Cockburn was born—on 26 October 1779—a prince of the country's *noblesse de robe*, which was recruited mainly from the landed gentry. This was an estate of lawyer-lairds reminiscent of the 'scholar gentry of medieval China. His father was a sheriff of Midlothian, a Baron of the Court of Exchequer, and a friend of the judge Lord Braxfield. Braxfield was no mandarin (Cockburn was to become rather like one), but something of a warlord temperamentally, and an aggressive defender of the landed interest. Cockburn's aunt married a potentate: Henry Dundas, later Lord Melville, Pitt the Younger's able ally and the outstanding Scottish manager or proconsul—"Harry the Ninth." Cockburn's kin were Tories, and they were also, in effect, the country's ruling dynasty. During his early years, spent in the government camp, there were blazings and bristlings at the spread of the French Revolutionary principles; but a worse threat to the authority of the Dundases lay in the gradual strengthening of support for political reform, which was interrupted by the Napoleonic Wars, but which assisted the accession to power in 1830 of the rival Whig patriciate.

After attending the High School and University of Edinburgh, he began in 1800 to practice as an advocate. Around 1807 family connections brought him a job as a Depute to the Lord Advocate (the Lord Advocate was a political appointee with extensive governmental responsibilities and a considerable power of patronage), but by that time he had broken with his father's politics and was already a renegade—that is, a Whig—and three years later he was dismissed from the post. At one point his opinions had been accounted by his kin "a mere youthful fervour," mere Whiggery-pokery. He writes revealingly in the *Memorials*: "My fear that they might think so had only made the fervour warmer."[4]

For Cockburn, as for many other Whigs both north and south of the border, Reform meant the enfranchisement of the prosper-

---

3. The *Reminiscences of Scottish Life and Character* reached their twenty-second edition in 1872 (Edinburgh and London). In that year Dean Ramsay died.
4. P. 240.

ous and intelligent, and the allaying of discontent in the country at large. It was a means of averting revolution. More ambitiously, he could also think of it as heralding a Scotch Millennium of social justice. That millennium never came. But, unlike many other Whigs, especially in England, where there was a marked tendency to see these measures in purely tactical terms, he was a convinced Reformer and, in earlier life, a sanguine one.

In general, however, for someone who often seemed pugnacious and despotic, Cockburn was an inveterate doubter: all the more so as he grew older. He was essentially a divided man, one whose life was composed of striking ambivalences—not least in relation to the past and to "the people." He wanted to change the Scotland in which he grew up, but he also loved it, and he poured out that love in the *Memorials*. He wanted a wider Parliamentary representation, but he did not want democracy. He even had doubts of a kind about the corruption of the Edinburgh Town Council in its oligarchic heyday, which he attacked in some of the most pugnacious words he ever wrote. A famous passage in the *Memorials* deals with their shabby, subterranean-seeming Council Chamber:

> Within this Pandemonium sat the town-council, omnipotent, corrupt, impenetrable. Nothing was beyond its grasp; no variety of opinion disturbed its unanimity, for the pleasure of Dundas was the sole rule for every one of them. Reporters, the fruit of free discussion, did not exist; and though they had existed, would not have dared to disclose the proceedings. Silent, powerful, submissive, mysterious, and irresponsible, they might have been sitting in Venice.[5]

For all his pugnacity, the exaggerations, exoticism, and flamboyance of this passage indicate that he is savoring and celebrating, as well as blaming, the behavior of the worthies whose authority he helped to supplant. It is worth remembering, too, that this was the Town Council that decreed the building of Edinburgh's beautiful New Town.

The government headed—or figureheaded—by the Doges was less despotic than he assumes, and he writes as if Venice were an object of special horror. Hostility to Venice was widespread then

5. Pp. 87–88.

in western Europe, and a book which could well have helped to promote a superstitious dread of that city arrived in Scotland at the time when he was engaged on the *Memorials*. In a letter of 1821,[6] the year Cockburn began writing, his friend Sir James Mackintosh discusses the *Histoire de la République de Venise* by Pierre, Comte Daru, which had lately been published in Paris. Mackintosh, whose *Vindiciae Gallicae* had argued against Burke on behalf of the French Revolution, mentions that the opening-up of the Venetian archives by Napoleon had given historians such as Daru "access to the most secret recesses of that tyrannical policy which was so long thought the model of wisdom." Wordsworth for one had thought well of Venice. His sonnet "On the Extinction of the Venetian Republic, 1802" proclaims her as formerly "the safeguard of the West": she was "the eldest Child of Liberty" who had held "the gorgeous East in fee."

Daru was Stendhal's cousin and one of Napoleon's staff officers; he is said to have been respected by Napoleon, and was given the unenviable task of planning the food supplies for the Russian campaign. The first volume of his history contains the words, *pour que ce gouvernement impénétrable n'eût plus de mystères*,[7] and it may be that this is where Cockburn got his "impenetrable" and "mysterious." Daru frequently deplores *les vices intérieurs de cet état inquisitorial*. This was the common coin of anti-Venetian invective in Europe, but there is a Gallic glitter here that should also be taken into account. The inquisitorial character imparted by Cockburn to the proceedings of the Edinburgh Town Council can fairly be called exotic in that it seems to have been partly derived from Napoleonic France's verdict on the Venetian oligarchy.

Renaissance Venice, the Venice antecedent to its eighteenth-century decline and fall, whose system lasted until the intervention of Napoleon, is thought once again, by some modern historians, to have been, if not the model of wisdom, at any rate a well-conducted and responsible society by the standards of its

6. The letter is printed in the *Memoir of Thomas Thomson, Advocate*, compiled by Cosmo Innes and published by the Bannatyne Club (Edinburgh, 1854), p. 173. Thomson was the recipient of the letter.
7. 2d ed., 8 vols. (Paris, 1821), 1:7.

time: as far as representation is concerned, it can probably bear comparison with the Scotland that succeeded the passing of the Reform Bill. But Cockburn was shocked by the very idea of Venice, and, for polemical purposes, turned its secret recesses into the dark and dirty den of the Edinburgh Town Council. Polemics and politics apart, he was greatly intrigued by the city, and went off in 1823 to gaze at its "queer old towers"[8] in the course of a Continental tour. An unpublished journal that he kept of the tour tells how he was struck by the funereal gondolas and the absence of courtesans, by the architectural splendors of this "old and fallen republic," and by the sense that its institutions and public buildings belonged to "the people"—"though the Venetian government, no doubt, was very bad in reality."[9] A kinder view than the one implied in the *Memorials*.

II

It is typical of the ambiguous Cockburn (though he was scarcely alone in this) that his tastes were both classical and estranged from classicism—both Roman and romantic. In 1811, the year after his dismissal from the government, he married and, in Horatian style, set up his rural household gods in the Pentland Hills some five miles from Edinburgh; he did so in a queer old tower of his own, unabashedly Gothic and feudal, which he had begun to build at Bonaly. His town house was in classical Charlotte Square, amid the crescents, circuses, straight streets, and "draughty parallelograms," as Robert Louis Stevenson called them, of the growing New Town, which Cockburn abhorred as unromantic, mercenary, and meanly mathematical.

It took him most of the remainder of his life to complete Bonaly Tower, and the place, Abbotsfordwise, proved of vital importance to him. At Bonaly, he played; in town, he worked and

8. From an anticipatory letter of 11 July 1823 to John Richardson, who was to accompany him on the tour. The letter is among the collection of Cockburn MSS in the National Library of Scotland.

9. The journal forms part of the Francis Jeffrey papers in the National Library of Scotland. Jeffrey was another of his companions on the tour, and so was Jeffrey's daughter Charlotte, who transcribed the journal.

did his duty. His seasons at Bonaly alternated with his sessions in town as reformer and iconoclast, as advocate and judge and Edinburgh eminence. The two habitations fostered a double life of sorts, which might appear to complete the other dualities and contradictions of his nature—those of an Anglophile Scottish patriot; of a patrician progressive; of someone at once convivial and grave, who could insist on how happy he had been, and was blamed for his pursuit of pleasure, but who was also capable of an altogether Presbyterian severity and who had his share of sufferings, certain of which he refused to divulge to his readership. His imagination was drawn, if not to the horizontals of the New Town plan, to the perpendicularities of towers and monuments and obelisks and walking-sticks; but it was also drawn to the hidden places, the secret recesses, of his Pentland haunts: so that the accommodation he effected between town and country was also an accommodation of sorts between male and female principles.

His "Pentlandising," as he called it, his walks and wanderings in the hills, was more of a religion than a recreation. Such pleasures were sublime: he worshiped the Pentlands and hailed them as his Paradise. I have gathered together a set of manuscript poems by Cockburn, almost all of which were written in his youth—though there is one about a lost walking-stick which belongs to his forties—and almost all of which are votive or devotional in character. They are hymns to his favorite hills, to their maternal hollows and declivities, to the groves, streams, and waterfalls of the blissful wilderness where this public man was able to lead a life that was, by turns, solitary and agreeably social. At Bonaly he could forget the pugnacities of politics and the law and be, as he described the golfers of St. Andrews, "gregarious without remorse."[10] Golf, I suppose, was a crude secular equivalent of Cockburn's magic game of sticks and springs.

In 1818 Raeburn painted a picture of his eminence in which the pleasure-lover is given a pensive look—a look that was to pass into somberness, on the evidence of the photographs that exist of him. This was, in fact, a bad year for Cockburn. His eldest

10. A phrase from his marvelous description of that leisured community in the *Journal*, 2:60–66.

daughter died at seven (a brood of ten children survived), one of his friends died, and his wife was seriously ill. Two years later, his father died. It is possible to guess that there had long been a coldness between them (there are hints, but no real disclosures on the subject), and he apparently preferred, and indeed revered, his mother. And it is possible to guess that his father's death, together with the foregoing crises, stirred or encouraged him to write the *Memorials*, which he then undertook to do. In that work he preaches the Whig gospel, glories in the Whig momentum of recent years and in the effacements of the past that were reckoned to lie ahead, and assails his father's friend, Lord Braxfield. The book performs a series of unfilial acts. But, in the tender telling of the story of his parents' Scotland and of its privileged caste, it also seems to seek, remorsefully, a measure of propitiation, as well as a maternal comfort similar to the blessings bestowed by the Pentlands. The 1820s were an exhilarating decade for the Scottish Whigs, and Cockburn's forties were a decisive period in his development, if not the time of his life.

He was a contributor to the *Edinburgh Review*, the forum of the eager new generation of Whig lawyers and thinkers, and an intimate friend of its editor, Francis Jeffrey. Among his confederates in criticism were Sydney Smith, something of a kindred spirit, and the unbearable Brougham, whom he distrusted as much as most people did and who was known to Cockburn's circle as The Evil—from a joke of Smith's about his being the true old Evil Principle. At the end of the 1820s Earl Grey became prime minister, with "Jeffrey and all high Whigs getting summoned into an Official career," as Carlyle expressed it in an account of the Scottish scene,[11] Jeffrey became Scotland's Lord Advocate, and Cockburn its Solicitor-General.

The *Memorials* concludes with the Whigs triumphantly in power. But Cockburn does not exult. Reform has yet to be achieved. Eventually, after months of commotion and uncertainty and talk of revolution, the laws were passed. The *Journal* discusses the sequel to Reform and, in depth, a second triumph of a different order—namely, the Disruption, when two-fifths of the Church of Scotland's ministers broke away to

11. *Reminiscences* (reprinted, London, 1972), p. 330.

form the Free Church, because of their opposition to lay patronage, or the preferment of ministers by local landowners, the
Crown, and others in possession of livings. The state in the shape
of the Court of Session (a civil court, whose judges also tried
criminal cases in the High Court of Justiciary), of which he was by
then a member, had attempted to coerce the Kirk—as he felt,
unwisely and unjustly. In one way, his sympathies were with
neither side: he was neither a Moderate, strictly speaking, nor an
Evangelical, though it was like him to lean, as he did, in both
directions. In another way, true to his rebellious form, his heart
was with the mutineer ministers. They were virtuous and courageous. The sighs and supplications of their followers breathed "the
very soul of Scotch Presbytery," and they themselves, with their
battlefields of Auchterarder and Strathbogie, were like the
Covenanters of old. If only for patriotic reasons, he was bound to
admire them. The collision between the commandments of
church and court was perceived as a gross and horrible embar-
rassment, but the ministers' departure was "the most honourable
fact for Scotland that its whole history supplies."[12]

The *Journal*, perhaps is drier than its first instalment,
the *Memorials*, but it is just as fine a work. It is less
of a gallery of portraits—which was how the *Memorials*
seems to have accumulated. The analyses of human behavior are as searching as ever, and more patiently conducted;
the instances and anecdotes are as well chosen. If the pace is
slower, the prose is still firm, clear, and incomparably witty: as
buoyant as a boat, as coercive as a Court of Session.

Earlier in his life, Cockburn had been one of the country's
most celebrated advocates. His *Examination of the Trials for
Sedition which have hitherto occurred in Scotland* is a viva-
cious description of the brutal treatment of a number of
radicals by Lord Braxfield and the Justiciary in the 1790s,
and of subsequent prosecutions of a similar kind when
Cockburn was among the defending counsel. On their retirement from politics, the Edinburgh Reviewers Cockburn and
Jeffrey were "benchified," joining the Court of Session. It isn't
every critic who is granted the ermine of a judge, or who deserves

12. *Journal*, 2:75 and 32.

to be. Literature had been a second string for the briefless Whig lawyer in former, Tory times, and in any case the two callings had long been rather closely linked. The Braxfieldian motto of the *Edinburgh Review—Judex damnatur cum nocens absolvitur—* was fair warning of the judicial temper of its literary criticism, but neither Cockburn nor Jeffrey was likely to prove a terror on the bench.

As a lawyer, Cockburn has been accounted a poor technician in civil matters (unlike Braxfield), and an unimpressive feudalist. The drafting of the Scotch Reform Bill has been criticized[13] for an ignorance of social conditions and established electoral practice in Scotland. The legal reforms for which he argued (for example, the abolition of the judge's right to pick the jury in criminal cases, and the introduction of jury trial in civil cases) tended to gain acceptance: by and large, they were the kind of things that a barrister, rather than a judge or jurist, might want accomplished. I have seen nothing to suggest that he failed as a judge, but there, too, he has had his disparagers, and his decisions were sometimes reversed by the other Lords of Session. He took pride in asserting, from the bench, the innocence of trade-union combinations, though he had long disapproved of their coercive or "concussive" tendencies. In his youth he wrote to a friend, the poet James Grahame: "It is *impossible* to defend a combination which is kept up by concussing me to join it."[14]

His experiences as a judge, and as a connoisseur of landscape and manners, are contained in the *Circuit Journeys*, a journal which appeared, as did the *Trials for Sedition*, in 1888. All his books were published in Edinburgh, and all but one were published posthumously. In addition, there are two books which include selections from his correspondence.[15] He died at Bonaly on 26 April 1854, and the *Memorials* came out two years later. In 1874 the *Journal* was issued in two volumes. In 1852 his interesting but encomiastic *Life of Lord Jeffrey* was published: this study of "the greatest of British critics"[16] can

13. By William Ferguson in "The Reform Act (Scotland) of 1832: Intention and Effect," *Scottish Historical Review* 45 (April 1966):105-14.

14. Cockburn MSS, National Library of Scotland (12 December 1808).

15. *Letters Chiefly Connected with the Affairs of Scotland* (London, 1874) consists for the most part of letters exchanged between Cockburn and Thomas

only seem uncommunicative when compared with Carlyle's superb rendering of Jeffrey in his *Reminiscences*, which may be said to call attention to the defects of Cockburn's Roman reticence. "You are so dreadfully in earnest!" the self-confident Jeffrey would exclaim to Carlyle, who, for his part, seems "to remember that I dimly rather felt there was something trivial, doubtful, and not quite of the highest type, in our Edinburgh admiration for our great Lights and Law Sages."[17] Elsewhere, though, he was warm about Cockburn, whom he felt to be the last of the old Scotch gentlemen.[18]

III

Cockburn—a small, wiry man, a talker, walker, swimmer, skater, bowls-player, and devotee of the open air—was certainly a great light in Edinburgh, very popular, an esteemed eccentric and sage. A society devoted to the protection of the Edinburgh environment was named after him, and he had a street named after him too (suitably precipitous and tortuous, almost a tower and almost a declivity). He spent time with the artists of the city, who were not averse to schism and had a Disruption of their own, and he was legal adviser to the Royal Scottish Academy. His friendship with the photographer Octavius Hill brought about some remarkable calotype pictures of the household at Bonaly. He helped to found a school, Edinburgh Academy, from which the Scots tongue, still spoken by himself, was expelled, and a bank, the Commercial Bank, which gave credit to those denied it on political grounds.

He was no dandy. His hat was alleged to be the worst in Edinburgh, and he designed his own very clumsy shoes. Evelyn

Kennedy of Dunure, a Treasury Lord in Earl Grey's government who worked on the Scottish Reform Bill. *Some Letters of Lord Cockburn* (Edinburgh, 1932), edited by his grandson Harry Cockburn, also includes pages from his original notebook which were omitted from the published *Memorials*, and a biographical commentary.

16. *Life of Lord Jeffrey*, p. 1.

17. *Reminiscences*, p. 313.

18. He says so in a passage from his journal quoted in J. A. Froude's *Thomas Carlyle: A History of His Life in London, 1834–1881*, 2 vols. (London, 1884), 2:158.

Waugh was a descendant of his (another is the Communist autobiographer and journalist, Claud Cockburn), and Waugh has this to say about the boots in his book of memoirs, *A Little Learning*: "Confirmation of this peculiarity in footwear comes from his granddaughter, my maternal grandmother. At the age of eight she was staying at Bonaly when the portrait which now hangs in the National Portrait Gallery of Scotland was being painted by Watson-Gordon. When asked her opinion by the painter, she replied after long and grave scrutiny: 'Well, it's *very* like his boots.' "[19] Queen Victoria and the Prince Consort visited Edinburgh in 1850, and Cockburn exclaimed in a letter: "Poor royal creature—she had never heard of the Pentland Hills!—on which she gazed with especial admiration. Think of a crowned head never having heard of the Pentland Hills! But her admiration shows that the head was not unworthy of a crown." As for Albert, "he particularly admired my shoes."[20]

The *Memorials* depicts an age of ceremonies and hilarities and holidays, succeeded by a discussing age, in which the intellectual standards of the earlier Enlightenment were in some measure maintained and renewed, and in which a mounting desire to protest and make progress was allied to a quite Venetian fondness for procession. Both were drinking ages, and dining ages. The cognoscenti—or the literati, or "eaterati," as Ramsay of Ochtertyre entitled them—made merry in their boisterous Edinburgh Eden. In these earlier times, Cockburn's urban haunts enjoyed their own state of bliss: the Flood of humanity had yet to cover the face of the earth; politically, the people had not yet arisen. The dinners of the literati were not yet troubled by the congested, cannibalistic world that he predicted in the somberness of his *Journal*.

He himself took part in their pleasures, entering his reservations, and his predictions, in his notebooks. In the country of cold winds, coughs and sore stomachs that is revealed in his unpublished correspondence, where a spell of sunny weather could seem paradisal, he advises a friend to be mindful of his

19. *A Little Learning* (London, 1964), pp. 11–12.
20. To Mrs. Sophia Rutherfurd, wife of Rutherfurd the Whig Lord Advocate, 31 August 1850, Cockburn MSS, National Library of Scotland.

viscera and to be Bacchanalian at least once a week. In a letter of 1840 he offers a partial but plausible explanation of the drinking habits of his native land: "The worst of Teetotalism is its cold. One freezes all night, even between eiderdown. An icicle in flannel is a type of me. Were it not for the glow at the heart, the blood would be solid."[21] But the face we see in the photographs is not that of a diner or a cheery dilettante: it is the face of his very darkest thoughts.

He did not quarrel with his society, which invested him with some of the "old excessive Edinburgh Hero-worship" referred to in Carlyle's *Reminiscences*.[22] There was nothing solitary or idiosyncratic about his dissenting politics earlier in his career: they were common form—and he saved his solitariness for the Pentlands. He criticized his society, however, for all he was worth and for the whole of his life; and with practically no exceptions, the objectives for which he worked do him honor. Contemptuous and compassionate, eminent and vagrant, an iconoclast who revered the past, to which, as to the Pentland Hills, he turned for refuge, he was the kind of man without whom the best societies would never come about, and without whom they would die.

Cockburn's contradictions were the life of him. The Roman god Janus, the god of doorways, whose two faces looked before him and behind, at the future and at the past, may be felt to have rated a shrine at Bonaly, among the dryads, and the dahlias and roses. He was a man who wanted to be king, and who wanted there to be no more kings. At the time of the Reform Bill, he writes to his political confederate, Kennedy of Dunure: "My old regal desire has been very strong of late." Three years previously, he had informed him: "I should like to see the world without kings, bishops, or standing armies, and with a new house at Bonaly."[23] In 1830 he said he would "eat my heart" if he and his associates did not achieve their political ends,[24] and—to abide by the metaphor—it may be that he had already eaten his father's. The *Almanach des Gourmands*, whose tomes the *Edinburgh*

21. To Mrs. Rutherfurd, 14 May 1840, Cockburn MSS, National Library of Scotland.

22. *Reminiscences*, p. 328.

23. *Letters Chiefly Connected with the Affairs of Scotland*, pp. 248, 203.

24. Ibid., p. 245.

Review did not disdain to notice, once praised a certain sauce: with such a sauce, *on mangerait son père*. And this, after a fashion, for Reform's sake, is what he did. But he was also a man who kept his taste for the solid fare of the unregenerate Scotland, an enemy of the lairds who was never to leave their ranks.

But if Cockburn was two-faced, both faces were benign. The *Edinburgh Review*'s review of the *Memorials* manages to evoke that benignity, together with the truce he established between his pugnacious politics and his dreams of the past and of the Pentlands. It says of Bonaly, with a period quaintness: "Those romantic grounds which he had reclaimed from the rugged Pentlands, he threw open to every holiday wanderer who loved fresh air and nature like himself. So would he have had it with all the political and social good which this world affords."[25] This is the encomium of a friend: Cockburn was no communist, and he was not as rashly hospitable as it claims. But few who read his books and study his life will dismiss these words as mere valedictory rhetoric.

The objectives for which he worked do him honor, and his books do him honor too, and should be better known. They are among the many elements of the Scottish Enlightenment which have been boorishly disregarded. It is not enough to think of him with nostalgia—in the manner that has become customary—as a kind of municipal pet: as a personification of the old Edinburgh, torn between the "heavenly Hanoverianism" of its New Town, in Burns's phrase,[26] and the heaven of his own creation in the hills, and as a charming dispenser of anecdotes and memories. It is not enough to think of him reading Tacitus all summer long in a cleft of the Pentlands—on the sunny side of the hill, no doubt. He is himself the Tacitus—though hardly the Horace—of Scotland.

IV

The present text of the *Memorials* is taken, with Cockburn's footnotes, from the edition of 1910 prepared by his grandson

25. *Edinburgh Review* 105 (January 1857): 242. The writer was Lord Moncreiff,

Harry Cockburn, who restored some passages (such as those concerning Henry Dundas, Henry Erskine, John Clerk, and the launching of the *Edinburgh Review*) which belonged, he says, to the original notebook, but which were omitted from the first edition by those responsible for it (two of Cockburn's trustees, both of them sheriffs, Thomas Cleghorn and Archibald Davidson) because they had been incorporated, with little change, in the *Life of Lord Jeffrey*. The *Memorials* has appeared in three editions, and in 1948 a digest was brought out in Edinburgh by W. Forbes Gray: there are useful antiquarian notes, but the text has been rewritten on grounds of taste—a latter-day literatus, W. Forbes Gray. Some literals and mistakes in the 1910 edition have been corrected, and a few unexplained minor digressions from the text of the first edition have been altered and the wording of that edition restored.

KARL MILLER

son of James Moncreiff and grandson of the Evangelical minister Sir Harry Moncreiff, both of whom are prominent in the *Memorials*. James Moncreiff and his son were both law lords.
26. From a letter to Mrs. Dunlop of 13 November 1788.

Recommended Reading

Three very good general histories of Scotland have appeared in recent years: William Ferguson's *Scotland 1689 to the Present* (Edinburgh and London, 1968); T. C. Smout's *A History of the Scottish People, 1560–1830* (London, 1969); and Rosalind Mitchison's *A History of Scotland* (London, 1970), the second and third of these books being particularly concerned with social and economic questions. A. J. Youngson's *The Making of Classical Edinburgh* (Edinburgh, 1966) and *After the Forty-Five* (Edinburgh, 1973) are important studies of the social background. John Clive's *Scotch Reviewers* (London, 1957) deals with the earlier history of the *Edinburgh Review* and gives an extremely useful account of Cockburn's acquaintance. Relevant material is also to be found in Clive's *Macaulay: The Shaping of the Historian* (London, 1973). *Lord Kames and the Scotland of His Day* by Ian Simpson Ross (London, 1972) contains a great deal of material that bears on the period recalled in the *Memorials*. Nicholas Phillipson's Cambridge University Ph.D. thesis (1967), "The Scottish Whigs and the Reform of the Court of Session, 1785 to 1830," breaks new ground with an analysis of the legal and political maneuvers of the time. L. J. Saunders's *Scottish Democracy, 1815–1840* (Edinburgh, 1950) is an enterprising study of the social background for the years in question. The Scottish Universities of the nineteenth century are the subject of an important book by George Davie, *The Democratic Intellect* (Edinburgh, 1961). Earlier works worth consulting include Henry

Meikle's *Scotland and the French Revolution* (Glasgow, 1912) and William Law Mathieson's *Church and Reform in Scotland* (Glasgow, 1916). There are no books on Cockburn himself.

MEMORIALS OF HIS TIME

CHAPTER I

I WAS born on the 26th of October 1779. This event
took place, I suspect, in one of the many flats of the
lofty range of dwelling-houses which then formed the
east side of the Parliament Close. If not there, it must
have been at Cockpen; * a small estate, about eight
miles south of Edinburgh, then belonging to my
father, but sold soon after this to the Earl of Dal-
housie. My terror at the apparition of a peacock in
one of the Cockpen walks, while I was still in petti-
coats, is the most distant recollection that I have.

My father was then Sheriff of the county of Midlothian; he was afterwards also Judge Admiral, and
finally a Baron of Exchequer. My mother was Janet
Rannie, one of the two daughters of Captain Rannie
of Melville. Her sister was married to Henry Dundas,
the first Viscount Melville; and besides this near
alliance by marriage, our family and that of the once
powerful house of Arniston were connected by blood,
and on habits of very friendly intimacy.

My father was a man of strong sense, and with no
aversion to a joke, whether theoretical or practical.

* *See* Introduction.

A

He was one of the many good fathers, who, from mere want of consideration and method, kept his children at a distance. My mother was the best woman I have ever known. If I were to survive her for a thousand years, I should still have a deep and grateful recollection of her kindness, her piety, her devotion to her family, and her earnest, gentle, and Christian anxiety for their happiness in this life and in the life to come.

After leaving Cockpen we removed to Hope Park. My father purchased the eastmost house on the south side of the Meadows; and there the next twenty-two or twenty-three years of my life were passed. We had about eight acres of ground, partly in lease and partly our own; and nearly the whole country to the south of us, though all private property, was almost quite open. There were very few fences south of the Meadows. The lands of Grange, Canaan, Blackford, Braid, Mortonhall, and many other now enclosed properties, were all, except in immediate connection with the mansion houses, unenclosed; and we roamed at pleasure till we reached the Pentlands, or the deserts of Peeblesshire. A delightful region for wild and active boys.* A part of the monastery of the nuns of Sienna (from which the neighbouring village, now part of Edinburgh, is called Sciennes or Sheens) stood in a field behind our house, which field my father always had in lease from Sir Andrew Lauder of Grange; and a fragment of the monastery still re-

* I do not mean to say that we ever held any of this space to be open to us, or to the public, as in right, but only that being unenclosed we used it freely. Yet many a time we were chased off, particularly from Blackford Hill.—H. C.

mains.* A large portion, including the great window, of the chapel of St Roque, on the northern base of Blackford Hill, then survived. There was a pond close beside it where I learned to skate—the most delightful of all exercises, and one which I have practised with unfailing ardour ever since.

In October 1787 I was sent to the High School. Having never been at a public school before, and this one being notorious for its severity and riotousness, I approached its walls with trembling, and felt dizzy when I sat down amidst above 100 new faces. We had been living at Leith, for sea-bathing, for some weeks before; and I was taken to school by our tutor. The only thing that relieved my alarm as he hauled me along was the diversion of crossing the arches of the South Bridge, which were then unfinished, on planks. The person† to whose uncontrolled discipline I was now subjected, though a good man, an intense student, and filled, but rather in the memory than in the head, with knowledge, was as bad a schoolmaster as it is possible to fancy. Unacquainted with the nature of youth, ignorant even of the characters of his own boys, and with not a conception of the art or of the duty of alluring them, he had nothing for it but to drive them; and this he did by constant and indiscriminate harshness.

* " This relic of the old monastery stood till 1871, when it was removed to make room for a semi-detached villa erected by his congregation for a Wesleyan Methodist minister. A tablet in the wall marks the site of the monastery."—Seton's *St Catherine of Sienna.*

† Mr, afterwards Professor, Christison, father of Sir Robert Christison. He was elected to the Chair of Humanity in the University in 1806.—Christison's *Autobiography.*

The effects of this were very hurtful to all his pupils. Out of the whole four years of my attendance there were probably not ten days in which I was not flogged, at least once. Yet I never entered the class, nor left it, without feeling perfectly qualified, both in ability and preparation, for its whole business; which, being confined to Latin alone, and in necessarily short tasks, since every one of the boys had to rhyme over the very same words, in the very same way, was no great feat. But I was driven stupid. Oh! the bodily and mental wearisomeness of sitting six hours a day, staring idly at a page, without motion and without thought, and trembling at the gradual approach of the merciless giant. I never got a single prize, and once sat *boobie* at the annual public examination. The beauty of no Roman word, or thought, or action, ever occurred to me! nor did I ever fancy that Latin was of any use except to torture boys.

After four years of this class, I passed on to that of the rector, Dr Alexander Adam, the author of the work on Roman Antiquities, then in the zenith of his reputation. He had raised himself from the very dust to that high position. Never was a man more fortunate in the choice of a vocation. He was born to teach Latin, some Greek, and all virtue. In doing so he was generally patient, though not, when intolerably provoked, without due fits of gentle wrath; inspiring to his boys, especially the timid and backward; enthusiastically delighted with every appearance of talent or goodness; a warm encourager by praise, play, and kindness; and constantly under the strongest sense of duty. The art of teaching has been so immeasurably improved in good Scotch schools since his time, that we can scarcely estimate his merits now. He had most of the usual peculiarities of a schoolmaster; but was so amiable and so artless, that no sensible friend would have wished one of them to be even softened. His private industry was appalling. If one moment late at school, he would hurry in, and explain that he had been detained " verifying a quotation "; and many a one did he verify at four in the morning. He told me at the close of one of his autumn vacations of six weeks, that, before it had begun, he had taken a house in the country, and had sent his family there, in order that he himself might have some rustic leisure, but that having got upon the scent of some curious passages (his favourite sport) he had remained with his books in town, and had never even seen the country house.*

He suffered from a prejudice likely to be injurious

* Dr Adam's early days at the University, like those of many other Scottish lads before and since, were a hard experience—one which might have readily discouraged him, and which a student now, through altered times and the Carnegie Trust, will never be called upon to face. The following account, from notes by Luke Fraser, is taken from an anonymous life of Dr Adam, published in 1810 :—" He lodged in a small room at Restalrig, then a suburb, for which he paid fourpence per week. All his meals, except dinner, uniformly consisted of oatmeal porridge, together with small beer, of which he allowed himself half a bottle at a time. When he wished to dine he purchased a penny loaf at the nearest baker's shop; and if the day was fair he would dispatch his meal in a walk to the Meadows ; but, if the weather was foul, he had recourse to some long and lonely stair, which he would climb, eating his dinner at every step. . . . When he was chill he used to run till his blood began to glow; and his studies were always prosecuted under the roof of some one or other of his companions."

in those days. He was no politician; insomuch that it may be doubted whether he ever knew one public measure or man from another. But a Latin and Greek schoolmaster naturally speaks about such things as liberty, and the people, and the expulsion of the Tarquins, and republics, and this was quite sufficient for the times; especially as any modern notions that he had were popular, and he was too honest, and too simple, to disguise them. This innocent infusion of classical patriotism into the mind of a man whose fancy dwelt in old Rome, made him be watched and traduced for several years. Boys were encouraged to bring home stories of him, and of course reported only what they saw pleased. Often, and with great agitation, did the worthy man complain of the injustice which tolerated these youthful spies; but his chief sorrow was for the corruption to which the minds of his pupils were exposed. I remained at the rector's class two years.

Some things happened during these six High School years, which, however insignificant now, made an impression on a boy.

In November 1789 we got a half holiday to see the foundation-stone of the new College laid, which was done with great civic and masonic pomp. Forty years more did not see the edifice completed. Only those who knew the adjoining grounds at this time can understand how completely its position has been since destroyed. With the exception of a few paltry and easily removable houses on the west and north, the ground all round it was entirely open. Nicolson Street

was partly, and College Street entirely, unbuilt; and
the College was so perfectly free on its east or front
side, that I saw the ceremonies both of laying the
foundation-stone, and of President Dundas's funeral
in 1787, from a window in the west wing of the Royal
Infirmary. The spaces now occupied by the various
buildings pressing on the College were then covered
with grass fields or gardens. How often did we stand
to admire the blue and yellow beds of crocuses rising
through the clean earth, in the first days of spring, in
the garden of old Dr Monro (the second), whose house
stood in a small field entering from Nicolson Street,
within less than a hundred yards south of the College.

Nicolson Street was the great haunt of the doctors
in those days. They clustered round the College and
the Infirmary. A pillar, in honour of a Lady Nicolson,
stood in the street named after her. It was placed just
at the top of the slope down to the South Bridge, and
was seen, I suppose, all the way from the General
Register House. It was destroyed soon after this,
because it was accused of narrowing the street—an
established piece of nonsense which has often done
much mischief in Edinburgh.

Dr Cullen died in 1790. I only learned his look from
the number of heads of him which, out of respect to
his memory, were instantly set up as signs for
druggists' shops; all representing him with a huge wig
and an enormous under lip.

The death of Sir George Ramsay,* who was killed

* Sir George Ramsay, sixth baronet of Bamff, and Lieut. Macrae
of Holmains, who lived at Marionville, near Edinburgh. The lieu-

at Musselburgh, in April 1790, by Lieut. Macrae, being the first event of the kind that we boys had heard of, made us all shudder at the idea of duelling. We were all strongly against Macrae. He was the survivor, and seemed to acknowledge his being in the wrong by absconding, and was a practised duellist.

They had the barbarity to make us be in school during summer at 7 in the morning. I once started out of bed, thinking I was too late, and got out of the house unquestioned. On reaching the High School gate, I found it locked, and saw the yards, through the bars, silent and motionless. I withdrew alarmed, and went near the Tron Church to see the clock. It was only about two or three. Not a creature was on the street; not even watchmen, who were of much later introduction. I came home awed, as if I had seen a dead city, and the impression of that hour has never been effaced.

Not one of the boys of my class has reached any great eminence; which indeed has been attained by only two boys who were at any of the classes of the High School in my time. These two were Francis Horner and Henry Brougham.

Horner, with whom I was at the rector's class for one year, was then exactly what he continued afterwards to be—grave, studious, honourable, kind; steadily pursuing his own cultivation; everything he did marked by thoughtfulness and greatness. Before leaving the school we subscribed for a book which we

tenant had beaten Lady Ramsay's servant for insolence, and because Sir George refused to dismiss him Lieut. Macrae challenged the baronet.

presented to the rector; a proceeding then unprecedented. It fell to Horner as the dux to give it, and he never acquitted himself better. It was on the day of the public examination; and after the prizes were distributed, and the spectators thought that the business was over, he stood forth with one volume of the book in his hand, and in a distinct though tremulous voice, and a firm but modest manner, addressed Adam in a Latin speech of his own composition, not exceeding three or four sentences, expressive of the gratitude and affection with which we all took leave of our master. The effect was complete, on Adam, on the audience, and on the boys. I was far down in the class, and can still recall the feeling of enthusiastic but despairing admiration with which I witnessed the scene. I thought Horner a god, and wondered what it was that made such a hopeless difference between him and me.

Brougham was not in the class with me. Before getting to the rector's class he had been under Luke Fraser, who, in his two immediately preceding courses of four years each, had the good fortune to have Francis Jeffrey and Walter Scott as his pupils. Brougham made his first public explosion while at Fraser's class. He dared to differ from Fraser, a hot, but good-natured old fellow, on some small bit of latinity. The master, like other men in power, maintained his own infallibility, punished the rebel, and flattered himself that the affair was over. But Brougham reappeared next day, loaded with books, returned to the charge before the whole class, and compelled honest Luke to acknowledge that he had been wrong. This made Brougham famous throughout the whole school. I remember as well as if it had been yesterday, having had him pointed out to me as " the fellow who had beat the master." It was then that I first saw him.

As mere school years, these six were very fruitlessly spent. The hereditary evils of the system and of the place were too great for correction even by Adam; and the general tone of the school was vulgar and harsh. Among the boys, coarseness of language and manners was the only fashion. An English boy was so rare, that his accent was openly laughed at. No lady could be seen within the walls. Nothing evidently civilised was safe. Two of the masters, in particular, were so savage, that any master doing now what they did every hour, would certainly be transported.

Before we left the school Adam made us a sensible and affecting address. In order to encourage us all to go on with our studies voluntarily and earnestly, he pointed out the opposite tendencies of early eminence, and of early obscurity, upon boys; warning those who had been distinguished against presumption, and those who had hitherto been unnoticed against despair; and explaining to both that, even in the very next stage, he had often known them change natures; the one from fancying that nothing more required to be done, the other from discovering that they had everything to do. I drank in every syllable of this well-timed discourse, and felt my heart revive. And a very few years proved its justice. The same powers that raise a boy high in a good school, make it probable that he will rise high in life. But in bad schools it is nearly the very reverse. And even in the most rationally conducted, superiority affords only a gleam of hope for the future. Men change, and still more boys. The High School distinctions very speedily vanished; and fully as much by the sinking of the luminaries who had shone in the zenith, as by the rising of those who had been lying on the horizon. I have ever since had a distrust of duxes, and thought boobies rather hopeful.*

I doubt if I ever read a single book, or even fifty pages, voluntarily, when I was at the High School. The *Spectator* was the first book I read, from the sheer pleasure of reading, after I left it.

Some of us, who lived near the Meadows, resolved to commemorate our final liberation from this hated school by erecting a pillar in what was then the little retired, wild, broomy glen between Braid and Blackford Hills. A long summer day was passed in piling stone upon stone " of lustre from the brook "; when, just as we were beginning to think that the edifice would do, the bank of the burn gave way, and in a moment the stream was glittering again over the fragments. We came away much mortified, and uttering what were probably our earliest reflections on the vanity of mortal hopes. To atone for this disaster, a tin box filled with precious coins (one of them being a new Glasgow halfpenny), was deposited in the crevice

* *See* Sir Robert Christison's *Autobiography*, vol. i. p. 17.

of a rock.* It lay undiscovered for above twenty years, when, seeing that it was in danger from the road trustees and their quarriers, who have now destroyed the whole rusticity of that beautiful and peaceful little valley, I rescued it, and have the relic at this hour.

I often think I see myself in my usual High School apparel, which was the common dress of other boys. It consisted of a round black hat; a shirt fastened at the neck by a black ribbon, and, except on dress days, unruffled; a cloth waistcoat, rather large, with two rows of buttons and of buttonholes, so that it could be buttoned on either side, which, when one side got dirty, was convenient; a single-breasted jacket, which in due time got a tail and became a coat; brown corduroy breeches, tied at the knees by a showy knot of brown cotton tape; worsted stockings in winter, blue cotton stockings in summer, and white cotton for dress; clumsy shoes made to be used on either foot, and each requiring to be used on alternate feet daily; brass or copper buckles. The coat and waistcoat were always of glaring colours, such as bright blue, grass green, and scarlet. I remember well the pride with which I was once rigged out in a scarlet

* Scott thus describes this spot :—"A natural alcove or hollow in the rock was a favourite retreat of the High School boys; who when tired with seeking birds' nests, or gathering wild berries, used to huddle themselves together in the cave, as it was called, and recount legends of the hermits who had dwelt there in Popish times, or one of the more recent adventures of covenanted martyrs, supposed to have sought refuge in this sequestered spot from the sword of persecution." This picturesque spot is now (1909) within the city boundary, and being directly under municipal control will surely preserve for future generations a large measure of its beauty and solitude.

waistcoat and a bright green coat. No such machinery as what are now termed braces or suspenders had then been imagined.

The valley of the Gala is associated with my earliest recollections, The old ale-house at Heriot was the first inn I ever entered. My father, who, I think, was then convener of the county of Edinburgh, went out to attend some meeting of road trustees, and he took a parcel of us with him. He rode; and we had a chaise to ourselves—happiness enough for boys. But more was in store for us; for he remained at the mansion-house of Middleton with his friend Mr Hepburn, and we went on, about four miles farther, to Heriot House, where we breakfasted and passed the day, fishing, bathing, and rioting. It was the first inn of most of the party. What delight! A house to ourselves, on a moor; a burn; nobody to interfere with us; the power of ringing the bell as we chose; the ordering of our own dinner; blowing the peat fire; laughing as often and as loud as we liked. What a day! We rang the hand-bell for the pure pleasure of ringing, and enjoyed our independence by always going out and in by the window. This dear little inn does not now exist, but its place is marked by a square of ash trees. It was a bright, beautiful August day.

We returned to the inn of Middleton, on our way home, about seven in the evening; and there we saw another scene. People sometimes say that there is no probability in Scott's making the party in Waverley retire from the Castle to the Howf; but these people were not with me at the inn at Middleton, about forty

years ago. The Duke of Buccleuch was living at
Dalkeith; Henry Dundas at Melville; Robert Dundas,
the Lord Advocate, at Arniston; Hepburn of Clerk-
ington at Middleton; and several of the rest of the
aristocracy of Midlothian within a few miles; all with
their families, and luxurious houses; yet had they, to
the number of twelve or sixteen, congregated in this
wretched ale-house for a day of freedom and jollity.
We found them roaring and singing, and laughing, in
a low-roofed room scarcely large enough to hold them,
with wooden chairs and a sanded floor. When their
own lacqueys, who were carrying on high life in the
kitchen, did not choose to attend, the masters were
served by two women. There was plenty of wine,
particularly claret, in rapid circulation on the table;
but my eye was chiefly attracted by a huge bowl of
hot whisky punch, the steam of which was almost
dropping from the roof, while the odour was enough
to perfume the whole parish. We were called in and
made to partake, and were very kindly used, particularly by my uncle, Harry Dundas. How they did
joke and laugh! with songs, and toasts, and disputation, and no want of practical fun. I don't remember
anything they said, and probably did not understand
it. But the noise, and the heat, and the uproarious
mirth—I think I hear and feel them yet. My father
was in the chair; and he having gone out for a little,
one of us boys was voted into his place, and the boy's
health was drank, with all the honours, as " the young
convener. Hurra! hurra! may he be a better man than
his father! hurra! hurra! " I need not mention that

they were all in a state of elevation; though there was
nothing like absolute intoxication, so far as I could
judge.

I have ever loved the Gala. But I think I should
have loved its pastoral valley without my early
attachment. It is bleak and wet no doubt; but so is
most of the pastoral scenery of Scotland, the whole of
which requires the attraction of a bright day. But
with such a day, the sparkling stream of the Gala,
the range of its wild unenclosed hills, and its impressive solitude, to say nothing of its coming in for a
share of the historical interest which belongs to the
whole of our southern border, give it powerful charms.
When I knew it first, Galashiels was a rural hamlet;
the house of Torwoodlee stood bare and staring; and
the high road ran on the west side of the valley. The
old laird of Torwoodlee survives to enjoy the reward
of his having planted judiciously, in seeing his now
beautiful place nearly buried in foliage. Galashiels
has become the Glasgow of Selkirkshire.

For many years almost all my Saturdays, Sundays,
and holidays, were passed at Niddrie, the seat of
Andrew Wauchope, Esq. I sighed over every holiday
as lost that was not. Part of the house is very old, but
it never had any architectural, or much historical
interest. But the garden! the garden! unseen and
unseeing, it was a world of its own. That unwalled
flat space, of only four or five acres, contained absolutely everything that a garden could supply for
" man's delightful use "; peaches and oaks, gravel
walks, and a wilderness " grotesque and wild," a burn

and a bowling-green, shade and sun, covert and lawn, vegetables and glorious holly hedges—everything delightful either to the young or the old. Eden was not more varied. And Eden is well worthy of its reputation if it was the scene of greater happiness. After a long and unbroken course of domestic security and pleasure, death began, about 1815, to extinguish, and circumstances to scatter, the gay and amiable family of which I was virtually a member; and I have since seldom revisited the generally silent walls. But the days of Niddrie are among the last I can forget.

My father was a friend of the Sir William Dick of Prestonfield who flourished when I was a boy; a great sportsman, handsome, good-natured, and (which goes a great way with me) a first-rate skater. We were the only boys (and how we were envied from the hillside!) who were always at liberty to play in his grounds, and to use his nice boat. So I knew the place thoroughly. The reeds were then regularly cut over, by means of short scythes with very long handles, close to the ground; and this made Duddingston Loch nearly twice its present size. All between the loch and the house was a sort of Dutch garden, admirably kept. Besides the invariable bowling-green, which formed the open-air drawing-room of all our old houses, it had several long smooth lanes of turf, anciently called bowling alleys, parterres and lawn interspersed, fountains, carved stone seats, dials, statues, and trimmed evergreen hedges. How we used to make the statues spout! There was a leaden Bacchus in particular, of whose various ejections it was impossible to tire. A very curious place.

Thus the dawn passed away.

In October 1793 I was sent to the College of Edinburgh.

My first class was for more of that weary Latin; an excellent thing if it had been got. For, all I have seen since, and all I felt even then, have satisfied me that there is no solid and graceful foundation for boys' minds like classical learning, grammatically acquired; and that all the modern substitutes of what is called *useful knowledge*, breed little beyond conceit, vulgarity, and general ignorance. It is not the mere acquaintance with the two immortal languages that constitutes the value, though the value of this is incalculable, but the early discipline of the mind, by the necessary reception of precise rules, of which the use and the reasonableness is in due time disclosed. But the mischief was that little Latin was acquired. The class was a constant scene of unchecked idleness and disrespectful mirth. Our time was worse than lost.

Andrew Dalzel, the author of *Collectanea Græca* and other academical books, taught my next class—the Greek. At the mere teaching of a language to boys, he was ineffective. How is it possible for the elements, including the very letters, of a language to be taught to one hundred boys at once, by a single lecturing professor? To the lads who, like me, to whom the very alphabet was new, required positive *teaching*, the class was utterly useless. Nevertheless, though not a good schoolmaster, it is a duty, and delightful, to record

B

Dalzel's value as a general exciter of boys' minds. Dugald Stewart alone excepted, he did me more good than all the other instructors I had. Mild, affectionate, simple, an absolute enthusiast about learning— particularly classical, and especially Greek; with an innocence of soul and of manner which imparted an air of honest kindliness to whatever he said or did, and a slow, soft, formal voice, he was a great favourite with all boys, and with all good men. Never was a voyager, out in quest of new islands, more delighted in finding one, than he was in discovering any good quality in any humble youth. His lectures (published injudiciously by somebody in 1820 or 1821) are an example of the difference between discourses meant to be spoken to boys, and those intended to be read by men. Yet our hearts bore witness how well they were conceived, at least as he read them, for moving youths. He could never make us actively laborious. But when we sat passive, and listened to him, he inspired us with a vague but sincere ambition of literature, and with delicious dreams of virtue and poetry. He must have been a hard boy whom these discourses, spoken by Dalzel's low, soft, artless voice, did not melt.

Dalzel was clerk to the General Assembly, and was long one of the curiosities of that strange place. He was too innocent for it. The last time I saw this simple and worthy man was very shortly before his death, the near approach of which he was quite aware of, at a house he had taken on the Bonnington road. He was trying to discharge a twopenny cannon for the amusement of his children; but his alarm and awkwardness only terrified them the more; till at last he got behind a washing-tub, and then, fastening the match to the end of a long stick, set the piece of ordnance off gloriously. He used to agree with those who say that it is partly owing to its Presbyterianism that Scotland is less classical than Episcopal England. Sydney Smith asserted that he had overheard the Professor muttering one dark night on the street to himself, " If it had not been for that confounded Solemn League and Covenant, we would have made as good longs and shorts as they."*

After being thus kept about nine years at two dead languages which we did *not* learn, the intellectual world was begun to be opened to us, by Professor Finlayson's lectures on what was styled Logic. He was a grim, firm-set, dark, clerical man; stiff and precise in his movements; and with a distressing pair of black, piercing, Jesuitical eyes, which moved slowly, and rested long on any one they were turned to, as if he intended to look him down, and knew that he could do so; a severe and formidable person. Though no speaker, and a cold, exact, hard reader, he surprised and delighted us with the good sense of his matter. Until we heard him, few of us knew that we had minds; and still fewer were aware that our intellectual operations had been analysed, and formed the subject of a science, the facts of which our own

* Dalzel was noted for his *bon mots*. Of the entrance to the old University from South College Street, to which many people objected, he remarked that "it was retained professedly for the professors, but principally for the Principal."

consciousness delighted to verify. Neither he nor his class were logical, in any proper sense of the word. But no exposition of the mere rules of reasoning could have been half so useful as the course which he adopted; which was first to classify and explain the nature of the different faculties, and then to point out the proper modes of using and improving them. This, though not logic, was the first thing that wakened our dormant powers. He did not work us half enough at composition.

After this we advanced to the Moral Philosophy of Dugald Stewart, which was the great era in the progress of young men's minds. His philosophy, and the general cast of his style and powers, are attested by his published works. His merit as a lecturer must depend on the recollection of those who heard him. His excellence in this very difficult and peculiar sphere was so great that it is a luxury to recall it.

He was about the middle size, weakly limbed, and with an appearance of feebleness which gave an air of delicacy to his gait and structure. His forehead was large and bald, his eyebrows bushy, his eyes grey and intelligent, and capable of conveying any emotion, from indignation to pity, from serene sense to hearty humour; in which they were powerfully aided by his lips, which, though rather large perhaps, were flexible and expressive. The voice was singularly pleasing; and, as he managed it, a slight burr only made its tones softer. His ear, both for music and for speech, was exquisite; and he was the finest reader I have ever heard. His gesture was simple and elegant, though not free from a tinge of professional formality; and his whole manner that of an academical gentleman.

Without genius, or even originality of talent, his intellectual character was marked by calm thought and great soundness. His training in mathematics, which was his first college department,* may have corrected the reasoning, but it never chilled the warmth, of his moral demonstrations. Besides being deeply and accurately acquainted with his own subject, his general knowledge, particularly of literature and philosophical history, was extensive, and all his reading well meditated. A strong turn for quiet humour was rather graced, than interfered with, by the dignity of his science and habits. Knowledge, intelligence, and reflection, however, will enable no one to reach the highest place in didactic eloquence. Stewart exalted all his powers by certain other qualifications which are too often overlooked by those who are ambitious of this eminence, and wonder how they do not attain it—an unimpeachable personal character, devotion to the science he taught, an exquisite taste, an imagination imbued with poetry and oratory, liberality of opinion, and the loftiest morality.

The tendency of these qualities, in a person of naturally an eloquent mind, to produce eloquence,

---

* He was elected joint-professor of Mathematics with his father, Dr Matthew Stewart, in 1775, and in 1778 undertook the work of the Moral Philosophy class for Professor Ferguson as well. In 1785, by arrangement with Professor Ferguson, there was an exchange of chairs—Stewart taking Moral Philosophy, and Ferguson, jointly with Playfair, that of Mathematics.

was increased by his avoiding certain things connected with his subject, which in dry hands have often made even the philosophy of morals repulsive. He dealt as little as possible in metaphysics, avoided details, and shrunk, with a horror which was sometimes rather ludicrous, from all polemical matter. Invisible distinctions, vain contentions, factious theories, philosophical sectarianism, had no attractions for him; and their absence left him free for those moral themes on which he could soar without perplexing his hearers, or wasting himself, by useless and painful subtleties.

Within this his proper sphere, with topics judiciously selected and views eloquently given, he was uniformly great and fascinating. The general constitution of moral and material nature, the duties and the ends of man, the uses and boundaries of philosophy, the connection between virtue and enjoyment, the obligations of affection and patriotism, the cultivation and the value of taste, the intellectual differences produced by particular habits, the evidences of the soul's immortality, the charms of literature and science, in short all the ethics of life— these were the subjects, in expatiating on which he was in his native element; and he embellished them all by a judicious application of biographical and historical illustration, and the happiest introduction of exquisite quotation. Everything was purified and exalted by his beautiful taste; not merely by his perception of what was attractive in external nature or in art, but by that moral taste which awed while it charmed, and was the chief cause of the success with which (as Mackintosh said) he breathed the love of virtue into whole generations of pupils.

He lectured standing; from notes which, with their successive additions, must, I suppose, at last have been nearly as full as his spoken words. His lecturing manner was professorial, but gentlemanlike; calm and expository, but rising into greatness, or softening into tenderness, whenever his subject required it. A slight asthmatic tendency made him often clear his throat; and such was my admiration of the whole exhibition, that Macvey Napier * told him, not long ago, that I had said there was eloquence in his very spitting. " Then," said he, " I am glad there was at least one thing in which I had no competitor."

There are some, and these good judges, who have depreciated his lectures, on account of what they call vagueness; by which they mean the absence of strict, and particularly of metaphysical, reasoning, which, they think, made his course evaporate in fruitless general declamation. The real import of this criticism is, that it was not prelections on the philosophy of morals that the critics desired. His generality and his indulgence in moral themes, which are what these hard-headed censors complain of, constituted the very charm of his course. A stronger infusion of dry matter, especially metaphysical, would have extinguished its magic. The breadth and simplicity of his views might, not unnaturally, have made him appear superficial to those who did not understand them. But he who, either in the business of life, or

* Succeeded Jeffrey as editor of the *Edinburgh Review*.

in the prosecution of philosophy, had occasion to recur to principles, always found that, either for study or for practice, Stewart's doctrines were his surest guide.

To me his lectures were like the opening of the heavens. I felt that I had a soul. His noble views, unfolded in glorious sentences, elevated me into a higher world. I was as much excited and charmed as any man of cultivated taste would be, who, after being ignorant of their existence, was admitted to all the glories of Milton, and Cicero, and Shakespeare. They changed my whole nature.

In short, Dugald Stewart was one of the greatest of didactic orators. Had he lived in ancient times, his memory would have descended to us as that of one of the finest of the old eloquent sages. But his lot was better cast. Flourishing in an age which requires all the dignity of morals to counteract the tendencies of physical pursuits and political convulsion, he has exalted the character of his country and his generation. No intelligent pupil of his ever ceased to respect philosophy, or was ever false to his principles, without feeling the crime aggravated by the recollection of the morality that Stewart had taught him.

A debating society was one of the natural results of these two classes. These institutions, which when ill managed are the hotbeds of conceit and petulance, and when managed tolerably well are powerfully productive of thought, of talent, and even of modesty, were in full operation at this time in the College of Edinburgh. It was a discussing age. Finlayson and

Stewart had touched our souls; and there were some ardent spirits among us. I never joined any of these societies except two—the Academical and the Speculative.

The Academical rose in 1796, and, after a short though very active life, died of decline about 1816. It met in Playfair's class-room, which was then the great receptacle of youthful philosophers and orators. There were more essays read, and more speeches delivered, by ambitious lads, in that little shabby place than in all Scotland. If it had been preserved it would have been near the centre of the new library. No part of my training did me so much good as this society. The Speculative, which I joined a few years later, was a higher and a more serious field; but it was the Academical plough that first opened the soil. It was here that I got my first notions of composition and debate, and that that delightful feeling of free doubting and independent discussion, so necessary for the expansion and manliness of young minds, was excited.

The change from ancient to modern manners, which is now completed, had begun some years before this, and was at this period in rapid and visible progress. The feelings and habits which had prevailed at the union, and had left so many picturesque peculiarities on the Scotch character, could not survive the enlarged intercourse with England and the world. It would be very interesting to trace the course of this alteration, provided the description was made intelligible by accounts of our curious men and our peculiar customs. But it cannot be done except by one who lived, and was in the practice of observing, and perhaps of noting, in the very scenes, and with the very men; and consequently it cannot be done by one who only came into action when the old suns were going down.*

The more immediate changes in Edinburgh proceeded chiefly from the growth of the city. The single circumstance of the increase of the population, and its consequent overflowing from the old town to the new, implied a general alteration of our habits. It altered the style of living, obliterated local arrangements, and destroyed a thousand associations, which nothing but the still preserved names of houses and of places is left to recall.†

It was the rise of the new town that obliterated our old peculiarities with the greatest rapidity and effect. It not only changed our scenes and habits of life, but, by the mere inundation of modern population, broke up and, as was then thought, vulgarised our prescriptive gentilities.

For example, Saint Cecilia's Hall ‡ was the only public resort of the musical, and besides being our most selectly fashionable place of amusement, was the best and the most beautiful concert-room I have ever yet seen. And there have I myself seen most of

* In so far as Edinburgh is concerned, there is a short but graphic view of the transformation by Scott, in a " General Account of Edinburgh," in the 5th No. of *The Provincial Antiquities and Picturesque Scenery of Scotland.*—H. C.

† Excellent accounts of these localities, and of the distinguished people who lived in them, and even of our curious street figures, have been preserved by Chambers, Paton, Wilson and others.—H. C.

‡ The building still stands (1909) at the foot of Niddry Street.

our literary and fashionable gentlemen, predominating with their side curls, and frills, and ruffles, and
silver buckles; and our stately matrons stiffened in
hoops and gorgeous satin; and our beauties with high-
heeled shoes, powdered and pomatumed hair, and
lofty and composite head-dresses. All this was in the
Cowgate! the last retreat nowadays of destitution and
disease. The building still stands, though raised and
changed, and is looked down upon from South Bridge,
over the eastern side of the Cowgate Arch. When I
last saw it, it seemed to be partly an old clothesman's
shop, and partly a brazier's. The abolition of this
Cecilian temple, and the necessity of finding accommodation where they could, and of depending for
patronage on the common boisterous public, of course
extinguished the delicacies of the old artificial parterre.

Our balls, and their manners, fared no better. The
ancient dancing establishments in the Bow and the
Assembly Close I know nothing about. Everything of
the kind was meant to be annihilated by the erection
(about 1787) of the handsome apartments in George
Street. Yet even against these, the new part of the
old town made a gallant struggle, and in my youth
the whole fashionable dancing, as indeed the fashionable everything, clung to George Square; where (in
Buccleuch Place, close by the south-eastern corner of
the square) most beautiful rooms were erected, which,
for several years, threw the New Town piece of presumption entirely into the shade. And here were the
last remains of the ball-room discipline of the preceding age. Martinet dowagers and venerable beaux

acted as masters and mistresses of ceremonies, and made all the preliminary arrangements. No couple could dance unless each party was provided with a ticket prescribing the precise place in the precise dance. If there was no ticket, the gentleman, or the lady, was dealt with as an intruder, and turned out of the dance. If the ticket had marked upon it—say for a country dance, the figures 3. 5; this meant that the holder was to place himself in the third dance, and fifth from the top; and if he was anywhere else, he was set right, or excluded. And the partner's ticket must correspond. Woe on the poor girl who with ticket 2. 7, was found opposite a youth marked 5. 9! It was flirting without a license, and looked very ill, and would probably be reported by the ticket director of that dance to the mother. Of course parties, or parents, who wished to secure dancing for themselves or those they had charge of, provided themselves with correct and corresponding vouchers before the ball day arrived. This could only be accomplished through a director; and the election of a pope sometimes required less jobbing. When parties chose to take their chance, they might do so; but still, though only obtained in the room, the written permission was necessary; and such a thing as a compact to dance, by a couple, without official authority, would have been an outrage that could scarcely be contemplated.*

* Goldsmith was struck with this. See his letter, 26th September, 1753.—*Prior's Life*, v. i. p. 141. The same restraint seems to have been in force at Bath in king Nash's time. It was a precaution, or perhaps rather an exercise of authority, natural to the days of compulsory decorum.—H. C.

Tea was sipped in side-rooms; and he was a careless beau who did not present his partner with an orange at the end of each dance; and the oranges and the tea, like everything else, were under exact and positive regulations. All this disappeared, and the very rooms were obliterated, as soon as the lately raised community secured its inevitable supremacy to the New Town. The aristocracy of a few predominating individuals and families came to an end; and the unreasonable old had nothing for it but to sigh over the recollection of the select and elegant parties of their youth, where indiscriminate public right was rejected, and its coarseness awed.

Yet, in some respects, there was far more coarseness in the formal age than in the free one. Two vices especially, which have been long banished from all respectable society, were very prevalent, if not universal, among the whole upper ranks—swearing and drunkenness. Nothing was more common than for gentlemen who had dined with ladies, and meant to rejoin them, to get drunk. To get drunk in a tavern seemed to be considered as a natural, if not an intended consequence of going to one. Swearing was thought the right, and the mark, of a gentleman. And, tried by the test, nobody, who had not seen them, could now be made to believe how many gentlemen there were. Not that people were worse tempered then than now. They were only coarser in their manners, and had got into a bad style of admonition and dissent. And the evil provoked its own continuance; because nobody who was blamed cared for

the censure, or understood that it was serious, unless
it was clothed in execration; and any intensity even
of kindness or of logic, that was not embodied in solid
commination, evaporated, and was supposed to have
been meant to evaporate, in the very uttering. The
naval chaplain justified his cursing the sailors,
because it made them listen to him; and Braxfield
apologised to a lady whom he damned at whist for
bad play, by declaring that he had mistaken her for
his wife. This odious practice was applied with particular offensiveness by those in authority towards
their inferiors. In the army it was universal by officers
towards soldiers; and far more frequent than is now
credible by masters towards servants.

The prevailing dinner hour was about three o'clock.
Two o'clock was quite common, if there was no
company. Hence it was no great deviation from their
usual custom for a family to dine on Sundays " between sermons "—that is between one and two. The
hour, in time, but not without groans and predictions, became four, at which it stuck for several years.
Then it got to five, which, however, was thought
positively revolutionary; and four was long and
gallantly adhered to by the haters of change as " the
good old hour." At last even they were obliged to give
in. But they only yielded inch by inch, and made a
desperate stand at half-past four. Even five, however,
triumphed, and continued the average polite hour
from (I think) about 1806 or 1807 till about 1820. Six
has at last prevailed, and half an hour later is not unusual. As yet this is the farthest stretch of London

imitation, except in country houses devoted to grouse
or deer, where the species called sportsmen, disdaining all mankind except themselves, glory in not dining
till sensible people have gone to bed. Thus, within my
memory, the hour has ranged from two to half-past
six o'clock; and a stand has been regularly made at
the end of every half-hour against each encroachment
and always on the same grounds—dislike of change
and jealousy of finery.

The procession from the drawing-room to the
dining-room was formerly arranged on a different
principle from what it is now. There was no such
alarming proceeding as that of each gentleman
approaching a lady, and the two hooking together.
This would have excited as much horror as the waltz
at first did, which never showed itself without
denunciations of continental manners by correct
gentlemen and worthy mothers and aunts. All the
ladies first went off by themselves, in a regular row,
according to the ordinary rules of precedence. Then
the gentlemen moved off in a single file; so that when
they reached the dining-room, the ladies were all
there, lingering about the backs of the chairs, till
they could see what their fate was to be. Then began
the selection of partners, the leaders of the male line
having the advantage of priority; and of course the
magnates had an affinity for each other.

The dinners themselves were much the same as at
present. Any difference is in a more liberal adoption
of the cookery of France. Ice, either for cooling or
eating, was utterly unknown, except in a few houses

of the highest class. There was far less drinking during
dinner than now, and far more after it. The staple
wines, even at ceremonious parties, were in general
only port and sherry. Champagne was never seen. It
only began to appear after France was opened by the
peace of 1815. The exemption of Scotch claret from
duty, which continued (I believe) till about 1780,
made it till then the ordinary beverage. I have heard
Henry Mackenzie and other old people say that, when
a cargo of claret came to Leith, the common way of
proclaiming its arrival was by sending a hogshead of
it through the town on a cart, with a horn; and that
anybody who wanted a sample, or a drink under
pretence of a sample, had only to go to the cart with a
jug, which, without much nicety about its size, was
filled for a sixpence. The tax ended this mode of
advertising; and, aided by the horror of everything
French, drove claret from all tables below the richest.

Healths and toasts were special torments; oppres-
sions which cannot now be conceived. Every glass
during dinner required to be dedicated to the health
of some one. It was thought sottish and rude to take
wine without this—as if forsooth there was nobody
present worth drinking with. I was present, about
1803, when the late Duke of Buccleuch took a glass of
sherry by himself at the table of Charles Hope, then
Lord Advocate; and this was noticed afterwards as a
piece of ducal contempt. And the person asked to take
wine was not invited by anything so slovenly as a look
combined with a putting of the hand upon the bottle,
as is practised by near neighbours now. It was a much

more serious affair. For one thing, the wine was very rarely on the table. It had to be called for; and in order to let the servant know to whom he was to carry it, the caller was obliged to specify his partner aloud. All this required some premeditation and courage. Hence timid men never ventured on so bold a step at all; but were glad to escape by only drinking when they were invited. As this ceremony was a mark of respect, the landlord, or any other person who thought himself the great man, was generally graciously pleased to perform it to every one present. But he and others were always at liberty to abridge the severity of the duty, by performing it by platoons. They took a brace, or two brace, of ladies or of gentlemen, or of both, and got them all engaged at once, and proclaiming to the sideboard—" A glass of sherry for Miss Dundas, Mrs Murray, and Miss Hope, and a glass of port for Mr Hume, and one for me," he slew them by coveys. And all the parties to the contract were bound to acknowledge each other distinctly. No nods or grins, or indifference; but a direct look at the object, the audible uttering of the very words— " Your good health," accompanied by a respectful inclination of the head, a gentle attraction of the right hand towards the heart, and a gratified smile. And after all these detached pieces of attention during the feast were over, no sooner was the table cleared, and the after-dinner glasses set down, than it became necessary for each person, following the landlord, to drink the health of every other person present, individually. Thus, where there were ten people, there

c

were ninety healths drunk. This ceremony was often slurred over by the bashful, who were allowed merely to *look* the benediction; but usage compelled them to look it distinctly, and to each individual. To do this well, required some grace, and consequently it was best done by the polite ruffled and frilled gentlemen of the olden time.

This prandial nuisance was horrible. But it was nothing to what followed. For after dinner, and before the ladies retired, there generally began what were called " *Rounds* " of toasts; when each gentleman named an absent lady, and each lady an absent gentleman, separately; or one person was required to give an absent lady, and another person was required to match a gentleman with that lady, and the pair named were toasted, generally with allusions and jokes about the fitness of the union. And, worst of all, there were " sentiments." These were short epigrammatic sentences, expressive of moral feelings and virtues, and were thought refined and elegant productions. A faint conception of their nauseousness may be formed from the following examples, every one of which I have heard given a thousand times, and which indeed I only recollect from their being favourites. The glasses being filled, a person was asked for his, or for her, sentiment, when this or something similar was committed—" May the pleasures of the evening bear the reflections of the morning." Or, " May the friends of our youth be the companions of our old age." Or, " Delicate pleasures to susceptible minds." " May the honest heart never feel distress." " May

the hand of charity wipe the tear from the eye of
sorrow." "May never worse be among us." There
were stores of similar reflections; and for all kinds of
parties, from the elegant and romantic, to the
political, the municipal, the ecclesiastic, and the
drunken.* Many of the thoughts and sayings survive
still, and may occasionally be heard at a club or a
tavern. But even there they are out of vogue as
established parts of the entertainment; and in some
scenes nothing can be very offensive. But the proper
sentiment was a high and pure production; a moral
motto; and was meant to dignify and grace private
society. Hence, even after an easier age began to sneer
at the display, the correct course was to receive the
sentiment, if not with real admiration, at least with
decorous respect. Mercifully, there was a large known
public stock of the odious commodity, so that nobody
who could screw up his nerves to pronounce the words
had any occasion to strain his invention. The conceited, the ready, or the reckless, hackneyed in the
art, had a knack of making new sentiments applicable
to the passing accidents, with great ease. But it was
a dreadful oppression on the timid or the awkward.
They used to shudder, ladies particularly—for nobody
was spared, when their turn in the *round* approached.
Many a struggle and blush did it cost; but this seemed
only to excite the tyranny of the masters of the craft;
and compliance could never be avoided except by

* Dean Ramsay gives a selection of these sentiments in "Scottish
Life and Character," taken from a volume published in 1777 under the
title of *The Gentleman's New Bottle Companion.*

more torture than yielding. There can scarcely be a
better example of the emetical nature of the stuff
that was swallowed than the sentiment elaborated by
the poor dominie at Arndilly. He was called upon, in
his turn, before a large party, and having nothing to
guide him in an exercise to which he was new, except
what he saw was liked, after much writhing and
groaning, he came out with—" The reflection of the
moon in the cawm bosom of the lake." It is difficult for
those who have been born under a more natural system, to comprehend how a sensible man, a respectable
matron, a worthy old maid, and especially a girl, could
be expected to go into company only on such conditions.

But a new generation gradually laughed the sentiments away; so that at last one could only be got as
a curiosity, from some old-fashioned practitioner.
They survived longer in male parties, especially of a
wild character. Yet Scott, in presiding even at the
grave annual dinners of the Bannatyne Club, always
insisted on rounds of ladies and gentlemen, and of
authors and printers, poets and kings, in regular
pairs. Of course in that toasting and loyal age, the
King was never forgotten, even though the company
consisted only of the host and his wife and children.

Early dinners begat suppers. But suppers are so
delightful that they have survived long after dinners
have become late. Indeed this has immemorially been
a favourite Edinburgh repast.* I have often heard

* According to Henry Mackenzie, the suppers of a Mr Alexander,
modelled on those of Paris, were "elegant and *enjoué*," and were
frequented by "all the literary and most of the fashionable persons of
the time. By those meetings some of the most distinguished members

strangers say, that Edinburgh was the only place where the people dined twice every day. It is now fading into paltry wine and water in many houses; but in many it still triumphs in a more substantial form. Lord Hermand was one of the great patrons of this Roman banquet. Almost all my set, which is perhaps the merriest, the most intellectual, and not the most severely abstemious, in Edinburgh, are addicted to it. I doubt if from the year 1811, when I married, I have closed above one day in the month, of my town life, at home and alone. It is always some scene of domestic conviviality, either in my own house or in a friend's. And this is the habit of all my best friends. The refection is beginning to be thought vulgar, or at least superfluous; which last, if mere hunger and thirst are to be considered, is certainly true. But its native force makes it keep its place even in polite societies. How could it fail? How many are the reasons, how strong the associations, that inspire the last of the day's friendly meetings! Supper is cheaper than dinner; shorter; less ceremonious; and more poetical. The business of the day is over; and its still fresh events interest. It is chiefly intimate associates that are drawn together at that familiar hour, of which night deepens the sociality. If there be any fun, or heart, or spirit, in a man at all, it is then, if ever, that it will appear. So far as I have seen social life, its brightest sunshine has been on the last repast of the day.

of the Select Society were more improved than by the debates at its meetings."

Tradition says that the suppers of Lord Monboddo were the most Attic in his day. But the Sunday suppers of Sir Henry Moncreiff are worthy of record. This most admirable, and somewhat old-fashioned, gentleman was one of those who always dined between sermons, probably without touching wine. He then walked back—look at him—from his small house in the east end of Queen Street to his church, with his bands, his little cocked hat, his tall cane, and his cardinal air; preached, if it was his turn, a sensible practical sermon; walked home in the same style; took tea about five; spent some hours in his study; at nine had family worship, at which he was delighted to see the friends of any of his sons; after which the whole party sat down to the roasted hens, the goblets of wine. and his powerful talk. Here was a mode of alluring young men into the paths of pious pleasantness. Those days are now passed, but the figure, and the voice, the thoughts, and the kind and cheerful manliness, of Sir Harry, as disclosed at those Sunday evenings, will be remembered with gratitude by some of the best intellects in Scotland.*

There is no contrast between those old days and the present that strikes me so strongly as that suggested by the differences in religious observances; not so much by the world in general, as by deeply religious people. I knew the habits of the religious very well, partly through the piety of my mother and her friends,

* Telling Mr T. F. Kennedy of Dunure of Sir Harry Moncreiff's death, Lord Cockburn elsewhere says that " Sir Harry's daughter, thinking her father gone, gave a short scream, when he looked up and said, ' No, no ! not so fast, Kate. We're not come that length yet ! ' "

the strict religious education of her children, and our connection with some of the most distinguished of our devout clergymen. I could mention many practices of our old pious which would horrify modern zealots. The principles and feelings of the persons commonly called evangelical were the same then that they are now; the external acts by which these feelings and principles were formerly expressed were materially different. In nothing do these differences appear more strikingly than in matters connected with the observance of Sunday. Hearing what is often confidently prescribed now as the only proper mode of keeping the Christian Sabbath, and then recollecting how it was recently kept by Christian men, ought to teach us charity in the enforcement of observances, which to a certain extent, are necessarily matters of opinion.

It is not unusual for certain persons to represent Scotland, but particularly Edinburgh, as having been about the beginning of this century very irreligious. Whenever any modern extravagance, under the name of piety, is attempted to be corrected by showing its inconsistency with the practice of the pious of the last age, this is sure to be met by the assertion that the last age was not merely irreligious, but generally infidel. There are some with whom this idea is suggested by the mere echo of the words David Hume. With others it is necessary for the promotion of a more ascetic system than the last age would have borne. And with many it is taken up from mere policy; as for example, when Established Churchmen, who maintain the necessity for college tests, are referred to the long success of the College of Edinburgh without tests, the answer is nearly certain to be that the College of Edinburgh used to be tainted by infidelity.

I attest that, so far as I ever saw or heard, this charge is utterly false. I am not aware of a single professor to whom it was ever applied, or could be applied, justly. Freedom of discussion was not in the least combined with scepticism among the students, or in their societies. I never knew or heard of a single student, tutor, or professor, by whom infidelity was disclosed, or in whose thoughts I believed it to be harboured, with perhaps only two obscure and doubtful exceptions. I consider the imputation as chiefly an invention to justify modern intolerance.

As to the comparative religiousness of the present and the preceding generation, any such comparison is very difficult to be made. Religion is certainly more the fashion than it used to be. There is more said about it; there has been a great rise, and consequently a great competition, of sects; and the general mass of the religious public has been enlarged. On the other hand, if we are to believe one half of what some religious persons themselves assure us, religion is now almost extinct. My opinion is that the balance is in favour of the present time. And I am certain that it would be much more so, if the modern dictators would only accept of that as religion which was considered to be so by their devout fathers.

Grown-up people talked at this time of nothing but

the French Revolution and its supposed consequences; younger men of good education were immersed in chemistry and political economy; the lower orders seemed to take no particular concern in anything. I heard a great deal that I did not then fully comprehend; but, even when not fully comprehending, boys are good listeners and excellent rememberers, and retain through life impressions that were only deepened by their vagueness and by their not flowing into common occupations. If the ladies and gentlemen who formed the society of my father's house believed all that they said about the horrors of French bloodshed, and of the anxiety of people here to imitate them, they must have been wretched indeed. Their talk sent me to bed shuddering. It was a relief to hear some younger persons talk of the new chemistry which Lavoisier had made fashionable, and of the economical doctrines so suitable for the country of Adam Smith. This, however, was a subject confined almost exclusively to young men. The middle-aged seemed to me to know little about the founder of the science, except that he had recently been a Commissioner of Customs, and had written a sensible book. The young, by which I mean the liberal young of Edinburgh, lived upon him. With Hume, Robertson, Millar, Montesquieu, Ferguson, and De Lolme, he supplied them with most of their mental food.

But this food of the liberal young was by no means relished by the stomachs of their seniors. It all tended towards awakening the intellect and exciting speculation, which were the very things that most of the minds that had been formed a little earlier thought dangerous. No young person who came to think for himself soon enough to keep what he heard in remembrance, can ever forget the painful impression made upon him by the intolerance of those times. No doubt the intolerance was justified, or at least provoked, by fright at first; but this soon became a pretence; and the hourly violence that prevailed was kept up chiefly as a factious engine. I lived in the midst of it. My father's house was one of the places where the leaders and the ardent followers of the party in power were in the constant habit of assembling. I can sit yet, in imagination, at the small side table, and overhear the conversation, a few feet off, at the established Wednesday dinner. How they raved! What sentiments! What principles! Not that I differed from them. I thought them quite right, and hated liberty and the people as much as they did. But this drove me into an opposite horror; for I was terrified out of such wits as they left me at the idea of bloodshed, and it never occurred to me that it could be avoided. My reason no sooner began to open, and to get some fair play, than the distressing wisdom of my ancestors began to fade, and the more attractive sense that I met with among the young men into whose company our debating societies threw me, gradually hardened me into what I became—whatever this was.

It has always been a pleasure to me to have seen some of the men of the retiring generation, who have done so much honour to Scotland by their literature and philosophy. I could not then value them on just grounds; but their reputation commanded the respect even of the young; and ever since I became acquainted with their merits, I have been glad that I saw them, and can recollect their figures, and such of their outward habits as a lad could observe.

Principal Robertson and his family were very intimate with the family of my father. The Principal dined in our house very often, and lived for the last two years of his life very near us, in the house of Grange, where he died in 1793. Many a happy summer day had his grandson John Russell and I in that house. The Doctor used to assist us in devising schemes to prevent the escape of our rabbits; and sometimes, but this was rarely, and with strict injunctions to us to observe that moderation which Mrs Robertson could never make himself practise, he permitted us to have a pull at his favourite cherry tree. He was a pleasant-looking old man; with an eye of great vivacity and intelligence, a large projecting chin, a small hearing trumpet fastened by a black ribbon to a buttonhole of his coat, and a rather large wig, powdered and curled. He struck us boys, even from the side-table, as being evidently fond of a good dinner; at which he sat, with his chin near his plate, intent upon the real business of the occasion. This appearance, however, must have been produced partly by his deafness; because, when his eye told him that there was something interesting, it was delightful to observe the animation with which he instantly applied his trumpet, when, having caught the scent, he followed it up, and was the leader of the pack.

Our neighbour on the east was old Adam Ferguson, the historian of Rome, and Stewart's predecessor in our moral chair—a singular apparition. In his younger years he was a handsome and resolute man. Being chaplain to the Black Watch, he could not be induced even by the positive orders of his commanding officer to remain in his proper place in the rear during an action, but persisted in being engaged in front.* Time and illness, however, had been dealing with him, and, when I first knew him, he was a spectacle well worth beholding. His hair was silky and white; his eyes animated and light blue; his cheeks sprinkled with broken red, like autumnal apples, but fresh and healthy; his lips thin, and the under one curled. A severe paralytic attack had reduced his animal vitality, though it left no external appearance, and he required considerable artificial heat. His raiment, therefore, consisted of half boots lined with fur, cloth breeches, a long cloth waistcoat with capacious pockets, a single-breasted coat, a cloth greatcoat also lined with fur, and a felt hat commonly tied by a ribbon below the chin. His boots were black; but with this exception the whole coverings, including the hat,

---

* Sir Robert Munro, the commanding officer, astonished to see the chaplain at the head of the column, desired him to go to the rear with the surgeons. This Adam Ferguson declined to do, when Sir Robert told him that his commission did not entitle him to be in the position he had assumed. " D—n my commission," said the warlike chaplain, throwing it towards his colonel.—Scott's *Miscellaneous Works*.

were of a Quaker grey colour, or of a whitish brown;
and he generally wore the furred greatcoat even
within doors. When he walked forth he used a tall
staff, which he commonly held at arm's length out
towards the right side; and his two coats, each
buttoned by only the upper button, flowed open
below, and exposed the whole of his curious and
venerable figure. His gait and air were noble; his
gesture slow; his look full of dignity and composed
fire. He looked like a philosopher from Lapland. His
palsy ought to have killed him in his fiftieth year; but
rigid care enabled him to live uncrippled, either in
body or mind, nearly fifty years more. Wine and
animal food besought his appetite in vain;* but huge
messes of milk and vegetables disappeared before
him, always in the never-failing cloth and fur. I never
heard of his dining out, except at his relation Dr
Joseph Black's, where his son Sir Adam (the friend of
Scott) used to say it was delightful to see the two
philosophers rioting over a boiled turnip. Domestically
he was kind, but anxious and peppery. His tempera-
ture was regulated by Fahrenheit; and often, when
sitting quite comfortably, he would start up and put
his wife and daughters into commotion, because his
eye had fallen on the instrument, and discovered that
he was a degree too hot or too cold. He always locked
the door of his study when he left it, and took the key
in his pocket; and no housemaid got in till the accumulation of dust and rubbish made it impossible to
put the evil day off any longer; and then woe on the

* He died in 1816 at the age of ninety-three.

family. He shook hands with us boys one day in summer 1793, on setting off, in a strange sort of carriage, and with no companion except his servant James, to visit Italy for a new edition of his history. He was then about seventy-two, and had to pass through a good deal of war; but returned in about a year, younger than ever.

Dr Joseph Black had, at one time, a house near us, to the west. He was a striking and beautiful person; tall, very thin, and cadaverously pale; his hair carefully powdered, though there was little of it except what was collected into a long thin queue; his eyes dark, clear, and large, like deep pools of pure water. He wore black speckless clothes, silk stockings, silver buckles, and either a slim green silk umbrella, or a genteel brown cane. The general frame and air were feeble and slender. The wildest boy respected Black. No lad could be irreverent towards a man so pale, so gentle, so elegant, and so illustrious. So he glided like a spirit through our rather mischievous sportiveness, unharmed. He died seated with a bowl of milk on his knee, of which his ceasing to live did not spill a drop; a departure which it seemed, after the event happened, might have been foretold of this attenuated philosophical gentleman.

I have known of some peaceful deaths not unlike this; but one that was even more than tranquil was that of Dr Henry the historian *—about 1790, I

* Dr Henry was one of Gilbert Stuart's victims. In 1775 Stuart wrote : " Poor Henry is on the point of death and his friends declare that I have killed him. I received the information as a compliment

think. I had the account of it from Sir Harry Moncreiff, who I believe was his favourite younger friend.
The Doctor was living at a place of his own in his
native county of Stirling. He was about seventy-two,
and had been for some time very feeble. He wrote to
Sir Harry that he was dying, and thus invited him for
the last time—" Come out here directly. I have got
something to do this week, I have got to die." Sir
Harry went, and found his friend plainly sinking, but
resigned and cheerful. He had no children, and there
was nobody with him except his wife. She and Sir
Harry remained alone with him for about three days,
being his last three; during a great part of which the
reverend historian sat in his easy chair, and conversed
and listened to reading, and dozed. While engaged in
this way, the hoofs of a horse were heard clattering
in the court below. Mrs Henry looked out and exclaimed that it was " that wearisome body," naming
a neighbouring minister, who was famous for never
leaving a house after he once got into it. " Keep him
out," cried the doctor, " don't let the cratur in here."
But before they could secure his exclusion, the cratur's
steps were heard on the stair, and he was at the door.
The Doctor instantly winked significantly, and signed
to them to sit down and be quiet, and he would pre-
tend to be sleeping. The hint was taken; and when the
intruder entered, he found the patient asleep in his
cushioned chair. Sir Harry and Mrs Henry put their

and begged they would not do me so much honour." But Henry and
his history outlived his unscrupulous critic.—*See* Disraeli's *Curiosities
of Literature.*

fingers to their lips, and pointing to the supposed slumberer as one not to be disturbed, shook their heads. The man sat down near the door, like one inclined to wait till the nap should be over. Once or twice he tried to speak, but was instantly repressed by another finger on the lip, and another shake of the head. So he sat on, all in perfect silence, for above a quarter of an hour; during which Sir Harry occasionally detected the dying man peeping cautiously through the fringes of his eyelids to see how his visitor was coming on. At last Sir Harry tired, and he and Mrs Henry pointing to the poor doctor, fairly waved the visitor out of the room; on which the doctor opened his eyes wide, and had a tolerably hearty laugh; which was renewed when the sound of the horse's feet made them certain that their friend was actually off the premises. Dr Henry died that night. A pious and learned man, with considerable merit in the execution, and complete originality in the plan, of his history.

Dr James Macknight, the colleague of Dr Henry, and the Harmonist (as he supposed) of the Four Gospels, lived in Nicolson Street, but crept round the Meadows almost every day. I think I see his large, square, bony visage, his enormous white wig, girdled by many tiers of curls, his old snuffy black clothes, his broad flat feet, and his threadbare blue greatcoat. His studies being very nocturnal, his morning walk began about two in the afternoon, and he rarely walked without reading. His elbows were stuck, immovably, to his haunches, on which they rested as on brackets, and enabled his arms to form a desk for his book. In this attitude he shuffled forward at the rate of half an inch each step; moving his rigid angular bulk straight forward, without giving place to any person or thing, or being aware indeed that there was anything in the world except himself and his volume. He died in 1800. He was one of the *Moderate* chiefs of his day, and boys stared at him for his queerness.

But Dr John Erskine! How everybody reverenced him! Though able and well read, his reputation rested on the better basis of a fine spirit, operating in all the walks in which liberal religion and active benevolence can be engaged. He lived at Lauriston, not far from us. No Edinburgh figure was better known. If stretched out he might probably have been of the average height but during his latter years he stooped so much that he was below it. He was one of the very few who in those days were not deformed by hair-powder, and he was distinguished by a neat, well-kept, jet-black wig, and plain but nice raiment. His face was small, pale, and active like; his figure that of a thin ardent creature. Stooping so low that it seemed as if he was looking for something on the ground, and hirpling along, with his hands in his sides, and his elbows turned outwards, he resembled a piece of old china with two handles. He was all soul, and no body. Never was there such a spectre, or such a spirit. There was nothing that this man would not do for truth or a friend. His language (like that of his colleague Princi-

D

pal Robertson) was good honest natural Scotch. We sat in his church; where he was so earnest, though with none of the Presbyterian roar or violence, that when his gown encumbered him, as it seemed often to do, he let it drop off, and went on almost erect with animation. His friend Henry Erskine had once some interest in a Fife election, but whether as a candidate or not I can't say, in which the Doctor had a vote. Being too old and feeble to bear the motion of a carriage or of a boat, he was neither asked nor expected to attend; but loving Henry Erskine, and knowing that victories depended on single votes, he determined to *walk* the whole way round by Stirling Bridge, which would have taken him at least a fortnight; and he was only prevented from doing so, after having arranged all his stages, by the contest having been unexpectedly given up. Similar sacrifices and exertions were familiar to the heroic and affectionate old gentleman. He died in 1803.

The Rev. Dr Carlyle must have had some substantial merit, for he was the associate of all the eminent men of his time, and is respectfully mentioned in most of their biographies. He was minister of Inveresk, where, from my being much in the family of the Hopes of Pinkie, I used often to visit him, and was always as kindly received as a lad generally is by the aged. Though known from his companions, he seems never to have done anything distinguished of his own, even in the very humble way of speaking, on behalf of his friend Principal Robertson's policy, in the General Assembly. His hold over his eminent comrades was derived from the charm of his private manners, which were graceful and kind. And he was one of the noblest looking old gentlemen I almost ever beheld.

John Robison, the Professor of Natural Philosophy, whose memory has been so beautifully embalmed in biography by Playfair, made himself remarkable, like others of his class at that time, by humouring his own taste in the matter of dress. A pig-tail so long and so thin that it curled far down his back, and a pair of huge blue worsted hose without soles, and covering the limbs from the heel to the top of the thigh, in which he both walked and lectured, seemed rather to improve his wise elephantine head and majestic person. A little hypochondria, induced by the frequent use of laudanum for the alleviation of pain, heightened the interest with which we gazed on a person who we knew combined such profound philosophy with such varied active life. He died in 1805.

Except Robison, these men were all great peripatetics, and the Meadows was their academic grove. There has never in my time been any single place in or near Edinburgh, which has so distinctly been the resort at once of our philosophy and our fashion. Under these poor trees walked, and talked, and meditated, all our literary and scientific, and many of our legal worthies. I knew little then of the grounds of their reputation, but saw their outsides with unquestioning and traditionary reverence; and we knew enough of them to make us fear that no such other race of men, so tried by time, such friends of each other and of learning, and all of such amiable manners and such spotless characters, could be expected soon to arise, and again ennoble Scotland. Though living in all the succeeding splendours, it has been a constant gratification to me to remember that I saw the last remains of a school so illustrious and so national, and that I was privileged to obtain a glimpse of the " skirts of glory " of the first, or at least of the second, great philosophical age of Scotland.*

There was a singular race of excellent Scotch old ladies. They were a delightful set; strong headed, warm hearted, and high spirited; the fire of their tempers not always latent; merry even in solitude; very resolute; indifferent about the modes and habits of the modern world; and adhering to their own ways, so as to stand out, like primitive rocks, above ordinary society. Their prominent qualities of sense, humour, affection, and spirit, were embodied in curious outsides; for they all dressed, and spoke, and

* Some curious anecdotes of these men will be found in an article in the seventy-first number of the *Quarterly Review*, by Scott, on the works of John Home. Some of the stories are trifling, but on the whole Sir Walter's account is tolerably correct. There is one complimentary blunder however. He talks of the strong subjection of Ferguson's "passions and feelings to the dominion of his reason." The statement would be nearer the truth if it were inverted. For though a most kind and excellent man, he was as fiery as gunpowder. *Kamtschatka*, Ferguson's residence, notwithstanding its internal comforts, was so called, Scott tells us, because of its insulated position at some distance from the town, and was hard by our house.—H. C.

did, exactly as they chose; their language, like their habits, entirely Scotch, but without any other vulgarity than what perfect naturalness is sometimes mistaken for.

There sits a clergyman's widow, the mother of the first Sir David Dundas,* the introducer of our German system of military manœuvres, and at one time commander-in-chief of the British Army. We used to go to her house in Bunker's Hill,† when boys, on Sundays between the morning and afternoon sermons, where we were cherished with Scotch broth and cakes, and many a joke from the old lady. Age had made her incapable of walking even across the room; so, clad in a plain black silk gown, and a pure muslin cap, she sat, half encircled by a high-backed black leather chair, reading; with silver spectacles stuck on her thin nose; and interspersing her studies, and her days, with much laughter, and not a little sarcasm. What a spirit! There was more fun and sense round that chair than in the theatre or the church. I remember one of her grand-daughters stumbling, in the course of reading

---

* Sir David Dundas's mother was Margaret, daughter of Robert Watson of Muirhouse, and his father, Robert Dundas, a merchant in Edinburgh. Sir David's brother was minister of Humbie. The ground on which St James's Square is built was the property of the Dundas family.

† "The first stone of the house in the south-east corner of the Square [James's] was laid on the day when the news of the battle of Bunker's Hill reached Edinburgh. . . . In the course of the potations, which at that period sanctified every occasion of business, the builders fell out between themselves, and before the ceremony was concluded most indecorously fell to and fought out the quarrel upon the spot in the presence of an immense assemblage of spectators. The name of Bunker's Hill was forthwith conferred upon the place."—Chambers' *Traditions of Edinburgh*.

the newspapers to her, on a paragraph which stated that a lady's reputation had suffered from some indiscreet talk on the part of the Prince of Wales. Up she of fourscore sat, and said with an indignant shake of her shrivelled fist and a keen voice—" The dawmed villain! does he kiss and tell!"

And there is Lady Arniston, the mother of Henry Dundas, the first Lord Melville, so kind to us mischievous boys on the Saturdays. She was generally to be found in the same chair, on the same spot; her thick black hair combed all tightly up into a cone on the top of her head; the remains of considerable beauty in her countenance; great and just pride in her son; a good representative in her general air and bearing of what the noble English ladies must have been in their youth, who were queens in their family castles, and stood sieges in defence of them. She was in her son's house in George Square, when it was attacked by the mob in 1793 or 1794,* and though no windows could be smashed at that time by the populace, without the inmates thinking of the bloody streets of Paris, she was perfectly firm, most contemptuous of the assailants, and with a heroic confidence in her son's doing his duty. She once wished us to go somewhere for her on an evening; and on one of us objecting that if we did, our lessons for next day could not be got ready—" Hoot, man!" said she, " what o' that? as they used to say in my day—it's only het hips and awa' again."

And Sophia—or, as she was always called, Suphy—

* " 57 George Square, on 5th June 1792."—*Arniston Memoirs.*

Johnston, of the Hilton family. There was an original!
Her father, from some whim,* resolved to see how it
would turn out, and gave her no education whatever.
Possessed of great natural vigour of mind, she passed
her youth in utter rusticity; in the course of which,
however, she made herself a good carpenter and a
good smith—arts which she practised occasionally,
even to the shoeing of a horse, I believe, till after the
middle of her life. It was not till after she became a
woman that she taught herself to read and write; and
then she read incessantly. She must have been about
sixty before I ever saw her, which was chiefly, and
often, at Niddrie. Her dress was always the same—a
man's hat when out of doors and generally when
within them, a cloth covering exactly like a man's
greatcoat, buttoned closely from the chin to the
ground, worsted stockings, strong shoes with large
brass clasps. And in this raiment she sat in any
drawing-room, and at any table, amidst all the
fashion and aristocracy of the land, respected and
liked. For her dispositions were excellent; her talk
intelligent and racy, rich both in old anecdote, and in
shrewd modern observation, and spiced with a good
deal of plain sarcasm; her understanding powerful;
all her opinions free, and very freely expressed; and

* "One day, after dinner, the Squire, having a mind to reason over
his bottle, turned the conversation on the folly of education." His
lady at first was inclined to dispute the question with him, but, "like
Mrs Shandy, she gave up the point, and as he strictly maintained his
argument they both agreed to make the experiment on the child she
was ready to produce, and mutually swore an oath that it never should
be taught anything from the hour of its birth, or ever have its spirit
broken by contradiction."—*Lives of the Lindsays.*

neither loneliness, nor very slender means, ever brought sourness or melancholy to her face or her heart.

Sitting, with her back to the light, in the usual arm-chair, by the side of the fire in the Niddrie drawing-room, with her greatcoat and her hat, her dark wrinkled face, and firmly-pursed mouth, the two feet set flat on the floor and close together, so that the public had a full view of the substantial shoes, the book held by the two hands very near the eyes, if the quick ear overheard any presumptuous folly, be it from solemn gentleman or fine lady, down went the volume, up the spectacles—"That's surely great nonsense, sir," though she had never seen him before; then, a little Quart and Tierce would begin, and the wight must have been very lucky if it did not end by his being smote.

Her own proper den was in a flat on the ground floor of a house in Windmill Street, where her sole companion was a single female servant. When the servant went out, which she generally took the liberty of doing for the whole of Sunday, Suphy's orders were that she should lock the door, and take the key with her. This saved Suphy the torment of always rising; for people went away when they found the house, as they thought, shut up. But she had a hole through which she saw them perfectly well; and, if she was inclined, she conversed through this orifice; and when tired of them told them to go away.

Though enjoying life, neither she nor any of those stout-hearted women had any horror of death. When

Suphy's day was visibly approaching, Dr Gregory prescribed abstinence from animal food, and recommended " spoon meat," unless she wished to die. " Dee, Doctor! odd—I'm thinking they've forgotten an auld wife like me up yonder! " However, when he came back next day, the doctor found her at the spoon meat—supping a haggis. She was remembered.*

The contrasts to these were Lady Don and Mrs Rochead of Inverleith: two dames of high aristocratic breed. They had both shone, first as hooped beauties in the minuets, and then as ladies of ceremonies, at our stately assemblies; and each carried her peculiar qualities and air to the very edge of the grave—Lady Don's dignity softened by gentle sweetness, Mrs Rochead's made more formidable by cold and rather severe solemnity.

Except Mrs Siddons in some of her displays of

* Several years after this attempt to describe Suphy Johnston another portrait by a far finer hand appeared. It is drawn by Lady Anne Barnard, one of the Balcarras family, and is to be found in Lord Lindsay's *Lives of the Lindsays*. Our two pictures agree substantially, though I have a higher opinion of Suphy than her relative, who must have known her best, seems to have had. When I knew her, which was only in advanced life and when she was probably shrunk, she was not at all " Amazonian." Lady Anne's saying that she " sung a man's song, in a bass voice, and was by many people suspected of being one," and that " she was a droll ingenious fellow," is all very graphic.—H. C.

Lady Anne Barnard concludes her description of Suphy Johnston with, " I scarce think any system of education could have made this woman one of the fair sex. Nature seemed to have entered into the jest and hesitated to the last whether to make her a boy or a girl. Her taste led her to hunt with her brothers, to wrestle with the stable boys and to saw wood with the carpenter. She worked well in iron, could shoe a horse quicker than the smith, made excellent trunks, played well on the fiddle, sung a man's song in a strong, bass voice, and was by many people suspected of being one" (*Lives of the Lindsays*).

magnificent royalty, nobody could sit down like the lady of Inverleith. She would sail like a ship from Tarshish, gorgeous in velvet or rustling in silk, and done up in all the accompaniments of fan, ear-rings and finger-rings, falling sleeves, scent bottle, embroidered bag, hoop and train—all superb, yet all in purest taste; and managing all this seemingly heavy rigging with as much ease as a full-blown swan does its plumage, she would take possession of the centre of a large sofa, and at the same moment, without the slightest visible exertion, would cover the whole of it with her bravery, the graceful folds seeming to lay themselves over it like summer waves. The descent from her carriage too, where she sat like a nautilus in its shell, was a display which no one in these days could accomplish or even fancy. The mulberry coloured coach, spacious but apparently not too large for what it carried—though she alone was in it; the handsome jolly coachman and his splendid hammer-cloth loaded with lace; the two respectful liveried footmen, one on each side of the richly-carpeted step; these were lost sight of amidst the slow majesty with which the lady came down, and touched the earth. She presided, in this imperial style, over her son's excellent dinners, with great sense and spirit, to the very last day almost of a prolonged life.

Lady Don (who lived in George Square) was still more highly bred, as was attested by her polite cheerfulness and easy elegance. The venerable faded beauty, the white well-coiled hair, the soft hand sparkling with old brilliant rings, the kind heart, the affectionate manner, the honest gentle voice, and the mild eye, account for the love with which her old age was surrounded. She was about the last person (so far as I recollect) in Edinburgh who kept a private sedan chair. Hers stood in the lobby, and was as handsome and comfortable as silk, velvet, and gilding could make it. And, when she wished to use it, two well-known respectable chairmen, enveloped in her livery cloaks, were the envy of their brethren. She and Mrs Rochead both sat in the Tron Church; and well do I remember how I used to form one of the cluster that always took its station to see these beautiful relics emerge from the coach and the chair.

Lady Hunter Blair too! and Mrs Murray of Henderland! Unlike, but both admirable. Lady Blair's elegance and sprightliness would have graced and enlivened the best society; but her tastes and virtues were entirely domestic, and made her the most delightful of household deities. Mild, affectionate, and cheerful, she attracted the love of all ages, and closed her many days without once knowing from personal consciousness what selfishness or want of charity meant.

Mrs Murray was stately, even to stiffness; but friendly and high minded; calm and ladylike in her dignity. The ceremonious formality of her air and demeanour was made graceful and appropriate by a once beautiful countenance still entire in its best features, but attenuated into such a death-like paleness, that, but for the unquenched light of a singularly radiant eye, she would have been a human statue.

Miss Menie Trotter, of the Mortonhall family, was of a later date. She was of the agrestic order. Her pleasures lay in the fields and long country walks. Ten miles at a stretch, within a few years of her death, was nothing to her. Her attire accorded. But her understanding was fully as masculine. Though slenderly endowed, she did, unnoticed, acts of liberality for which most of the rich would expect to be advertised. Prevailing loneliness gave her some entertaining habits, but never impaired her enjoyment of her friends, for whom she had always diverting talk, and occasionally " a bit denner." Indeed she generally sacrificed an ox to hospitality every autumn, which, according to a system of her own, she ate regularly from nose to tail;* and as she indulged in him only on Sundays, and with a chosen few, he feasted her half through the winter. This was at Blackford Cottage, a melancholy villa on the north side of Blackford Hill, where the last half, at the least, of her life was passed. I remember her urging her neighbour, Sir Thomas Lauder, not long before her death, to dine with her next Sunday—" For, eh! Sir Thammas! we're terrible near the tail noo." She told me that her oldest friends were the Inneses of Stow and the Scotts of Malleny—families she had known for above eighty-five years. They and the Mortonhall family had each

---

* Dean Ramsay tells a similar story of Lord Polkemmet, the Scottish judge. One day at dinner when the covers were removed the dishes were seen to consist entirely of veal cooked in different ways. Observing a look of surprise on his guests' faces he explained, "Ou, ay, it's a cauf; when we kill a beast we just eat it up ae side an' doon the tither."

a mansion-house in town; two of them being the two corner houses at the lower end of a close leading from the High Street down to the Cowgate, and the third one of the corner houses opposite, at the lower end of the close leading from the Cowgate southwards; each of the three houses looking into both the Cowgate and the close. The Cowgate has now lost half its character by getting a large sewer under ground; but before this innovation " the Coogate Strand," as it was called, when in flood was a great torrent, not filling the cellars merely, but almost the whole canal of the street. I remember a station on its banks, near Holyrood, where there was a regular net fishery, to catch what the stream brought down, particularly corks. Miss Trotter described the delight of the children of these families in wading in that gutter when it was safe.

On one of her friends asking her, not long before her death, how she was, she said, " Very weel—quite weel. But, eh, I had a dismal dream last night! a fearfu' dream!" " Aye! I'm sorry for that—what was it? " " Ou! what d'ye think? Of a' places i' the world, I dreamed I was in heeven! And what d'ye think I saw there? Deil ha'et but thoosands upon thoosands, and ten thoosands upon ten thoosands, o' stark naked weans! That wad be a dreadfu' thing! for ye ken I ne'er could bide bairns a' my days! "

It is remarkable that though all these female Nestors were not merely decorous in matters of religion, but really pious, they would all have been deemed irreligious now. Gay hearted, and utterly devoid of every tincture of fanaticism, the very freedom and cheerfulness of their conversation and views on sacred subjects would have excited the horror of those who give the tone on these matters at present. So various are the opinions of what constitutes religiousness.

There were some curious tests of loyalty in those days.

One was dress. The dignified rigidity of the old fashion was obstinately adhered to by one set of people and was of course outraged by the disdain of others, who were profane in the matter of shorts, silks, and buckles. Old Niddrie would hardly admit any one who came to his hospitable house in trousers or gaiters, which he described as Jacobinical. This feeling lingered in some tastes so long, that after the year 1820 I have heard old loyalists thanking God that they had always stuck to the Constitution and to buckles. In nothing was the monarchical principle more openly displayed or insulted than in the adherence to, or contempt of, hair-powder. The reason of this was, that this powder, and the consequent enlargement and complexity of the hair on which it was displayed, were not merely the long-established badges of aristocracy, but that short and undressed crops had been adopted in France. Our loyal, therefore, though beginning to tire of the greasy and dusty dirt, laid it on with profuse patriotism, while the discontented exhibited themselves ostentatiously in all the Jacobinism of clean natural locks.

Another was *keeping* the King's birthday. This day

was the 4th of June, which for the sixty years that
the reign of George the III. lasted gave an annual
holiday to the British people, and was so associated
in their habits with the idea of its being a free day,
that they thought they had a right to it even after
his Majesty was dead. And the established way of
keeping it in Edinburgh was, by the lower orders and
the boys having a long day of idleness and fireworks,
and by the upper classes going to the Parliament
House, and drinking the royal health in the evening,
at the expense of the city funds. The magistrates who
conducted the banquet, which began about seven,
invited about 1500 people. Tables, but no seats except
one at each end, were set along the Outer House.
These tables, and the doors and walls, were adorned
by flowers and branches, the trampling and bruising
of which increased the general filth. There was no
silence, no order, no decency. The loyal toasts were let
off, in all quarters, according to the pleasure of the
Town Councillor who presided over the section, without any orations by the Provost, who, seated in his
robes, on a high chair, was supposed to control the
chaos. Respectable people, considering it all as an
odious penance, and going merely in order to show
that they were not Jacobins, came away after having
pretended to drink one necessary cup to the health of
the reigning monarch. But all sorts who were worthy
of the occasion and enjoyed it, persevered to a late
hour, roaring, drinking, toasting, and quarrelling.*

* The character of the Lord Provost's entertainment to the representative citizens on the King's birthday must have somewhat degenerated
by Lord Cockburn's time. Arnot (about 1779), referring to a pulpit and

They made the Court stink for a week with the wreck
and the fumes of that hot and scandalous night. It
was not unusual at old Scotch feasts for the guests,
after drinking a toast, to toss their glasses over their
heads, in order that they might never be debased by
any other sentiment. The very loyal on this occasion
availed themselves of this privilege freely, so that
fragments of glass crunched beneath the feet of the
walkers. The infernal din was aggravated by volleys
of musketry, fired very awkwardly by the Town
Guard, amidst the shouts of the mob, in the Parliament Close. The rabble, smitten by the enthusiasm
of the day, were accustomed, and permitted, to think
license their right, and exercised their brutality without stint. Those who were aware of what might take
place on the street, retired from the banquet before
the spirit of mischief was fully up. Those who came out
so late as ten or even nine of the evening, if observed
and unprotected, were fortunate if they escaped
rough usage, especially if they escaped being " *Burgh-
ered*," or made to " *Ride the Stang*," a painful and
dangerous operation, and therefore a great favourite
with the mob. I forget when this abominable festival
was given up. Not, I believe, till the poverty, rather
than the will, of the Town Council was obliged to
consent. In 1798 these civic fathers passed a self-
denying ordinance, by which they resolved to ruin

gallery standing in Parliament Hall which had been used for worship,
during the sittings of the Scots Parliament, says : " These now serve no
other purpose but to accommodate the band of music which performs
on His Majesty's birthday, when the Lord Provost of Edinburgh is entertaining the nobility and gentry with wine and sweetmeats."

France by abstaining from claret at this and all other municipal festivals. The vow, however, was not kept; and so the French were not ruined.

Another patriotic criterion, which, however, was necessarily limited, consisted in joining what was called the *Gentlemen Volunteers*, the only voluntary regiment that we then had. Such establishments became universal afterwards, and, as there was then real danger, were put on a military footing. But the original long blue-coated regiment was a merely political association, which persons willing to attest their principles and to pay for a uniform, were expected to join. It was a respectable, though rather pretending, body; composed of comfortable privates, and middle-aged officers, selected on the ground of their station in the world, and the intensity of their public intolerance. They were an assiduous and well-fed corps, and made a grand figure parading in Bruntsfield Links or Heriot's Green; but a march to Haddington would have dissolved it. Charles Hope, who afterwards became their Lieutenant-Colonel, was almost the only ardent spirit among them. This first appearance of private citizens in uniforms and arms was portentous to us, who had never been accustomed to any militia. The whole kingdom was soon afterwards a camp.

In the years 1795 and 1796 there was a greater dearth than has ever since visited the British Islands. On the 4th of March 1795 about eleven thousand persons, being probably about an eighth of the population, were fed by charity in Edinburgh. I have

E

never forgotten that famine, perhaps because it was the first I had seen. A public proclamation specified the exact quantity of bread which each family ought to consume, being a loaf, if I recollect rightly, for each individual weekly. An odd proceeding; but it gave a measure, and a ground for economy, which were useful. Then was the triumph, and the first introduction, of public kitchens, Count Rumfords,* and cooking committees. Chemistry strained itself to extract nutriment from everything. One ingenious sacrifice in wealthy houses was to produce an appearance of wheat at table without the reality. So dishes were invented which in shape and colour resembled the forbidden articles, and the knife often struck on what seemed good pie-crust but was only clay. Jacobins had a great advantage in having their heads set up already on an economical system. Some paltry Tories took this opportunity of saving the powder tax; only cautiously announcing that this was done on no revolutionary principle, but solely in order that the stomach might get what would be wasted on the hair. This assimilation to disloyalty, however, was thought dangerous; and therefore the correct course was still to whiten the head, but to make the powder of chalk or any other substance not usually eaten.

* Count Rumford, Benjamin Thompson, an American, who came to England about 1776 and was elected Fellow of the Royal Society in 1779. Later, in Austria, he was created a Count of the Holy Roman Empire, taking the title Rumford from an American township. Returning to London he applied himself to the discovery of methods of curing smoky chimneys and to the improvement of fireplaces. Hence Lord Cockburn's phrase, "Count Rumfords."

The state of people's knowledge of political economy at this period may be judged of from the fact, that punishing what were held to be the crimes of Forestalling and Regrating was deemed one of the cures of this long-continued dearth; and this with the entire approbation of the public. The same idea prevailed in England. The extent, indeed, to which the freedom of trade was interfered with, by even petty authority, is scarcely credible now. Whenever prices rose higher than purchasers liked, there was a cry for legal interference; and this cry was very often successful. The price of bread was directly and habitually regulated within burgh, and indirectly beyond it, by the magistrates, who for many years after this issued periodical proclamations " setting the assize of bread." The charge for post-horses was regulated in the same way. No letter of horses could demand more from the hirer than what Town Councils or Justices of the Peace prescribed. All this, I believe, was agreeable to law; for the Court of Session sustained it, and sometimes even acted directly as a regulator of prices. But the wonder is how such a system could be enforced, for at least thirty years after the publication of the *Wealth of Nations*.

In November 1799 I entered the Speculative Society; an institution which has trained more young men to public speaking, talent, and liberal thought, than all the other private institutions in Scotland. The society had never been in such glory as during the immediately preceding years. I forget the exact origin of the disputes that had convulsed it; but they all grew out of the proceedings connected with the expulsion of Mr Emmett, then implicated in the Irish rebellion, and afterwards leading counsel at New York—an able and excellent man, and with a proposal for dissolving some literary connection which had long subsisted between the Speculative and a similar society in Dublin. This (as was secretly intended) introduced the whole politics of the day. The agitation brought back the old members; who, headed by Charles Hope and David Hume, of course tried to bear down the younger, who, led by Brougham, Jeffrey, Horner, Lord Henry Petty, and Lord Kinnaird, were as defying in their Whiggism as their opponents in their Toryism. Their contest produced animated debates and proceedings, which did not occupy the society alone, but the whole College, and indeed all Edinburgh, for nearly an entire session. Hume being supposed to have applied some offensive imputation to the junior party, it was arranged (by lot, I believe) that Jeffrey should require an explanation. This was given; but still they were bound over to keep the peace. At last the seniors were defeated; and some of them made the victory clearer by resigning.

No better arena could possibly have been provided for the exercise of the remarkable young men it excited. In a few years after this Petty was Chancellor of the Exchequer. He had left the Society before I joined it; but Kinnaird, an able man and an excellent speaker, continued to attend occasionally; and Brougham, Horner, Jeffrey, James Moncreiff, and other powerful persons, attended regularly, and took an active part in the business, throughout all the three years during which I was an ordinary member. The only defect was, that the recent discussions turned away many of the good Tory youths, and that the usual audience was not large enough for such speakers. However, there were some of them on whom this had little effect. Brougham, in particular, whose constitutional keenness made him scent the future quarry, gave his whole soul to this preparatory scene, and often astonished us by the vigour with which, even to half a dozen of lads, he could abandon himself to his subject, and blaze as if he had been declaiming against Cicero in the forum. Moncreiff has improved very greatly since then; but Jeffrey, Horner, and Brougham were as good writers and speakers then as they have ever been since; and each in the very same style he afterwards retained. Of all those who attempted to speak, I was then decidedly the worst and the most unpromising; worse perhaps than even Charles and Robert Grant, both of whom have since risen to high station in Parliament and in public life.* In so far as I was personally concerned, however, the Speculative completed what the Academical had

---

* Charles Grant, Lord Glenelg, and his brother, Sir Robert, were born in India. The former represented Inverness and Fortrose burghs, and later succeeded his father in the representation of the County of Inverness from 1818 until raised to the peerage in 1835. As Colonial Secretary he saw the total abolition of slavery in the West Indies, but his administration of Canada was sharply criticised. Sir Robert entered Parliament as member for Elgin burghs and again for Inverness burghs. He was appointed Governor of Bombay in 1834 and died in 1839. Lord Glenelg died in 1866.

begun; and together they did me more good than all the rest of my education. And I must attest that their moral benefits were fully more important than their intellectual. They inspired a high tone of virtue.

An exposition of things not merely true, but provable, and yet incredible, would be a very curious work. And few countries could supply better materials for it than Scotland, where modern changes have been so numerous and so striking.

For example, there are few people who now know that so recently as 1799 there were slaves in this country. Twenty-five years before, that is, in 1775, there must have been thousands of them; for this was then the condition of all our colliers and salters. They were literally slaves. They could not be killed nor directly tortured; but they belonged, like the serfs of an older time, to their respective works, with which they were sold as a part of the gearing. With a few very rigid exceptions, the condition of the head of the family was the condition of the whole house. For though a child, *if never entered* with the work, was free, yet entering was its natural and almost certain destination; for its doing so was valuable to its father, and its getting into any other employment in the neighbourhood was resisted by the owner. So that wives, daughters, and sons went on from generation to generation under the system which was the family doom. Of course it was the interest of a wise master to use them well, as it was to use his other cattle well. But, as usual, the human animal had the worst of it.

It had rights, and could provoke by alluding to them. It could alarm and mutiny. It could not be slain, but it had no protection against fits of tyranny or anger. We do not now know much of their exact personal or domestic condition. But we know what their work makes them, even when they are free, and within the jealous benevolence of a softer age. We know that they formed a separate and avoided tribe, as to a great extent they still do, with a language and habits of their own. And we know what slavery even in its best form is, and does. The completeness of their degradation is disclosed by one public fact. The statue passed in 1701, which has been extolled as the Scotch Habeas Corpus Act, proceeds on the preamble that " Our Sovereign Lord, considering it is the interest of all his good subjects that the liberty of their persons be duly secured." Yet, while introducing regulations against " wrongous imprisonment, and undue delays in trials,—" the statute contains these words—" And sicklike it is hereby provided and declared that this present act is noways to be extended to colliers or salters." That is, being slaves, they had no personal liberty to protect.

These facts enable us to understand the hereditary blackguardism, which formed the secondary nature of these fixed underground gipsies, and the mysterious horror with which they were regarded, and which, in a certain degree, attaches to all subterranean labourers.

The first link of their chain was broken in 1775, by the 15th act of George Third, chap. 28. It sets out on the preamble that " many colliers and salters *are in a state of slavery and bondage.*" It emancipates *future* ones entirely, that is, those who after the 1st of July 1775 " *shall begin* to work as colliers and salters." But the existing ones were only liberated gradually; those under 21 in 7 years; those between 21 and 35 in 10 years. The liberation of the father was declared to liberate his family. And the freed were put under the act 1701. But this measure, though effective in checking new slavery, was made very nearly useless in its application to the existing slaves by one of its conditions. Instead of becoming free by mere lapse of time, no slave obtained his liberty unless he instituted a legal proceeding in the Sheriff Court, and incurred all the cost, delay, and trouble of a lawsuit; his capacity to do which was extinguished by the invariable system of masters always having their workmen in their debt. The result was that, in general, the existing slave was only liberated by death.

But this last link was broken in June 1799 by the 39th George Third, chap. 56, which enacted that from and after its date " all the colliers in Scotland who were bound colliers at the passing of the 15th George Third, chap. 28, *shall be free from their servitude.*" This annihilated the relic.

These two statutes seem to have been neither the effect nor the cause of any public excitement. I do not see either of them even mentioned in the *Scots Magazine.* People cared nothing about colliers on their own account, and the taste for improving the lower orders had not then begun to dawn.

CHAPTER II

IN December 1800 I entered the Faculty of Advocates; and, with a feeling of nothingness, paced the Outer House.

Being now of an age and in a position to observe things intelligently, I can speak of Edinburgh, and through it of Scotland, then and since, with the knowledge of a witness, and indeed of an actor in most of its occurrences. It is necessary, towards a right perception of the progress of the place, that its general condition at this period should be understood.

Everything rung, and was connected with the Revolution in France; which, for above 20 years, was, or was made, the all in all. Everything, not this or that thing, but literally everything, was soaked in this one event.

Yet we had wonderfully few proper Jacobins; * that is, persons who seriously wished to introduce a republic into this country, on the French precedent. There were plenty of people who were *called* Jacobins; because this soon became the common nickname which was given, not only to those who had admired the dawn of the French liberation, but to those who were known to have any taste for any internal reform

* The revolutionary party in France. So called because their meetings were held in the Jacobin convent.

of our own. There was a short period, chiefly in 1793 and 1794, during which this imputation was provoked by a ridiculous aping of French forms and phraseology, and an offensive vaunting of the superior excellence of everything in that country. But the folly, which only appeared in a few towns, was very soon over, cured by time, by the failure of the French experiment, and by the essential absurdity of the thing itself; and it had never been patronised by a single person of sense and public character or influence. Firm, but mild and judicious, treatment, and a little reliance on the tendency of time to abate epidemic follies, would have made the British Constitution popular, and the proceedings in France odious, everywhere. Scotch Jacobinism did not exist.

But Scotch Toryism did, and with a vengeance. This thing, however, must not be considered as exactly the same with pure Toryism in England. It seldom implies anything with us except a dislike of popular institutions; and even this chiefly on grounds of personal advantage. A pure historical and constitutional Tory is a very rare character in this country.

This party engrossed almost the whole wealth, and rank, and public office, of the country, and at least three-fourths of the population. They could have afforded, therefore, to be just and well-tempered. But this, as it appeared to them, would have endangered their supremacy, which they were aware was upheld by their opponents being believed to entertain alarming principles and ends. Hence the great Tory object was, to abuse everybody but themselves, and in particular to ascribe a thirst for bloodshed and anarchy, not merely to their avowed public opponents, but to the whole body of the people. It is frightful even to recollect the ferocious bitterness and systematic zeal with which this principle was acted upon; and this under the direct sanction of Government. No one ever heard of a check being given, even by a hint, from headquarters, with a view to arrest intolerance or to encourage charity.* Jacobinism was a term denoting everything alarming and hateful, and every political objector was a Jacobin. No innovation, whether practical or speculative, consequently no political or economical reformer, and no religious dissenter, from the Irish Papist to our own native Protestant Seceder, could escape from this fatal word. This misrepresentation, and the natural tendency of the traduced to provoke and frighten by rather extenuating some of the French proceedings, might make the reader of an account of those days suppose that the revolutionary infection had spread far enough and deep enough to justify the proscription it met with. But, unquestionably, this was not the fact. The chief object at which our discontented aimed was parliamentary reform. But this and other home-bred ends were hid by a cloud of foreign follies, which the Tories exhibited as

* "It is hardly possible to credit now, save as having been uttered in jest, the things gravely said, and as gravely believed, at that time in Edinburgh concerning those who were generally held to be on the wrong side in politics. That our mother had provided herself with a small guillotine, and exercised the same in beheading poultry, or perhaps 'rats and mice and such small deer,' in order to be expert when French principles and practice in accordance should prevail in our land, was one of them."—Mrs Fletcher's *Autobiography*.

demonstrations that the correction of domestic abuses was a pretence and Jacobinism the truth. On this foundation they represented the whole lower orders as hostile to our institutions; from which the desired and comfortable inference was, that there was no salvation for the country except in the predominance of their own party.

The real *Whigs* were extremely few. Self-interest had converted some, and terror more; and the residue, which stood out, consisted of only the stronger-minded men of the party. The adherence of these men to rational opinions was attended with very considerable personal risk in Scotland, where the result of a political prosecution did not admit of the very slightest doubt. They were treated as the causes and the shields of the popular delusions; and belonging mostly to the bar, they were constantly and insolently reminded that the case of their brother Thomas Muir, transported for sedition, was intended for their special edification. But though the condition of Parliament made their carrying any practical measure impossible, their constancy to their principles kept their friends from despair; and this was the chief good that they did, or could have done. Though on the whole very united, yet, during the hottest fit of the revolutionary fever, the moderate were disturbed by the intemperance of the wild; two classes into which all parties are apt to arrange themselves, but which were particularly repulsive to each other at this crisis, when the slightest wildness was alarming to the moderate, and all moderation contemptible to the wild.

The principal leaders of the true Whig party were Henry Erskine, who had recently been Lord Advocate; Adam Gillies, John Clerk, and David Cathcart, all afterwards Judges; Archibald Fletcher, Malcolm Laing, James Grahame, and John Macfarlane, Advocates; and James Gibson, Writer to the Signet [Sir James Gibson-Craig of Riccarton, Bart.]. Some brighter names, especially that of Jeffrey, had not yet come into action; and there were a few stout-hearted brethren, who, though too obscure to be now named, formed a rear rank on whom those in advance could always rely. The profession of these men armed them with better qualities than any other avocation could supply in a country without a Parliament—with talent, the practice of speaking, political knowledge, and public position; but their personal boldness and purity marked them out still more conspicuously for popular trust. It was among them accordingly that independence found its only asylum. It had a few silent though devoted worshippers elsewhere, but the Whig counsel were its only open champions. The Church can boast of Sir Harry Moncreiff alone as its contribution to the cause; but he was too faithful to his sacred functions to act as a political partisan. John Allen and John Thomson, of the medical profession, were active and fearless. And the College gave Dugald Stewart, John Playfair, and Andrew Dalzel. Of these three, mathematics, which was his chair, enabled Playfair to come better off than his two colleagues; for Dalzel had to speak of Grecian liberty, and Stewart to explain the uses of liberty in general;

and anxiously were they both watched. Stewart, in particular, though too spotless and too retired to be openly denounced, was an object of great secret alarm. Not only virtuous, but eloquent in recommending virtue to the young, he united Nero's objections both to Virginius the rhetorician and Rufus Musonius the philosopher—" Virginium Flavum et Musonium Rufum claritudo nominis expulit. Nam Virginius studia juvenum eloquentiâ, Musonius præceptis sapientiæ, fovebat." (Tacitus—An. Lib. 15, cap. 71.) A country gentleman with any public principle except devotion to Henry Dundas was viewed as a wonder, or rather as a monster. This was the creed also of almost all our merchants, all our removable office-holders, and all our public corporations. So that, literally, everything depended on a few lawyers; a class to which, in modern times, Scotland owes a debt of gratitude which does not admit of being exaggerated. Nor have any men, since our revolution, been obliged to exercise patriotism at greater personal risk or sacrifice. Could there have been the slightest doubt of their purity or courage, public spirit must have been extinguished in Scotland. The real strength of their party lay in their being right, and in the tendency of their objects to attract men of ability and principle.

With the people put down and the Whigs powerless, Government was the master of nearly every individual in Scotland, but especially in Edinburgh, which was the chief seat of its influence. The infidelity of the French gave it almost all the pious;

their atrocities all the timid; rapidly-increasing taxa-
tion and establishments all the venal; the higher and
middle ranks were at its command, and the people at
its feet. The pulpit, the bench, the bar, the colleges,
the parliamentary electors, the press, the magistracies,
the local institutions, were so completely at the
service of the party in power, that the idea of independence, besides being monstrous and absurd, was
suppressed by a feeling of conscious ingratitude. And
in addition to all the ordinary sources of Government
influences, Henry Dundas, an Edinburgh man, and
well calculated by talent and manner to make despotism popular, was the absolute dictator of Scotland,
and had the means of rewarding submission and of
suppressing opposition beyond what were ever exercised in modern times by one person in any portion of
the empire.

The true state of things and its effects may be better
seen in a few specific facts, than in any general
description.

As to our *Institutions*—there was no popular representation; all town-councils elected themselves; the
Established Church had no visible rival; persons were
sent to the criminal courts as jurymen very nearly
according to the discretion of the Sheriff of their
county; and after they got there, those who were to
try the prosecution were picked for that duty by the
presiding judge, unchecked by any peremptory
challenge. In other words, we had no free political
institutions whatever.

The consequences of this were exactly what might

have been expected, and all resolved into universal prostration. The town-councils who elected the burgh members of Parliament, and the 1500 or 2000 freeholders who elected the county members formed so small a body, that a majority, and indeed the whole, of them were quite easily held by the Government strings; especially as the burgh electors were generally dealt with on a principle which admitted of considerable economy. Except at Edinburgh, there was only one member for what was termed a *district* of four or five burghs. Each town-council elected a delegate; and these four or five delegates elected the member; and instead of bribing the town-councils, the established practice was to bribe only the delegates, or indeed only one of them, if this could secure the majority. Not that the councils were left unrefreshed, but that the hooks with the best baits were set for the most effective fishes. There was no free, and consequently no discussing, press. For a short time two newspapers, the *Scots Chronicle* and the *Gazetteer*, raved stupidly and vulgarly, and as if their real object had been to cast discredit on the cause they professed to espouse. The only other newspapers, so far as I recollect, were the still surviving *Caledonian Mercury*, the *Courant*, and the *Advertiser*; * and the only other periodical publication was the doited *Scots Magazine*. This magazine and these three newspapers actually formed the whole regular produce of the Edinburgh periodical press. Nor was the absence of a free public press compensated by any

* See *The Periodical Press of Edinburgh*, by W. J. Couper, 2 vols.

freedom of public speech. Public *political* meetings could not arise, for the elements did not exist. I doubt if there was one during the twenty-five years that succeeded the year 1795. Nothing was viewed with such horror as any political congregation not friendly to existing power. No one could have taken a part in the business without making up his mind to be a doomed man. No prudence could protect against the falsehood or inaccuracy of spies; and a first convic_ tion of sedition by a judge-picked jury was followed by fourteen years' transportation. *As a body to be deferred to,* no *public* existed. Opinion was only recog- nised when expressed through what were acknow- ledged to be its legitimate organs; which meant its formal or official outlets. Public bodies therefore might speak each for itself; but the general commun- ity, as such, had no admitted claim to be consulted or cared for. The result, in a nation devoid of popular political rights, was, that people were dumb, or if they spoke out, were deemed audacious. The wishes of the people were not merely despised, but it was thought and openly announced, as a necessary precaution against revolution, that they should be thwarted. I knew a case, several years after 1800, where the seat- holders of a town church applied to Government, which was the patron, for the promotion of the second clergyman, who had been giving great satisfaction for many years, and now, on the death of the first minis- ter, it was wished that he should get the vacant place. The answer, written by a member of the Cabinet, was, that the single fact of the people having interfered so far

F

as to express a wish was conclusive against what they desired; and another appointment was instantly made.

This condition of the country was not owing to anything like tyranny on the part of its rulers. They did not create the circumstances in which they were obliged to act. Their error was that, instead of trying to mitigate these circumstances, they did what they could to aggravate them; and this for party purposes. There was no need for tyranny where the people had no public rights. But it would have been better, if the efforts of popular leaders to get them public rights had not been sternly repressed. However, in the circumstances, this party use of what existed is not much to be wondered at in party men. It was not owing to any positive despotism that there was no discussion by the press or by public meetings, but to the general abasement of the community, among which free habits could not at once arise. This community consisted of a people that was prostrate, a few brave but powerless individuals, and an overwhelming faction exercising the whole influence of the Government, on party principles, and without control.

This necessarily produced great personal bitterness. Even in private society, a Whig was viewed somewhat as a Papist was in the days of Titus Oates. There were a few exceptions, in the case of persons too attractive or too powerful to be ill used; but in general Whigs had to associate solely with Whigs. Very dear friendships were in many instances broken,* and although

* In 1801 Lord Jeffrey was a candidate for a vacant collectorship (reporter of decisions of the Court), and Lord Glenlee's intimacy with

the parties may have survived till age and changed times made longer severance absurd, the reconcilement was always awkward and never true. This incompatibility of public difference with private cordiality is the most painful recollection that I have of those days, and the most striking evidence of their hardness.

Fox's birthday was generally celebrated by a dinner every year. But only a very few of the best Whigs could be got to attend, or were wished for. It was not safe to have many; especially as great prudence was necessary in speaking and toasting. Yet even the select, though rarely exceeding a dozen or two, were seldom allowed to assemble without sheriff's officers being sent to take down the names of those who entered.* This turned away some, but others never hesitated to say what they thought of so base a hint. James Gibson and John Clerk used to tell them to hold up their lanterns, and to be quite sure that they knew them; and then would give the officers their

his father and himself led him to ask for that judge's influence to secure the appointment. "But his lordship took this occasion to tell him plainly that, in consequence of his politics, he could befriend him no more. They parted and scarcely exchanged words for nearly twenty-five years."—Lord Cockburn's *Life of Lord Jeffrey*.

* "Lord Daer gave a dinner in Hunter's Tavern, Writers Court, to about twenty of the leading Liberals, of whom Allen, Thomson and I were part. In the tavern were two rooms parallel, separated by a wooden partition. What passed in one room could easily be heard in the other. The party met in one room and adjourned to the other for dinner. After dinner one of the party, leaving, went into the next room to get his hat, and almost instantly returned, saying, 'Be on your guard in what you say; the Sheriff of the County and a celebrated Professor of Law (naming him) are in the next room without wine before them, listening to what is going on.' (Hume was the professor)."—Letter of Sir James Gibson-Craig quoted in *Edinburgh Review*, January 1857.

cards, with orders to be sure to deliver them with their compliments, and an invitation to their masters to attend next year.

Even the Whig lawyers who had secured their footing at the bar, or were plainly irrepressible, had hard enough work to keep their places. The juniors who dared to begin in this line were put under a severe proscription, and knew it. Every official gate was shut against them, and in the practice of their profession the judges were unkind, and agents therefore kept their fees for those of the safer faith. The prospects of no young man could be more apparently hopeless than of him who, with the known and fatal taint of a taste for popular politics, entered our bar. But they were generally well warned. If not overlooked for their significance, a *written test* was for some years presented to them, and a refusal to subscribe it set a black mark upon him who refused. I have heard George Cranstoun say that the test was put to him, and by a celebrated Professor of Law acting for the Tory party.* It was rejected; and Cranstoun found it convenient to leave the bar, and spend some time, chiefly in Ireland, as an officer in

* A writer in the *Edinburgh Review* for January 1857 quotes the following from further MSS. of Lord Cockburn, written in 1829: " Dining as usual at Craigcrook one Saturday this session, Cranstoun was contrasting these times with those when he came to the Bar ; and told us that a day or two after he put on his gown, a person, whom he only knew by sight and station, came to his lodgings and tendered him a written Tory test and a requisition to sign it on pain of such proscription as that party could inflict in the year 1793—a pretty serious threat. I had heard him say this before, but never till then heard him give the name. It was David Hume." Nephew of the Historian and Professor of Scots Law, afterwards Baron of Exchequer.

a regiment of fencible cavalry, commanded by his friend the Earl of Ancrum.

Henry Erskine, the brightest ornament of the profession, was Dean of the Faculty of Advocates. Considering the state of the times, the propriety of his presiding at a public meeting to petition against the war may be questioned.* The official head of a public body should consider what is due to the principles and the feelings of those he may be supposed to represent; and to the great majority of the Faculty Erskine's conduct must have been deeply offensive. Still, the resolution to dismiss him was utterly unjustifiable. It was nearly unprecedented, violent, and very ungrateful. He had covered the Faculty with the lustre of his character for several years; and, if wrong, had been misled solely by a sense of duty.† Nevertheless, on the 12th of January 1796 he was turned out of office. Had he and the Faculty alone been concerned in this intemperate proceeding it would not have occurred. But it was meant, and was taken, as a warning to all others to avoid the dangers of public meet-

---

* "At that meeting Mr Erskine, who, it would appear, was not the chairman, was called upon to move the resolutions, nine in number." —Fergusson's *Henry Erskine and his Kinsfolk.* "James Mansfield of Midmar, Esq., banker in Edinburgh, was called to the chair, which, however, he left for the moment, that the Hon. Henry Erskine, who was called to it, might move a vote of thanks to the chairman."— *Caledonian Mercury.*

† Replying to the letter stating the reasons for raising opposition to his re-election as Dean of Faculty, Henry Erskine wrote: "In my opinion the highest honour that can be enjoyed by a virtuous mind is the reflection of having allowed no personal consideration to stand between it and the firm, manly and independent performance of public duty."—Fergusson's *Henry Erskine and his Kinsfolk.*

ings on the wrong side. The efforts made to prevent young men from yielding to their conviction in Erskine's favour is another striking mark of the times. Jeffrey, Cranstoun, and Thomas Thomson were ardent to vote for him, and never were easy in their minds for not having done so. But Thomson was obliged to yield to the wishes of George Ferguson, afterwards Lord Hermand; Jeffrey to those of his father and Lord Glenlee; and Cranstoun to those of the Duke of Buccleuch; and none of them voted at all.* The forbearance of these young men was in accordance with the gentleness and propriety of their whole future lives. But what a condition men's minds must have been in when good men, who had selected them for patronage because they loved them, were not ashamed to exact such sacrifices.†

Almost everything in the city was under the control of the town-council; not merely what was properly magisterial, but most things conducive to the public economy, which are always managed now by independent guardians. Our light, water, education, paving, trade, including the port of Leith, the

* The conduct of Robert Ferguson, afterwards of Raith, and of George Joseph Bell, both eminent at last in the Whig party, has often been misunderstood. But the truth is, that the Whiggism of Bell, who voted against Erskine, had not then come upon him ; and that Ferguson, who gave no vote, was abroad.—H. C.

† Only one of Erskine's personal and political associates deserted his principles and opposed him—a man of great worth and learning, and who afterwards rose deservedly high, but whose respectable future life never effaced this sad stain from the memory of either friends or foes. When his name was called and he gave his vote, the clock happened to strike three ; on which John Clerk said, with great intensity, " When the cock crew thrice Peter denied his master."—H. C.

poor, the police, were all in the hands of the great civic corporation. Hence in Edinburgh, as in all other royal burghs, the character of the municipal magistracy was symptomatic of the whole place.

It met in a low, dark, blackguard-looking room, entering from a covered passage which connected the north-west corner of the Parliament Square with the Lawnmarket. At its Lawnmarket end this covered passage opened out on the south side of " The Heart of Midlothian." If that passage existed now, it would cross the present opening somewhere between the south-west corner of St Giles' Cathedral and the north-east corner of the Writers' [Signet] Library. The shop of George Heriot was said to have stood within it; and I certainly remember seeing, after 1805,* a horizontal stone lintel over a door there, with the words " *George Heriot* " carved upon it. But it was removed; and unless some antiquary saved it by a judicious theft, it was probably broken when the whole collection of interesting relics that encumbered the spot was cleared away. The Council Chamber entered directly from this passage, and, if it had remained, would have been in the east end of the Writers' Library. The chamber was a low-roofed room, very dark, and very dirty, with some small dens off it for clerks.

Within this Pandemonium sat the town-council, omnipotent, corrupt, impenetrable. Nothing was beyond its grasp; no variety of opinion disturbed its

* George Heriot's workshop existed till 1809. The forge and bellows with which he operated were found when the building was taken down.

unanimity, for the pleasure of Dundas was the sole rule for every one of them. Reporters, the fruit of free discussion, did not exist; and though they had existed, would not have dared to disclose the proceedings. Silent, powerful, submissive, mysterious, and irresponsible, they might have been sitting in Venice. Certain of the support of the Proconsul, whom they no more thought of thwarting than of thwarting Providence, timidity was not one of their vices. About the year 1799 a solitary schism amazed the public, by d sclosing the incredible fact that the town-council might contain a member who had an opinion of his own. A councillor, named Smith, electrified the city by a pamphlet showing that the burgh was bankrupt.* Time has put it beyond all doubt that he was right; and fortunate would it have been for the city and its creditors if this had been acknowledged at the time, instead of being aggravated by years of subsequent extravagance and concealment. But his rebellion drove Mr Smith out of the place.

The council's two great organs were John Gray and James Laing. Gray was city clerk; a judicious man,

* Bailie Smith's address called forth the usual crop of pamphlets—the favourite method in those days of bringing forward one's views on public matters. One of these takes the form of a satirical poem addressed to the Bailie, in which occurs the verse :

> " What business has the vulgar rabble
> To ken what's done on Council table?
> Or whether they keep books ava?
> Or books be free frae stain or flaw?
> What signify the debts increasing?
> It's no on individuals pressing.
> The wheels are ay kept tight and greasy
> An' Councillors ride fast and easy."

with a belly, white hair, and decorous black clothes; famous for drinking punch, holding his tongue, and doing jobs quietly; a respectable and useful officer, with an exclusive devotion to the town-council, but with such municipal wisdom, and such an intimate acquaintance with their affairs, that he was oftener the master than the slave. There was a person of this class in almost every royal burgh. If Gray was the head of the Council, Laing was its hand. He was one of the clerks, and managed such police as we then had, and, though not an officer in the old Town Guard, could, as representing the magistrates, employ it as he chose. It is incredible now how much power this man had, and how much he was feared. His masters, to whom he was all apparent obeisance, felt that they could not do without his activity and experience. He knew this, and adventured accordingly; and the result was, that with sagacity enough to keep clear of offensive excess towards them, he did almost anything else that he chose. He had more sense than to meddle with the rich, but over the people he tyrannised to his heart's content. For example—about the year 1795, six or eight baker lads of good character, and respectable though humble parentage, being a little jolly one night, were making a noise on the street. This displeased Mr Laing, who had a notion that nobody could be drunk with safety to the public except himself. So he had the lads apprehended; and as they did not appear in the morning, their friends became alarmed, and applied to Mr (afterwards Sir Henry) Jardine, a zealous partizan of Government, who took

an interest in the family of one of them. Mr Jardine
told me that next morning he inquired about them,
when Laing told him that he need give himself no
trouble, because " *they are all beyond Inchkeith by this
time.*" And so they were. He had sent them on board
a tender lying in Leith Roads, which he knew was to
sail that morning. This was done by his own authority,
without a conviction, or a charge, or an offence. They
had been troublesome, and this was the very way of
dealing with such people. Such proceedings were far
from uncommon, especially during the war, when the
navy and the army were the convenient receptacles of
all it was comfortable to get quit of summarily. Legal
redress was very seldom resorted to. Laing had an
incomprehensible reverence for Dugald Stewart.
Stewart used to tell, how he was walking in the
Meadows very early one morning, when he saw a
number of people within the enclosure seemingly
turning up the turf, and that upon going up to them
he found his friend Jamie Laing, who explained that
in these short light nights there was nothing going on
with the blackguards, " and so, ye see, Mr Professor,
I ve just brought oot the constables to try oor hands
at the moudieworts."

Though I had little personal knowledge of any other
town-council, there is no reason to believe that, in
general, they were a whit better than that of Edinburgh. On the contrary, as Edinburgh was under the
eye and the influence of higher men, the probability is
that they were worse; and many of the small ones
were in the lowest possible condition both of public

and private morality. In general, they were sinks of political and municipal iniquity, steeped in the baseness which they propagated, and types and causes of the corruption that surrounded them.

But by far the most frightful, and the justest, idea of the spirit of those times is to be found in the proceedings of the Supreme Criminal Court in the Sedition Trials of 1793 and 1794. These cannot be seen in detail without a minute examination of the reports, and indeed they are very faintly given even in the State Trials.

They were political prosecutions, during a period of great political excitement; and therefore, however faction might have raged, everything done by the Court ought to have been done calmly, impartially, and decorously. The general prevalence of public intemperance was the very circumstance that ought to have impressed more deeply upon judges the duty of steady candour, and of that judicial humanity which instinctively makes every right-minded occupier of the judgment seat interpose between a prisoner and prejudice. The Court does not seem to have been unduly inflamed by the official accuser.* The madness of the people, if it existed, would have been best allayed by giving them reason to rely on the administration of justice. But I fear that no impartial censor can avoid detecting, throughout the whole course of the trials, not mere casual indications of bias, but absolute straining for convictions. With all

* Robert Dundas, son of the second Lord President Dundas, and nephew of Lord Melville.

their prepossessions the judges were not cruel, nor even consciously unfair. But being terrified, and trying those who were causing their alarm, they could scarcely be expected to enter the temple of justice in a state of perfect composure.* If ever there was an occasion when a judge might have shone, simply by being just, this was one. But the bench was the place upon which political passions, not aggravated by the prosecutor, and distressing to many of the jurymen, settled and operated. Little depended upon erroneous decision. But what shall be held to be sedition always resolves, to a far greater extent than in other crimes, into mere opinion, and therefore everything depended upon candour of construction. Hence, all the sources of prejudice ought to have been at least attempted to be excluded.† Fair play ought to have been given to claims of constitutional right, and particularly to supposed privileges of public discussion. No juryman ought to have been able to excuse any party spirit that he felt coming over him by the contagion of the bench. Yet the fact is, that in every case sentiments

---

* "At the trial of Gerald, objection was made to Lord Braxfield remaining on the Bench, because he had, the previous evening, while dining with Rocheid of Inverleith, one of the jurymen trying the case, expressed views indicating that in his mind the question of the prisoner's guilt was already settled. The objection was repelled by the other judges."—Mackenzie's *Life of Muir.*

† "In the early part of 1793 the Lord Provost in his civic capacity attended the court and "delivered an address to the judges on the excellence of the constitution and the wickedness of those who found any fault or blemish in it ; this was answered by a long homily from the Lord President, in which the wickedness of innovation and the dangers of sedition were duly urged for the benefit of the lieges."—Craik's *Century of Scottish History.*

were avowed implying the adoption of the worst current intemperance. If, instead of a Supreme Court of Justice, sitting for the trial of guilt or of innocence, it had been an ancient commission appointed by the Crown to procure convictions, little of its judicial manner would have required to be changed.

When the verdicts were returned, the Court had to exercise a discretionary power in fixing upon the sentence; which discretion ranged, as these judges decided, from one hour's imprisonment to transportation for life. Assuming transportation to be lawful, it was conceded not to be necessary, and it was not then, nor at any time, used in England as a punishment of sedition. At that period it implied a frightful voyage of many months, great wretchedness in the new colony, an almost complete extinction of all communication with home, and such difficulty in returning, that a man transported was considered as a man never to be seen again. Nevertheless, transportation for a first offence was the doom of every one of these prisoners.

All this was approved of no doubt, not only by the Tories, but by Parliament advised by the Lord Chancellor. But this never satisfied judicious men, and it can neither silence nor pervert history. It will remain true that, in order to find a match for the judicial spirit of this Court, at this period, we must go back to the days of Lauderdale and Dalzell.

It has been said, in defence of the Court, that the times were dangerous. So they were. But these are the very times in which the torch of justice should burn most purely. It has also been said that the prisoners were all guilty. Holding this to be true, had they not a right to be fairly tried? And lastly, it has been said, that after these trials there was no more sedition. The same thing might be said though they had been tried by the boot, and punished by fire. Jeffreys and Kirke put down sedition, for the day, by their bloody assizes. But our exhibitions of judicial vigour, instead of eradicating the seditious propensity, prolonged its inward vitality. Future outbreaks were only avoided by the course of events, which turned men's passions into other channels.

These trials, however, sunk deep not merely into the popular mind, but into the minds of all men who thought. It was by these proceedings, more than by any other wrong, that the spirit of discontent justified itself throughout the rest of that age. It was to them that peaceful reformers appealed for the practical answer to those who pretended to uphold our whole Scotch system as needing no change. One useful lesson to be sure, they taught, though in the wrong way—namely, that the existence of circumstances, such as the supposed clearness and greatness of their guilt, tending to prejudice prisoners on their trials, gives them a stronger claim than usual on that sacred judicial mildness, which, far more than any of the law's terrors, procures respect for authority, and without which courts, let them punish as they may, only alienate and provoke.

Such was the public condition of Edinburgh in 1800, and for the preceding ten years. It was a condition of great pain and debasement, the natural consequence of bad times operating on defective political institutions. The frightful thing was the personal bitterness. The decent appearance of mutual toleration, which often produces the virtue itself, was despised, and extermination seemed a duty. This was bad enough in the capital; but far more dreadful in small places, which were more helplessly exposed to persecution. If Dugald Stewart was for several years not cordially received in the city he adorned, what must have been the position of an ordinary man who held liberal opinions in the country or in a small town, open to all the contumely and obstruction that local insolence could practise, and unsupported probably by any associate cherishing kindred thoughts. Such persons existed everywhere; but they were always below the salt. Their merit therefore was great. Under insult and cold unkindness, and constant personal loss, they adhered throughout many dark years to what they thought right; and such of them as lived to be old men had the reward of seeing the regeneration, which had depended so much on their spirit and firmness.

This was the first time that Scotland had ever been agitated by discussions upon general principles of liberty. Neither the Union, nor the two Rebellions, nor even the Revolution, had any of this matter in them. The course of this our first conflict of constitutional opinions has been very distinctly marked. With no improvement in their public education, habits, or institutions, with all power in the hands of those with whom change was in itself an ultimate evil, and with reason superseded by dread of revolution, the cause of the people was put down, and could not possibly have been then raised up. The only hope was in the decline of the circumstances that had sunk it. What had to be waited for was, the increase of numbers and of wealth, the waning of the revolutionary horror, the dying out of the hard old aristocracy, the advance of a new generation, and the rise of new guides. The gradual introduction and operation of these redeeming circumstances has been very interesting, and illustrates, by the example of a single place, the general principles which regulate the improvement of the world.

In 1800 the people of Edinburgh were much occupied about the removal of an evil in the system of their Infirmary; which evil, though strenuously defended by able men, it is difficult now to believe could ever have existed. The medical officers consisted at that time of the whole members of the Colleges of Physicians and of Surgeons, who attended the hospital by a monthly rotation; so that the patients had the chance of an opposite treatment, according to the whim of the doctor, every thirty days. Dr James Gregory, whose learning extended beyond that of his profession, attacked this absurdity in one of his powerful, but wild and personal, quarto pamphlets. The public was entirely on his side; and so at last were the managers, who resolved that the medical officers should be appointed permanently, as they have ever since been. Most of the medical profession, including the whole private lecturers, and even the two colleges, who all held that the power of annoying the patients in their turn was their right, were vehement against this innovation; and some of them went to law in opposition to it.

Gregory, descended from an illustrious line, was a curious and excellent man, a great physician, a great lecturer, a great Latin scholar, and a great talker; vigorous and generous; large of stature, and with a strikingly powerful countenance. The popularity due to these qualities was increased by his professional controversies, and the diverting publications by which he used to maintain and enliven them. The controversies were rather too numerous; but they never were for any selfish end, and he was never entirely wrong. Still, a disposition towards personal attack was his besetting sin.

Mr John Bell, the best surgeon that Scotland had then produced, a little vigorous creature, who wrote well and with intense professional passion, was generally put forward by his brethren to carry on the Gregorian battles. Perhaps he had the best both of the argument and of the clever writing; but the public sided with the best laugher; and so Gregory was generally held to have the victory.

When I first knew it, the Parliament House, both outside and in, was a curious and interesting place. No one who remembers the old exterior can see the new one without sorrow and indignation. The picture

G

which recalls the old edifice most distinctly to my mind, is the one in Arnot's *History of Edinburgh*. The Parliament Square (as foppery now calls it, but which used, and ought, to be called the Parliament *Close*) was then, as now, enclosed on the north by St Giles Cathedral, on the west by the Outer House, and on the south, partly by courts and partly by shops, above which were very tall houses, and on the east by a line of shops and houses of the same grand height. So that the courts formed the south-west angle of the Close. The old building exhibited some respectable turrets, some ornamental windows and doors, and a handsome balustrade. But the charm that ought to have saved it, was its colour and its age, which, however, were the very things that caused its destruction. About 170 years had breathed over it a grave grey hue. The whole aspect was venerable and appropriate; becoming the air and character of a sanctuary of Justice. But a mason pronounced it to be all " *Dead Wall*." The officials to whom, at a period when there was no public taste in Edinburgh, this was addressed, believed him; and the two fronts were removed in order to make way for the bright freestone and contemptible decorations that now disgrace us. The model having been laid down, has been copied on all subsequent occasions; till at last the old Parliament Close would not be known by the lawyers or senators who walked through it in the days of the Stuarts, or of the first two of the Guelphs. I cannot doubt that King Charles tried to spur his horse against the Vandals when he saw the profanation begin. But there was such an utter absence of public spirit in Edinburgh then, that the building might have been painted scarlet without anybody objecting.

The auctioneers and pawnbrokers had their quarters in the Horse Wynd, where I remember genteel families living in most excellent houses.* The potters and candlemakers congregated in the Rows which still bear their names. I don't know the former seat of the shoemakers, but about the beginning of the century they took possession of the new made Leith Terrace, which was then thought a very fine thing, as well it might, being the only place in Edinburgh, or perhaps in Scotland, with a street above the roofs of houses. The sons of Crispin occupied both the shops below this street and those in it—two rows of shops. As soon as the South Bridge was built it was taken possession of by the haberdashers. The Parliament Close was the haunt of the jewellers, some watchmakers, and a few booksellers, which last, however, flowed more over into the High Street. A wooden partition, about fifteen feet high, was drawn across the Outer House, cutting off apparently about twenty-five or thirty feet of its northern end, but with a small central opening into the public hall. Arnot says that this space was occupied by booksellers' stalls when he published his book in 1788.† These stalls must have disappeared, or been greatly diminished, very soon after this; for I was there for

* It was one of the very few wynds that were wide enough to let a horse through them ; when it got unfashionable the fops used to call it " *Cavalry Lane.*"—H. C.

† The first edition was published in 1779.

the first time about 1792 or 1793, and observed none of them. The whole space seemed to be occupied as a jeweller's and cutler's shop. My first pair of skates was bought there; and I remember my surprise at the figures with black gowns and white wigs walking about among the cutlery.

But the delightful place was *The Krames*. It was a low narrow arcade of booths, crammed in between the north side of St Giles Cathedral and a thin range of buildings that stood parallel to the Cathedral, the eastmost of which buildings, looking down the High Street, was the famous shop of William Creech the bookseller. Shopless traffickers first began to nestle there about the year 1550 or 1560, and their successors stuck to the spot till 1817, when they were all swept away. In my boyhood their little stands, each enclosed in a tiny room of its own, and during the day all open to the little footpath that ran between the two rows of them, and all glittering with attractions, contained everything fascinating to childhood, but chiefly toys. It was like one of the Arabian Nights' bazaars in Bagdad. Throughout the whole year it was an enchantment. Let any one fancy what it was about the New Year, when every child had got its handsel, and every farthing of every handsel was spent there. The Krames was the paradise of childhood.*

Scarcely a year passed since the time I am referring to without some change in the internal arrangement of the Outer House. Doors, chimneys, screens,

* The word "*Kraimery*" occurs in some ancient deeds to denote the articles sold in the Krames.—H. C.

windows, benches, and Lords Ordinary's bars, have wandered round and round the whole hall, exactly as has suited the taste of the official improver of the day. After much temporary deformity, and many alarming escapes, the result on the whole has been good, because the recent taste has been to remove obstructions, and to introduce art.

The modern accommodation for the courts is so ample that it is curious to recollect its amount, and how it looked before 1808,* when the judges began to sit in two separate chambers. The den called *The Inner House* then held the whole fifteen judges. It was a low square like room, not, I think, above from thirty to forty feet wide. It stood just off the southeast corner of the Outer House; with the Exchequer, entering from the Parliament Close, right above. The Barons being next the sky, had access to the flat leaden roof, where I have seen my father, who was one of them, walking in his robes. The Inner House was so cased in venerable dirt that it was impossible to say whether it had ever been painted; but it was all of a dark brownish hue. There was a gallery over the bar, and so low that a barrister in a frenzy was in danger of hitting it. A huge fire-place stood behind the Lord President's chair, with one of the stone jambs cracked, and several of the bars of the large grate broken. That grate was always at least half full of dust. It probably had never been completely cleared since the institu-

* Exactly one hundred years later changes have been made on the courts, and, to quote Lord Cockburn's words, "the modern accommodation" is now "so ample that it is curious to recollect" how they looked before 1908.

tion of the Court in the sixteenth century. The hearth-stone, the fender, and the chimney-piece were all massive, and all undisturbed by any purification. On the one side of that fireplace there was fixed in a wooden frame the Lord's Prayer, and on the other side the Ten Commandments; each worked in faded gold thread letters into a black velvet ground. George Cranstoun used to propose adding a Scriptural verse to be set over the head of each judge, and had culled the texts.

Dismal though this hole was, the old fellows who had been bred there never looked so well anywhere else; and deeply did they growl at the spirit of innovation which drove them from their accustomed haunt. The cave indeed had an antique air. It was Durie's Reports. Very little fancy was necessary to make one see the ancient legal sages hirpling through its dim litigious light.

Of the fifteen judges of those days, some of course were " heads without names." Of the others, Monboddo, Swinton, and Braxfield had left the scene shortly before I entered the Faculty.

Classical learning, good conversation, excellent suppers, and ingenious though unsound metaphysics were the peculiarities of Monboddo. He was reputed a considerable lawyer in his own time; and his reports show that the reputation was well founded. Some offence had made him resolve never to sit on the same bench with President Dundas; and he kept this vow so steadily that he always sat at the clerk's table even after Dundas was gone. I never saw him sitting anywhere else. This position enabled him to get easily out and in; and whenever there was a pause he was sure to slip off, gown and all, to have a talk in the Outer House, where I have often seen the shrivelled old man walking about very cheerfully. He went very often to London, almost always on horseback, and was better qualified than most of his countrymen to shine in its literary society. But he was insufficiently appreciated; and he partly justified and indeed provoked this, by taking his love of paradox and metaphysics with him, and dealing them out in a style of academical formality; and this even after he ought to have seen, that all that people cared about his dogmas was to laugh at their author. It is more common to hear anecdotes about his maintaining that men once had tails,* and similar follies, than about his agreeable conversation and undoubted learning. All who knew him in Edinburgh concur in describing his house as one of the most pleasant in the place.

I knew Lord Swinton as much as a youth can know an old man, and I have always been intimate with his family. He was a very excellent person; dull, mild, solid, and plodding; and in his person large and heavy. It is only a subsequent age that has discovered his having possessed a degree of sagacity, for which he

* Dr Johnson said of him, "Most men endeavour to hide their tails, but Lord Monboddo is as vain of his as a squirrel." And Dean Ramsay tells a story of Lord Kames yielding precedence to Lord Monboddo with the remark, "You must walk first that I may *see your tail.*"

did not get credit while he lived. So far back as 1765 he published an attack on our system of entails; in 1779 he explained a scheme for a uniform standard of weights and measures; and in 1789 he put forth considerations in favour of dividing the Court of Session into more courts than one, and of introducing juries for the trial of civil causes. All these improvements have since taken place, but they were mere visions in his time; and his anticipation of them, in which, so far as I ever heard, he had no associate, is very honourable to his thoughtfulness and judgment. Notwithstanding the utter dissimilarity of the two men, there was a great friendship between him and Henry Erskine, which it is to the honour of Swinton's ponderous placidity that Erskine's endless jokes upon him never disturbed.*

But the giant of the bench was Braxfield. His very name makes people start yet.

Strong built and dark, with rough eyebrows, powerful eyes, threatening lips, and a low growling voice, he was like a formidable blacksmith. His accent and his dialect were exaggerated Scotch; his language, like his thoughts, short, strong, and conclusive.

Our commercial jurisprudence was only rising when he was sinking, and, being no reader, he was too old both in life and habit to master it familiarly; though

---

* When Cranstoun temporarily left the bar he consulted Lord Swinton about joining the Austrian Army, where it was said officers were liable to be flogged. His lordship, who had a sound horror of a Jacobin, replied, "'Deed, Mr George, ye wad be muckle the better o' being whuppit."

even here he was inferior to no Scotch lawyer of his time except Ilay Campbell, the Lord President. But within the range of the feudal and the civil branches, and in every matter depending on natural ability and practical sense, he was very great; and his power arose more from the force of his reasoning and his vigorous application of principle than from either the extent or the accuracy of his learning. I have heard good observers describe with admiration how, having worked out a principle, he followed it in its application, fearlessly and triumphantly, dashing all unworthy obstructions aside, and pushed on to his result with the vigour and disdain of a consummate athlete. And he had a colloquial way of arguing, in the form of question and answer, which, done in his clear abrupt style, imparted a dramatic directness and vivacity to the scene.

With this intellectual force, as applied to law, his merits, I fear, cease. Illiterate and without any taste for refined enjoyment, strength of understanding, which gave him power without cultivation, only encouraged him to a more contemptuous disdain of all natures less coarse than his own. Despising the growing improvement of manners, he shocked the feelings even of an age, which, with more of the formality, had far less of the substance of decorum than our own. Thousands of his sayings have been preserved, and the staple of them is indecency; which he succeeded in making many people enjoy, or at least endure, by hearty laughter, energy of manner, and rough humour. Almost the only story of him I ever heard

that had some fun in it without immodesty, was when
a butler gave up his place because his lordship's wife
was always scolding him. " Lord! " he exclaimed,
" ye've little to complain o': ye may be thankfu' ye're
no married to her."

It is impossible to condemn his conduct as a criminal judge too gravely, or too severely. It was a disgrace to the age. A dexterous and practical trier of
ordinary cases, he was harsh to prisoners even in his
jocularity, and to every counsel whom he chose to dislike. I have heard this attempted to be accounted for
and extenuated by the tendency which the old
practice of taking all the evidence down in writing, by
judicial dictation, had to provoke a wrangle between
the court and the bar every moment, and thus to excite mutual impatience and hostility. No doubt there
was something in this; but not much. And Braxfield,
as might have been expected from his love of domineering, continued the vice after its external cause,
whatever it may have been, had ceased. It may be
doubted if he was ever so much in his element as when
tauntingly repelling the last despairing claim of a
wretched culprit, and sending him to Botany Bay or
the gallows with an insulting jest; over which he
would chuckle the more from observing that correct
people were shocked.* Yet this was not from cruelty,
for which he was too strong and too jovial, but from
cherished coarseness.

This union of talent with a passion for rude pre-

* " As Lord Braxfield once said to an eloquent culprit at the bar—
' Ye're a vera clever chiel, man, but ye wad be nane the waur o' a
hanging.' "—Lockhart's *Life of Scott*, chap. 48.—H. C.

domination, exercised in a very discretionary court, tended to form a formidable and dangerous judicial character.* This appeared too often in ordinary cases; but all stains on his administration of the common business of his court disappear in the indelible iniquity of the political trials of 1793 and 1794. In these he was the Jeffreys of Scotland. He, as the head of the Court, and the only very powerful man it contained, was the real director of its proceedings. The reports make his abuse of the judgment seat bad enough; but his misconduct was not so fully disclosed in formal decisions and charges, as it transpired in casual remarks and general manner. " Let them bring me prisoners, and I'll find them law," used to be openly stated as his suggestion, when an intended political prosecution was marred by anticipated difficulties. If innocent of this atrocious sentiment, he was scandalously ill-used by his friends, by whom I repeatedly heard it ascribed to him at the time, and who, instead of denying it, spoke of it as a thing understood, and rather admired it as worthy of the man and of the times. Mr Horner (the father of Francis), who was one of the jurors in Muir's case, told me that when he was passing, as was often done then, behind the bench to get into the box, Braxfield, who knew him, whispered —" Come awa, Maister Horner, come awa, and help us to hang† ane o' thae daamned scoondrels." The re-

* One of his brother judges having advanced rather novel doctrines on a question under discussion, Lord Braxfield asked where he had got that law. "From Lord Stair," replied the judge. "No, no," said Braxfield, "that canna be, for there is nae nonsense to be found in Lord Stair."

† *Hang* was his phrase for all kinds of punishment.—H. C.

porter of Gerald's case could not venture to make the prisoner say more than that " Christianity was an innovation." [*State Trials*, vol. xxiii. p. 972.] But the full truth is, that in stating this view he added that all great men had been reformers, " even our Saviour himself." " Muckle he made o' that," chuckled Braxfield in an under voice, " he was hanget." Before Hume's *Commentaries* had made our criminal record intelligible, the forms and precedents were a mystery understood by the initiated alone, and by nobody so much as by Mr Joseph Norris, the ancient clerk. Braxfield used to quash anticipated doubts by saying, " Hoot! just gie me Josie Norrie and a gude jury and I'll do for the fallow." He died in 1799, in his seventy-eighth year.*

Of the older judges still on the bench in 1800, but who soon left it, there were two who ought not to be allowed to perish. These were the Lord Justice-Clerk Rae and the Lord President Campbell.

David Rae, Lord Eskgrove, succeeded Braxfield as

---

* When Lord Kames, an indefatigable and speculative but coarse man, tried Matthew Hay, with whom he used to play at chess, for murder at Ayr in September 1780, he exclaimed, when the verdict of guilty was returned, "That's checkmate to you, Matthew!" Besides general and uncontradicted notoriety, I had this fact from Lord Hermand, who was one of the counsel at the trial, and never forgot a piece of judicial cruelty which excited his horror and anger.

Scott is said to have told this story to the Prince Regent. If he did so, he would certainly tell it accurately, because he knew the facts quite well. But in reporting what Sir Walter had said at the royal table, the Lord Chief Commissioner Adam confused the matter and called the judge Braxfield, the crime forgery, and the circuit town Dumfries; and this inaccurate account was given by Mr Lockhart in his first edition of *Scott's Life* (chap. 34). Braxfield was one of the judges at Hay's trial, but he had nothing to do with the checkmate.—H. C.

head of the Criminal Court; and it is his highest
honour that he is sometimes mentioned as Braxfield's
judicial rival. In so far as law and political partiality
went they were pretty well matched; but in all other
respects they were quite different men.

Eskgrove was a very considerable lawyer; in
mere knowledge probably Braxfield's superior. But
he had nothing of Braxfield's grasp or reasoning,
and in everything requiring force or soundness of
head, he was a mere child compared with that practical Hercules. Still he was cunning in old Scotch
law.

But a more ludicrous personage could not exist.
When I first knew him he was in the zenith of his
absurdity. People seemed to have nothing to do but
to tell stories of this one man. To be able to give an
anecdote of Eskgrove, with a proper imitation of his
voice and manner, was a sort of fortune in society.
Scott in those days was famous for this particularly.
Whenever a knot of persons were seen listening in the
Outer House to one who was talking slowly, with a
low muttering voice and a projected chin, and then
the listeners burst asunder in roars of laughter, nobody thought of asking what the joke was. They were
sure it was a successful imitation of Esky; and this
was enough. Yet never once did he do or say anything
which had the slightest claim to be remembered for
any intrinsic merit. The value of all his words and
actions consisted in their absurdity.

He seemed, in his old age, to be about the average
height; but as he then stooped a good deal, he might

have been taller in reality. His face varied, according
to circumstances, from a scurfy red to a scurfy blue;
the nose was prodigious; the under lip enormous, and
supported on a huge clumsy chin, which moved like
the jaw of an exaggerated Dutch toy. He walked with
a slow stealthy step—something between a walk and
a hirple, and helped himself on by short movements
of his elbows, backwards and forwards, like fins. The
voice was low and mumbling, and on the bench was
generally inaudible for some time after the movement
of the lips showed that he had begun speaking; after
which the first word that was let fairly out was generally the loudest of the whole discourse. It is unfortunate that, without an idea of his voice and manner,
mere narrative cannot describe his sayings and doings
graphically.

One of his remarks on the trial of Mr Fysche Palmer
for sedition—not as given in the report of the trial,
but as he made it—is one of the very few things he
ever said that had some little merit of its own. Mr
John Haggart, one of the prisoner's counsel, in defending his client from the charge of disrespect of the
king, quoted Burke's statement that kings are naturally lovers of low company. " Then, sir, that says very
little for you or your client! for if kinggs be lovers of
low company, low company ought to be lovers of
kinggs! "*

* Whenever a name could be pronounced in more ways than one,
he gave them all; and always put an accent on the last syllable. For
example, syllable he called syllabill. And when a word ended with the
letter G, this letter was pronounced, and strongly. And he was very
fond of meaningless successions of adjectives. A good man would be

Nothing disturbed him so much as the expense of the public dinner for which the judge on the circuit has a fixed allowance, and out of which the less he spends the more he gains. His devices for economy were often very diverting. His servant had strict orders to check the bottles of wine by laying aside the corks. His lordship once went behind a screen at Stirling, while the company was still at table, and seeing an alarming row of corks, got into a warm altercation, which everybody overheard, with John; maintaining it to be " impossibill " that they could have drunk so much. On being assured that they had, and were still going on—" Well, then, John, I must just protect myself! " On which he put a handful of the corks into his pocket and resumed his seat.

Brougham tormented him, and sat on his skirts wherever he went, for above a year. The Justice liked passive counsel who let him dawdle on with culprits and juries in his own way; and consequently he hated the talent, the eloquence, the energy, and all the discomposing qualities of Brougham. At last it seemed as if a court day was to be blessed by his absence, and the poor Justice was delighting himself with the prospect of being allowed to deal with things as he chose; when, lo! his enemy appeared—tall, cool, and resolute. " I declare," said the Justice, " that man Broom

described as one excellent, and worthy, and amiabill, and agreeabill, and very good man. The article A was generally made into *one*, and he generally cut a word of three syllables into two separate words, the first of two syllables and the last of one, and even divided a word of two syllables into two words. Thus, I met a young friend as I was walking in the Canongate, was converted by him into, " I met one youngg friend as I was walk-ing in the Canon-gate."—H. C.

or Broug-ham is the torment of my life!" His revenge, as usual, consisted in sneering at Brougham's eloquence by calling it or him *the Harangue*. " Well, gentle-men, what did the Harangue say next? Why, it said this " (misstating it) ; " but here, gentle-men, the Harangue was most plainly wrongg, and not intelligibill."

As usual, then, with stronger heads than his, everything was connected by his terror with republican horrors. I heard him, in condemning a tailor to death for murdering a soldier by stabbing him, aggravate the offence thus, " and not only did you murder him, whereby he was berea-ved of his life, but you did thrust, or push, or pierce, or project, or propell, the le-thall weapon through the belly-band of his regimen-tal breeches, which were his Majes-ty's! "

In the trial of Glengarry for murder in a duel, a lady of great beauty was called as a witness.* She came into Court veiled. But before administering the oath Eskgrove gave her this exposition of her duty— " Youngg woman! you will now consider yourself as in the presence of Almighty God, and of this High Court. Lift up your veil; throw off all modesty, and look me in the face."

Sir John Henderson of Fordell, a zealous Whig, had long nauseated the civil court by his burgh politics. Their Lordships had once to fix the amount of some discretionary penalty that he had incurred. Eskgrove began to give his opinion in a very low voice, but loud

* Miss Forbes of Culloden (Mrs Hugh Duff of Muirtown).

enough to be heard by those next him, to the effect
that the fine ought to be fifty pounds; when Sir John,
with his usual imprudence, interrupted him, and
begged him to raise his voice, adding that if judges did
not speak so as to be heard, they might as well not
speak at all. Eskgrove, who could never endure any
imputation of bodily infirmity, asked his neighbour,
" What does the fellow say? " " He says that, if you
don't speak out, you may as well hold your tongue."
" Oh, is that what he says? My Lords, what I was sayingg was very simpell. I was only sayingg that in my
humbell opinyon, this fine could not be less than two
hundred and fifty pounds, sterlingg "—this sum being
roared out as loudly as his old angry voice could
launch it.

His tediousness, both of manner and matter, in
charging juries was most dreadful. It was the custom
to make juries stand while the judge was addressing
them; but no other judge was punctilious about it.
Eskgrove, however, insisted upon it; and if any one of
them slipped cunningly down to his seat, or dropped
into it from inability to stand any longer, the unfortunate wight was sure to be reminded by his Lordship that " these were not the times in which there
should be any disrespect of this High Court, or even of
the law." Often have I gone back to the Court at mid-
night, and found him, whom I had left mumbling
hours before, still going on, with the smoky unsnuffed
tallow candles in greasy tin candlesticks, and the poor
despairing jurymen, most of the audience having retired or being asleep; the wagging of his lordship's

H

nose and chin being the chief signs that he was still *char-ging*.

A very common arrangement of his logic to juries was this—" And so, gentle-men, having shown you that the pannell's argument is utterly impossibill, I shall now proceed for to show you that it is extremely improbabill.'

He rarely failed to signalise himself in pronouncing sentences of death. It was almost a matter of style with him to console the prisoner by assuring him that, " whatever your religi-ous persua-shon may be, or even if, as I suppose, you be of no persua-shon at all, there are plenty of rever-end gentle-men who will be most happy for to show you the way to yeternal life."

He had to condemn two or three persons to die who had broken into a house at Luss, and assaulted Sir James Colquhoun and others, and robbed them of a large sum of money. He first, as was his almost constant practice, explained the nature of the various crimes, assault, robbery, and hamesucken—of which last he gave them the etymology; and he then reminded them that they attacked the house and the persons within it, and robbed them, and then came to this climax—" All this you did; and God preserve us! joost when they were sitten doon to their denner!"

But a whole volume could easily be filled with specimens of his absurdities. Scott, not by invention but by accurate narration, could have done it himself. So could Jeffrey; and William Clerk; and William Erskine; and indeed everybody who had eyes and ears. He was the staple of the public conversation;

and so long as his old age lasted (for of his youth I know nothing) he nearly drove Napoleon out of the Edinburgh world. He died in 1804, in his eightieth year; and had therefore been put at the head of the Court when he had reached the age of seventy-six: an incredible appointment; for his peculiarities had been in full flourish long before that. It would have been a pity if the public had lost them; but it was unfortunate that a judicial chair was necessary for their complete exhibition. A story of Eskgrove is still preferred to all other stories. Only, the things that he did and said every day are beginning to be incredible to this correct and flat age.

Besides great experience and great reputation in every legal sphere, Ilay Campbell, the Lord President, had had his mind enlarged by the office of Lord Advocate, which had introduced him to Parliament and to public administration. These opportunities were not lost upon his working and intelligent intellect. As a lawyer, and in every department of the science, he was inferior to none of his brethren in depth or learning, and was greatly superior to them all in a genuine and liberal taste for the law's improvement. Of all the old judges he was the only one whose mind was thoroughly opened to the comprehension of modern mercantile jurisprudence. Though grave and sound, ingenuity was perhaps his prevailing power. Fineness in a piece of reasoning had far greater attractions for him than plainness: the reality of a distinction was rather improved by its not being obvious. I forget whether it was Thurlow or Lough-borough who described this logical delicacy by saying, that if the question was, whether a wine was Sherry or Madeira, he would refer it to Wight; but that if it was whether the wine was one kind of either, or another kind, he would rely upon Campbell. This habit of active refinement is often unfavourable to correctness of judgment. But this tendency was avoided in him by the practical nature of the ends and of the means to which his life was devoted. His sagacity upon these matters was too strong to be misled by the subtlety which he reserved for the logic of professional argument.

His forensic writing, which was the form in which the argumentation of the bar was then mostly conducted, was admirable. And well was he practised in it; because during a considerable period of his career, he was believed to have furnished at least one *Session Paper* every day. They were models, as everything he wrote was, of clearness and brevity. His speaking, always admirable in matter, was the reverse of attractive. He could only be severely argumentative, and the painfulness of this was increased by the minuteness of his elaboration, and the dryness of his manner. His voice was low and dull, his face sedate and hard. Even when heaving internally with strong passion, externally he was like a knot of wood.

There was one part of his Presidential duty which he performed better than any one in that chair has ever done. He was accessible to every individual, and to every scheme, having the improvement of the law for their object; and not content with a formal and gracious tolerance of legal authors or reformers, he listened with the sincere patience of one who liked the subject, read every line of their manuscripts, discussed every point, and gave them the full aid of his station and experience. Bell's recorded acknowledgments of the assistance he derived from him, in the construction of his great work, are not merely complimentary, but express the simple fact. He did not go, and could not have gone, so far in legal reform as Parliament and the public have since done; and no wise man, whatever his opinions might have been, would have attempted to do so in his day. But he went far enough to evince great enlargement of mind, and a complete superiority to that adherence to established abuses which is most unjustly ascribed to all professional lawyers. I can sympathise with his lingering attachment to that judicial discretion, termed the *nobile officium*, of the Court, which though dangerous, and seldom mentioned now except with a sneer, was necessary long ago, and was frequently appealed to and exercised for several years after I came to the bar. His collection of the rarer Acts of Sederunt was made and published chiefly in order to defend this authority by showing how beneficially it had been administered. It is a power that can never be safe; but it was natural, and indeed indispensable, in old Scotland: where Prætorian equity was at least better than anything that was to be expected from subservient Parliaments or profligate Privy Councils.

The only shade ever attempted to be cast over Sir

Ilay's memory was by an insinuation that as Lord President he was tricky. That he was ambitious of having a prevailing influence over his brethren was true of him, as of every other Chief Justice. None of them ever like to be in a minority in their own court. But there was no ground for believing that he attempted to secure this honourable predominance by improper management. We must consider the circumstances of his situation. When a court consists, as the Court of Session then did, of a mob of fifteen judges, meeting without previous consultation, and each impatient for independent eminence, and many of them liable to be called away and to return irregularly in the course of the same day, the decorum of the tribunal often compels the head to exercise an indirect control, which is liable to be mistaken for manœuvring dexterity. The necessity for anything of the kind has been extinguished by reducing the Court to a small number of fixed judges. But so long as it might consist of fifteen, and might at every moment vary between fifteen and nine, President Campbell managed it exactly as all other Presidents had been obliged to do. Had there been more in his manner and general reputation to render this charge improbable, it would never have been made. Blair would have put it down by a look. But Campbell was known to have a turn for managing, and to hide beneath his calm steady appearance a deep and artful spirit. That he allowed it, however, to obstruct his Presidential correctness I do not believe.

His private life was useful and respectable. Beloved

by his family, and looked up to by a large circle of
friends, he passed his time in town mostly in his
library, and in the country on his farm; and wherever
he was, he was always a hospitable gentleman. Few
houses saw more or better company than his. He had
an excellent Presidential custom of giving substantial
and agreeable evening parties to the young men at the
bar. Many have I seen. Not stiff and vapid formalities,
nor impracticable mobs, but manageable meetings of
from ten to twenty, where he presided, in his single-
breasted coat and a wig, over solid food, and free talk,
and copious claret. But these were in the supper days.

Of the younger judges, who belonged to the generation with which I was now connected, the most
remarkable were Lord Glenlee,* Lord Hermand, Lord
Meadowbank, and Lord Cullen; all of whom I knew
personally.

I was so intimately connected, as a relation and
friend, with Lord Kilkerran's son George Fergusson,
Lord Hermand, that it may perhaps be supposed that
I cannot speak candidly about him. But he has often
been described in a way neither agreeable to truth,
nor respectable for himself. His celebrity arose entirely from his personal character. For although he
attained considerable practice at the bar, and was
a quick and vigorous judge, and took a keen part in
all the public measures of his time, he was not so important in these spheres as to have been a man of
mark in them, independently of his individual

* *See* Cockburn's *Life of Jeffrey.*

peculiarities. But these made him one of the most singular, and indeed incredible of our old originals. They often threw even Eskgrove into the shade during that person's life, and after he died, no Edinburgh man, by worth and singularity alone, belonged so much as Hermand did to the public.

His external appearance was as striking as everything else about him. Tall and thin, with grey lively eyes, and a long face, strongly expressive of whatever emotion he was under, his air and manner were distinctly those of a well-born and well-bred gentleman. His dress for society, the style of which he stuck to almost as firmly as he did to his principles, reminded us of the olden time, when trousers would have insulted any company, and braces were deemed an impeachment of nature. Neither the disclosure of the long neck by the narrow bit of muslin stock, nor the outbreak of the linen between the upper and nether garments, nor the short coat sleeves, with the consequent length of bare wrist, could hide his being one of the aristocracy. And if they had, the thin and powdered grey hair, flowing down into a long thin gentleman-like pig-tail, would have attested it. His morning raiment in the country was delightful. The articles, rough and strange, would of themselves have attracted notice in a museum. But set upon George Fergusson, at his paradise of Hermand, during vacation, on going forth for a long day's work—often manual—at his farm with his grey felt hat and tall weeding hoe—what could be more agrestic or picturesque.

Till about the age of thirty, when he began to get into practice, he was a pretty regular student; and he was always fond of reading, and being read to, but not methodically, nor in any particular line. He had thus gathered a respectable chaos of accidental knowledge. Of his various and very respectable mental powers, acuteness was perhaps the most striking. His affections were warm and steady; his honour of the highest and purest order.

But all this will not produce a curious man. What was it that made Hermand such an established wonder and delight? It seems to me to have been the supremacy in his composition of a single quality—intensity of temperament, which was so conspicuous that it prevented many people from perceiving anything else in him. He could not be indifferent. Repose, except in bed, where however he slept zealously, was unnatural and contemptible to him. It used to be said that if Hermand had made the heavens, he would have permitted no fixed stars. His constitutional animation never failed to carry him a flight beyond ordinary mortals. Was he in an argument, or at whist, or over his wine; in Court, or at an election, or a road meeting; consulting with a ploughman, or talking with a child; he was sure to blaze out in a style that nobody could have fancied, or could resist enjoying. Those who only saw the operation of this ardour in public conflict, were apt to set him down as a frenzied man, with rather a savage temper, an impression that was increased by what the Scotch call the *Birr*, which means the emphatic energy, of his pronunciation.

Beholding him in contention, they thought him a tiger.*

But to those who knew him personally, the lamb was a truer type. When removed from contests which provoke impatience, and placed in the private scene, where innocent excesses are only amusing, what a heart! what conversational wildness! made more delightful by the undoubting sincerity of the passing extravagance. There never was a more pleasing example of the superiority of right affections over intellectual endowments in the creation of happiness. Had he depended on his understanding alone, or chiefly, he would have been wrecked every week. But honesty, humanity, social habits, and diverting public explosions, always kept him popular; and he lived about eighty-four years, with keen and undisguised feelings and opinions, without ever being alienated from a friend, or imagining a shabby action, devoted to rural occupations, keeping up his reading, and maintaining his interest in the world by cultivating the young. Instead of sighing over the departure of former days, and grumbling at change, he zealously patronised every new project, not political; and at last mellowed away, amidst a revering household, without having ever known what a headache is, with no decay of his mental powers, and only a short and gentle physical feebleness.

* "Or Hermand, as fierce as a tiger offended,
    Is muttering his curses not loudly but deep."
From Richardson's parody of Scott's *Helvellyn*. Lord Cockburn explains, "Richardson did not know Lord Hermand when he wrote these lines ; they were great friends afterwards."

With very simple tastes, and rather a contempt of
epicurism, but very gregarious, he was fond of the
pleasures, and not the least of the liquid ones, of the
table; and he had acted in more of the severest scenes
of old Scotch drinking than any man at last living.
Commonplace topers think drinking a pleasure; but
with Hermand it was a virtue. It inspired the excitement by which he was elevated, and the discursive
jollity which he loved to promote. But beyond these
ordinary attractions, he had a sincere respect for
drinking, indeed a high moral approbation, and a
serious compassion for the poor wretches who could
not indulge in it; with due contempt of those who
could, but did not. He groaned over the gradual disappearance of the *Fereat* days of periodical festivity,
and prolonged the observance, like a hero fighting
amidst his fallen friends, as long as he could. The
worship of Bacchus, which softened his own heart,
and seemed to him to soften the hearts of his companions, was a secondary duty. But in its performance
there was no violence, no coarseness, no impropriety,
and no more noise than what belongs to well-bred
jollity unrestrained. It was merely a sublimation of
his peculiarities and excellences; the realisation of
what poetry ascribes to the grape. No carouse ever
injured his health, for he was never ill, or impaired his
taste for home and quiet, or muddled his head; he
slept the sounder for it, and rose the earlier and the
cooler. The cordiality inspired by claret and punch
was felt by him as so congenial to all right thinking,
that he was confident that he could convert the Pope

if he could only get him to sup with him. And certainly his Holiness would have been hard to persuade, if he could have withstood Hermand about the middle of his second tumbler.

The public opinions of this remarkable person were very decided and not illiberal; for he combined strong Tory principles with stronger Whig friendships, and a taste for Calvinism, under the creed of which he deemed himself extremely pious, with the indulgence of every social propensity.

Like many other counsel, not of the highest class, he owed his professional practice chiefly to the fervour of his zeal. His other qualities would have carried him a considerable way, but they would never have raised him to the height he reached and retained, without his honest conviction that his client was always right, and always ill-used. When it was known that he was to speak, the charm of the intensity which this belief produced never failed to fill the Court. His eagerness made him froth and sputter so much in his argumentation that there is a story to the effect, that when he was once pleading in the House of Lords, the Duke of Gloucester, who was about fifty feet from the bar, and always attended when " Mr George Fergusson, the Scotch counsel " was to speak, rose and said with pretended gravity, " I shall be much obliged to the learned gentleman if he will be so good as to refrain from spitting in my face." The same animation followed him to the bench, where he moderated no view from prudence, and flinched from no result, and never saw any difficulty. President Campbell once delivered one of his deep and nice opinions, full of qualifications and doubts. The instant he was done, Hermand sprang upon him by a judgment beginning —" My Lords,* thank God, I never doubted!"

He was very intimate at one time with Sir John Scott, afterwards Lord Eldon. They were counsel together in Eldon's first important Scotch entail case in the House of Lords. Eldon was so much alarmed that he wrote his intended speech, and begged Hermand to dine with him at a tavern, where he read the paper, and asked him if he thought it would do. " Do, Sir? It is delightful—absolutely delightful! I could listen to it for ever! It is so beautifully written! And so beautifully read! But, Sir, it's the greatest nonsense! It may do very well for an English Chancellor; but it would disgrace a clerk with us." He told me the blunder, and though gross for a Scotch lawyer, it was one that an English counsel would readily commit. Many a bottle of port did he and Eldon discuss together.

Bacon advises judges to draw their law " out of your books, not out of your brain." Hermand generally did neither. He was very apt to say " My Laards, I *feel* my law—*here*, my Laards," striking his heart. Hence he sometimes made little ceremony in disdaining the authority of an Act of Parliament, when he and it happened to differ. He once got rid of one which Lord Meadowbank (the first), whom he did not particularly like, was for enforcing because the Legisla-

* He pronounced this word as if it had been *Laards*—with a prolonged quiver of intensity, and many others in the same way.—H. C.

ture had made it law, by saying, in his snorting, contemptuous way, and with an emphasis on every syllable—" But then we're told that there's a statute against all this. A statute! What's a statute? Words. Mere words! And am *I* to be tied down by words? No, my Laards; I go by the law of *right reason*." Lord Holland noticed this in the House of Peers as a strange speech for a judge. Lord Gillies could not resist the pleasure of reading Holland's remark to Hermand, who was generally too impetuous to remember his own words. He entirely agreed with Lord Holland, and was indignant at the Court suffering " from the rashness of fools." " Well, my Lord, but who could Lord Holland be alluding to? " " Alluding to? who *can* it be but that creature Meadowbank? "

In giving his opinion on the validity of a qualification to vote for a member of Parliament, after it had been sustained both here and in the House of Lords, he declared that, nevertheless, it was not only bad, but so bad that " I defy Omnipotence to make it good." " Then," said the quiet philosophic Playfair, " it must be very bad indeed; for his Lordship assured me, in a conversation about Professor Leslie's case, that he had no difficulty at all in conceiving God to make a world where twice three was not six."

There was a case about a lease, where our Court thought itself entitled in equity to make a new contract for parties, different from the one which the parties had made for themselves. The Lord Chancellor (Eldon) was of opinion that a clear clause in a contract ought always to be enforced, and remitted the matter to the Court below for reconsideration. The result of Hermand's reconsideration was this—"Why, my Lords, I beg to put a very simple question to the House of Lords. Suppose that the tenant had engaged to hang himself at the end of the lease, would their Lordships enforce that?" Upon a second appeal, after reading the question aloud, Eldon, with ludicrous gravity, said "that he would endeavour to make up his mind upon the very important question put, when the case should come before their Lordships in regular form;" and added, that he had great pleasure in remembering when his friend George Fergusson and he used to do battle at this bar in Scotch causes, but that, if he recollected right, his learned friend had not then the admiration of the Court of Session that he seemed to have acquired since. Hermand was pleased with the recognition, and exclaimed, "And if he knew the truth, sir,—though this is a secret—he would find that I had not got it yet."

Two young gentlemen, great friends, went together to the theatre in Glasgow, supped at the lodgings of one of them, and passed a whole summer night over their punch. In the morning a kindly wrangle broke out about their separating or not separating, when by some rashness, if not accident, one of them was stabbed, not violently, but in so vital a part that he died on the spot. The survivor was tried at Edinburgh, and was convicted of culpable homicide. It was one of the sad cases where the legal guilt was greater than the moral; and, very properly, he was sentenced to only a short imprisonment. Hermand, who felt that discredit had been brought on the cause of drinking, had no sympathy with the tenderness of his temperate brethren, and was vehement for transportation. " We are told that there was no malice, and that the prisoner must have been in liquor. In liquor! Why, he was drunk! And yet he murdered the very man who had been drinking with him! They had been carousing the whole night; and yet he stabbed him; after drinking a whole bottle of rum with him; Good God, my Laards, if he will do this when he's drunk, what will he not do when he's sober? "

His love of children was warm-hearted and unaffected. He always treated them seriously, exactly as if they were grown up. Few old men's speeches are more amiable than his about his grandnephew who happened to be his partner in a match at bowls, " No wonder that that little fellow and I are such friends— there are just seventy years between us." He was eighty, the boy ten.

But when a boy happened to be a sailor, he was irresistible. A little English midshipman being violently attacked by a much bigger lad in Greenock, defended himself with his dirk, and by an unfortunate, if not accidental, thrust killed the assailant. He was tried for this at Glasgow, and had the good luck to have Hermand for his judge; for no judge ever fought a more gallant battle for a prisoner. The boy appeared at the bar in his uniform. Hermand first refused " to try a child." After this was driven out of him, the indictment, which described the occurrence and said that the prisoner had slain the deceased

" wickedly and feloniously," was read; and Hermand then said, " Well, my young friend, this is not true, is it? Are you guilty or not guilty? " " Not guilty, my Lord." " I'll be sworn you're not! " In spite of all his exertions, his young friend was convicted of culpable homicide; for which he was sentenced to a few days' imprisonment.

Allan Maconochie, Lord Meadowbank, was a curious and able man. His true merits were obscured, while he lived, by certain accidental oddities which obstructed the perception of them. He took great pleasure in exercising his own mind, and in making people wonder at the singularity of his views; into which, as into his language, he never failed to infuse as much metaphysical phraseology and argument as he could. Though not really conceited, he was apt to put on an air of pretension, which, though it was chiefly in the manner, was often misunderstood. There could scarcely be better evidence of the vigour of his intellect, than that he was able, by it alone, to triumph over his defects.

For he was a person of great mental activity and acuteness, an independent and original thinker, and of very considerable learning. His knowledge reached every subject—legal, scientific, historical, and literary and consequently was perhaps more varied than accurate; and under his ceaseless industry, his information increased hourly. I used to go circuits with him, and he seemed to me to be equally at home in divinity or agriculture, or geology, in examining mountains, or

I

demonstrating his errors to a farmer, or refuting the dogmas of the clergyman; though of all his occupations, the last perhaps gave him the greatest pleasure. For his peculiar delight, and his peculiar power, was in speculation; chiefly as applied to the theoretical history of man and of nations. He acquired great skill in the use of his metaphysical power, both as a sword and as a shield, in the intellectual contests in which it was his delight to be always engaged. He questioned every thing; he demonstrated every thing; his whole life was a discussion. This, though sometimes oppressive, was generally very diverting, and gave him a great facility in detecting and inventing principles, and in tracing them to their sources, and to their consequences. Jeffrey described this well when he said that while the other judges gave the tree a tug, one on this side and one on that, Meadowbank not only tore it up by the roots, but gave it a shake which dispersed the earth and exposed the whole fibres.

In the higher quality of calm soundness he was not equally eminent. Indeed before he spoke it would often have been a fair wager, whether what he said would be reasonable or extravagant. All that was certain was, that even his extravagance would be vigorous and original. Soundness indeed had no great attraction for a spirit eager for victory, but still more eager for conflict. He had more pleasure in inventing ingenious reasons for being wrong, than in being quietly right. Thus, with powers which made all anxious to listen, he had few followers as a safe leader.

Sir Harry Moncreiff, who was present at his marriage, and I believe performed the ceremony, told me that the knot was tied about seven in the evening, and that at a later hour the bridegroom disappeared; and, on being sought for, was found absorbed in the composition of a metaphysical essay " on pains and penalties."

Mr Thomas Walker Baird was, in a dull technical way, stating a dry case to his Lordship, who was sitting single. This did not please the judge, who thought that his dignity required a grander tone. So he dismayed poor Baird, than whom no man could have less turn for burning in the Forum, by throwing himself back in his chair, and saying, " Declaim, Sir! why don't you declaim? speak to me as if I were a popular assembly! "

Robert Cullen, a son of the great physician, was a gentleman-like person in his manner, and learned in his profession, in which however he was too indolent and irregular to attain steady practice. His best professional achievement was his written argument for Lord Daer, in support of the right of the eldest sons of Scotch peers to sit in the House of Commons; and his best political one was, the bill for the reform of the Scotch representation in 1785, which he drew, and his share in the measures connected with that project.

But the truth is, that he had the misfortune to possess one power which seems to exclude the exercise of all others. He was a mimic; and one of the very highest order. Dugald Stewart somewhere calls him

" the most perfect of all mimics." His skill was not confined to imitations of voices, looks, manners, and external individualities; but he copied the very words, nay the very thoughts of his subjects. He was particularly successful with his friend Principal Robertson, whose character he once endangered in a tavern by indecorous toasts, songs, and speeches, given with such a resemblance of the original, that a party on the other side of the partition, suspecting no trick, went home, believing that they had caught the reverend historian unawares. On another occasion, the Principal announced his determination to administer a severe lecture to a young Englishman,* who was boarding with him, the next time that he stayed out too late at night. He soon transgressed again, probably in Cullen's company. Cullen, knowing what was likely to happen, went to the Principal's early next morning, and walked up to the youth's room, with an exact resemblance of the doctor's step on the stair, and then, seating himself behind the curtain, gave a long and formal admonition to the headachy penitent; after which he retired with the same foot-tread. In fulfilment of his threat, the Principal approached some time afterwards, sat down, and began. After he had gone on a certain time, the culprit, who could not understand why he should get it twice, confesséd his sin, and reminded the doctor, that when he had been with him before, he had assured him that he would not err in the same way again. " Oh ho! " said the Principal, " so that dog Cullen has been before me! "

* The Hon. James Stuart Wortley. *Jupiter Carlyle's Autobiography.*

He could not tell a story without disclosing his power
—a fee-less faculty.

Though these few were those most spoken of, the
Bench contained several other learned and worthy
judges, but not one whose public ideas went beyond
the passing hour, or who saw any duty or object for
that hour except an adoption and promotion of its
intolerance. Cullen, and Bannatyne Macleod, an
honest merry old gentleman, were so far disenthralled
that they disclaimed exclusive fealty to Henry Dundas, to whom by some accident they did not directly
owe their appointments. With these two shades of
immaterial exception, there probably were not fifteen
other men in the island to whom political independence was more offensive than to these fifteen judges.

CHAPTER III

THE Bar, upon which the condition of Scotland has always so much depended, was rich in talent, and its public lines were deeply marked. It was divided into Whigs and Tories, with an overwhelming numerical majority in favour of the latter. The seniors—meaning by this term those who had secured, or had begun to secure, practice prior to the decided outbreak of the French Revolution in 1790—could not be then turned off the professional course by politics. The public favour was strongly with the Tories; who had also the much more valuable advantage of the very undisguised favour of the Bench. But still the Whigs, having started, could not be prevented going on with the race. But all hope of official preferment, and even of any professional countenance that power could show them, was sternly and ostentatiously closed against them. A sacrifice of principle would have relaxed the interdiction; but in no one instance was the sacrifice made or imagined.

Of the juniors—by whom I mean those who came to the Bar between 1790 and 1804, the hot stage of our political fever, which our second war cooled—very nearly the whole junior practice, and absolutely the whole of everything else that patronage could confer, was engrossed by the Tories. Their Whig brethren were practically proscribed. They liberated themselves ultimately, and vindicated their proper places; but it was under proscription, with all its privations and bitterness, that their course began.

This single and most blessed fact explains important distant results. Certainty of easy success, paraded, not too modestly, as triumphant evidence of superior merit, deeply and irrecoverably injured the Government juniors, on whom, far more than on the seniors, the coming times were to depend. There was such a crowd of candidates for favour, that the eager mendicants had no such obvious way of pushing their claim as by excess of party zeal and party service. This is common in all parties. But it was unfortunate for these men that the policy of the party which they had to promote was not connected with enlightened objects or principles. The only duty presented to them was one, which, the better they practised it, was the worse for themselves. All they had to do was " to maintain the cause of good order," which meant to resist change, to uphold whatever was, and to abuse as democrats all who differed from them; a task not calculated to liberalise the mind. Their worst qualities were most fostered. The consequence scarcely requires to be stated. They produced several most excellent men and very respectable lawyers, but not one person except Walter Scott, who rose to distinction in literature, and not one who was looked up to by the country as its guide or instructor in public affairs or in any branch of political philosophy. There never was a period during which in these fields the Tory side of the Bar was so barren.

Those on the opposite side, who saw themselves excluded from everything that power could keep from them, reaped the natural advantages of this position. It gave them leisure; persecution cherished elevation of character and habits of self-dependence. Being all branded with the same mark, and put under the same ban, they were separated into a sect of their own, within which there was mirth and friendship, study and hope, ambition and visions. There was a particular place at the north end of the Outer House which was the known haunt of these doomed youths. And there did they lounge session after session, and year after year, employed sufficiently now and then by a friendly agent to show what was in them, but never enough to make them feel that they were engaged in a fair professional competition: reconciled however to their fate; and not at all depressed by their bad character. The most important among them (besides other meritorious, though humbler, names) were John Macfarlan, Archibald Fletcher, James Grahame, George Joseph Bell, Thomas Thomson, Francis Jeffrey, James Moncreiff, Henry Brougham, George Cranstoun, and Francis Horner. These names indicate a greater amount of accomplished talent, and greater public service in literature, in policy, and in law, than has ever distinguished any era of the Scotch Bar.

This was the general condition of the Bar. The individuals most remarkable on account of their professional eminence, and their public importance, were—on the popular side, Erskine, Clerk, and Gillies; on the Government side, Blair, Hope, and Dundas. The three last, though followed by a large shoal of younger fry, had no leviathans in their party greater than themselves. The three first had several persons in their wake not at all inferior to themselves in solidity and spirit, and their superiors at last in general reputation; but these three were the leaders in the meantime.

Henry Erskine's name can no sooner be mentioned than it suggests ideas of wit, with which, in many memories, the recollection of him is chiefly associated. A tall and rather slender figure, a face sparkling with vivacity, a clear sweet voice, and a general suffusion of elegance, gave him a striking and pleasing appearance. He was nearly the same in private as in public, the presence of only a few friends never diminishing his animation, nor that of the largest audience his naturalness. No boisterousness ever vulgarised, no effort ever encumbered, his aerial gaiety. Though imposing no restraint upon himself, but always yielding freely to the radiant spirit within him, his humour was rendered delightful by its gentleness and safety. Too good-natured for sarcasm, when he was compelled to expose, there was such an obvious absence of all desire to give pain, that the very person against whom his laughing darts were directed generally thought the wounds compensated by the mirth and by the humanity of the cuts. Yet those will form a

very erroneous conception of him who shall suppose
that the mere display of wit was his principal object.
In society, of course, his pleasure was to please his
friends. But in public he scarcely ever uttered a joke
merely for the sake of the laugh. He was far above this
seducing vulgarity. His playfulness was always an
argumentative instrument. He reasoned in wit; and
untempted by the bad taste and the weakness of de-
siring to prolong it for his own sake, it ceased the very
instant that the reasoning was served. Nevertheless,
notwithstanding the fascination it threw around him
he had better have been without the power. It allured
him into a sphere below that to which his better
faculties would have raised him, and established obstructing associations of cheerfulness, whenever he
appeared, in the public mind. For he was intuitively
quick in apprehension, and not merely a skilful, but a
sound reasoner;—most sagacious in judgment; and
his speaking had all the charms that these qualities,
united to a copious but impressive language, and to a
manner of the most polished and high-born graceful-
ness, could confer. Hence, though naturally, perhaps,
his intellect was rather rapid and acute than deep or
forcible, he could discharge himself of all his lightness
when necessary, and could lead an audience, in the
true tone, and with assured success, through a grave or
distressing discussion.

In his profession he was the very foremost. There
were some, particularly Blair, afterwards the head of
the Court, who surpassed him in deep and exact legal
knowledge. But no rival approached him in the variety,

extent, or brilliancy of his general practice. Others
were skilled in one department, or in one court. But
wherever there was a litigant, civil, criminal, fiscal,
or ecclesiastic, there there was a desire for Harry
Erskine;—despair if he was lost—confidence if he
was secured. And this state of universal requisition
had lasted so long, that it could only have proceeded
from the public conviction of his general superiority.
He had been Lord Advocate during the coalition
administration, but not long enough to enlarge his
public views; and when Jeffrey was first honoured by
his notice, his brethren had, for eight successive
years, chosen him for their Dean, or official head. His
political opinions were those of the Whigs; but a
conspicuous and inflexible adherence to their creed
was combined with so much personal gentleness, that
it scarcely impaired his popularity. Even the old
judges, in spite of their abhorrence of his party,
smiled upon him; and the eyes of such juries as we
then had, in the management of which he was agreeably despotic, brightened as he entered. He was the
only one of the marked Edinburgh Whigs who was not
received coldly in the private society of their opponents. Nothing was so sour as not to be sweetened
by the glance, the voice, the gaiety, the beauty, of
Henry Erskine. He and his illustrious brother Lord
Erskine have sometimes been compared. There is
every reason for believing that, in genius, Thomas
was the superior creature. But no comparison of two
men so differently placed is of any value. It is scarcely
possible even to conjecture what each might have been

in the other's situation. All that is certain is that each was admirable in his own sphere. Cast as his lot was, our Erskine shone in it to the utmost! and it is no deduction from his merits that no permanent public victories, and little of the greatness that achieves them, are connected with his name. He deserves our reverence for every virtue and every talent that could be reared in his position; by private worth and un-sullied public honour—by delightful temper, safe vivacity, and unmatched professional splendour.

John Clerk, son of Clerk of Eldin (a man whose science and originality, whether he first propounded the modern system of naval tactics or not, were far above that idea), had been Solicitor-General under the Whig Government of 1805 and 1806, and had since risen into great practice. It is difficult to describe a person whose conditions in repose and action—that is, in his private and in his professional life—almost amounted to the possession of two natures.

A contracted limb, which made him pitch when he walked, and only admitted of his standing erect by hanging it in the air, added to the peculiarity of a figure with which so many other ideas of oddity were connected. Blue eyes, very bushy eyebrows, coarse grizzly hair always in disorder, and firm, projecting features, made his face and head not unlike that of a thorough-bred shaggy terrier. It was a countenance of great thought and great decision.

Had his judgment been equal to his talent, few powerful men could have stood before him. For he had a strong, working, independent, ready head; which had been improved by various learning, extending beyond his profession into the fields of general literature, and into the arts of painting and sculpture. Honest, warm-hearted, generous, and simple, he was a steady friend, and of the most touching affection in all domestic relations. The whole family was deeply marked by an hereditary caustic humour, and none of its members more than he.

These excellences, however, were affected by certain peculiarities, or habits, which segregated him from the whole human race.

One of these was an innocent admiration both of his own real merits and achievements, and of all the supposed ones which his simplicity ascribed to himself. He was saved from the imputation of vanity in this, by the sincerity of the delusion. Without any boasting or airs of superiority, he would expatiate on his own virtues with a quiet placidity, as if he had no concern in the matter, but only wished others to know what they should admire. This infantine self-deification would have been more amusing, had it not encouraged another propensity, the source of some of his more serious defects—an addiction, not in words merely, but in conduct, to paradox. He did not announce his dogmas, like the ordinary professors of paradox, for surprise or argument, but used to insist upon them with a calm, slow, dogged obstinacy, which at least justified the honesty of his acting upon them. And this tendency was aggravated, in its turn, by a third rather painful weakness; which, of all the parts in his character, was the one which his friends would have liked most to change—jealousy of rivalship, and a kindred impatience of contradiction. This introduced the next stage, when confidence in his own infallibility ascribed all opposition to doubts of his possessing this quality, and thus inflamed a spirit which, however serene when torpid, was never trained to submission, and could rise into fierceness when chafed.

Of course it was chafed every moment at the bar; and accordingly it was there that his other and inferior nature appeared. Every consideration was lost in eagerness for the client, whose merit lay in this, that he has relied upon me, John Clerk. Nor was his the common zeal of a counsel. It was a passion. He did not take his fee, plead the cause well, hear the result, and have done with it; but gave the client his temper, his perspiration, his nights, his reason, his whole body and soul, and very often the fee to boot. His real superiority lay in his legal learning and his hard reasoning. But he would have been despicable in his own sight had he reasoned without defying and insulting the adversary and the unfavourable judges; the last of whom he always felt under a special call to abuse, because they were not merely obstructing justice, but thwarting him.* So that pugnacity was his

* One of the judges of the Court of Session, whose father had been a distinguished member of the Bench under the same title, on one occasion petulantly interrupted Clerk with the remark that they could not listen all day to reiteration of "also and likewise." Clerk promptly replied that his lordship seemed to consider the two words synonymous but they were not so. " Your lordship's father was lord ; you are lord *also*, but I doubt if you are *likewise*."

line. His whole session was one keen and truceless conflict; in which more irritating matter was introduced than could have been ventured upon by any one except himself, whose worth was known, and whose intensity was laughed at as one of the shows of the court.

Neither in speaking, nor in anything else, was he at all entangled with the graces; but his manner was always sensible and natural. An utterance as slow as minute guns, and a poor diction, marked his unexcited state, in one of his torpid moods. But when roused, which was his more common condition, he had the command of a strong, abrupt, colloquial style, which either for argument or for scorn, suited him much better than any other sort of eloquence would have done. Very unequal, no distinguished counsel made so many bad appearances. But then he made many admirable ones, and always redeemed himself out of the bad ones by displays of great depth and ability. And his sudden rallies, when, after being refuted and run down, he stood at bay, and either covered his escape or died scalping, were unmatched in dexterity and force. A number of admirably written arguments, on profound legal difficulties, will sustain his reputation in the sight of every lawyer who will take the very useful trouble of instructing himself by the study of these works. It was his zeal, however, which of all low qualities is unfortunately the one that is most prized in the daily market of the bar, that chiefly upheld him when in his glory; and as this fiery quality must cool with age, he declined some years before he withdrew.

His popularity was increased by his oddities. Even in the midst of his frenzies he was always introducing some original and quaint humour;* so that there are few of the lights of the court of whom more sayings and stories are prevalent. Even in his highest fits of disdainful vehemence, he would pause—lift his spectacles to his brow—erect himself—and after indicating his approach by a mantling smile, would relieve himself, and cheer the audience, by some diverting piece of Clerkism—and then, before the laugh was well over, another gust would be up. He, and his consulting room, withdrew the attention of strangers from the cases on which they had come to hear their fate. Walls covered with books and pictures, of both of which he had a large collection; the floor encumbered by little ill-placed tables, each with a piece of old china on it; strange boxes, bits of sculpture, curious screens, and chairs, cats and dogs (his special favourites), and all manner of trash, dead and living, and all in confusion;—John himself sitting in the midst of this museum,—in a red worsted night cap, his crippled limb resting horizontally on a tripod stool,—and many pairs of spectacles and antique snuff-boxes on a small table at his right hand; and there he sits—perhaps dreaming awake—probably

---

* When pleading in the House of Lords he, as usual, repeatedly pronounced the word enough " enow," when the Lord Chancellor interposed with, " Pardon me, Mr Clerk, but we pronounce ' ough ' as ' uff.'" " Well, my lord," proceeded Clerk, " there was a ' pluff-gate ' of land belonging to my client. A ' pluff-gate,' my lord, is as much land as a single ' pluffman ' can ' pluff ' in a day." " Mr Clerk," rejoined the Lord Chancellor, " you may as well resume your ' enow.' "

descanting on some of his crotchets, and certainly abusing his friends the judges—when recalled to the business in hand; but generally giving acute and vigorous advice.

Except in his profession, and as an ardent partizan, he was little of a public character. Resolute in his Whig principles, which he delighted to shake in the face of his adversaries during the fulness of their power, and entering hotly into all the movements of his party, inexperience of public management, and some impracticability, disqualified him from originating measures, and occasionally made him a little dangerous even as their defender. In these matters, indeed, his friends could not have the confidence in his judgment which friends would have liked to have had in one so upright, and with so muscular a mind.

Robert Blair, the son of the reverend author of *The Grave*, was a species of man not very common in Scotland. He had a fine manly countenance, a gentleman-like portly figure, a slow dignified gait, and a general air of thought and power. Too solid for ingenuity, and too plain for fancy, soundness of understanding was his peculiar intellectual quality. Within his range nobody doubted, or could doubt, Blair's wisdom. Nor did it ever occur to any one to question his probity. He was all honesty. The sudden opening of the whole secrets of his heart would not have disclosed a single speck of dishonour. And all his affections, personal and domestic, were excellent and steady.

K

He had one quality, or rather habit, so marked that it was the only one by which some people knew him, and which affected all his proceedings. It was generally called laziness, but was perfectly distinct from the ignoble sloth and the apathetic indifference which this term is meant to describe. He was strong in principle, and grudged no exertion that principle required; and his feelings were warm, and his temper hot. These are not the attributes of laziness. But he had certainly a great taste for contemplative repose, and a magnificent disdain of the paltry distractions and low pursuits by which the self-possession of repose is so commonly disturbed. This of course implied a considerable extinction of vulgar labour, and a great aversion to many of the efforts that public men are often required to make, and to many of the occupations in which they are often expected to engage. Instead of impairing Blair's usefulness, as it used to be said to do, this dislike of disturbance greatly promoted it. It disinclined him from meddling with the thousand little teasing and degrading affairs in which men of influence get involved, and tended to secure his purity and independence. Hence he never stooped to act in scenes unworthy of him, and passed through a life beset by competitions, without being ever drawn, so much as for a moment, from his high even path by any contemptible object. In dignity, sense, honesty, and, when not excited, in repose he was an absolute rock.

But he was very apt to be excited. And I have no doubt that he took refuge in repose in order to keep down the tendency; though its having this effect may be questioned. His temperament was inflammable. The great check to such a constitution arises out of the suppression produced by the necessities of human intercourse. But Blair's indolence avoided these. He exposed himself so seldom to opposition, that, instead of being practised into coolness by it, its friction made him blaze. It is rare to find a fiery disposition and a strong love of ease combined. In Blair each promoted the other. The interruption of the ease raised the fire; the irritation of the fire made a relapse into ease delicious.

Amidst almost boundless general admiration, persons who thought themselves more discriminating used to underrate his learning and his speaking; but this depreciation was almost always provoked by the exaggeration of injudicious friends. The exact truth admits of no doubt. He was very learned as a lawyer, and respectably learned as a practical gentleman. Science, as such, either moral or physical, he had never studied. But besides English literature, he read French, Greek, and Latin; and on the whole was a liberally intelligent man.* The merit of his speaking lay in two things—in luminous exposition of legal views, and in the effect with which his warmth, manliness, and sincerity enabled him to express moral

* John Playfair, one of his great friends, published an account of Blair immediately after his death, which was republished at the end of No. 139 of the *Edinburgh Review* (vol. lxix. p. 281). He there mentions Blair's " profound erudition." This was one of the imprudences of friendly compliment, which made some people maintain that he was positively ignorant. The praise and the blame were equally groundless.—H. C.

emotion, chiefly indignation. Neither his position nor his taste had ever required him to cultivate the higher and more general habits of language and of thought that can only be generated in spheres superior to courts of law. There is therefore no sense in describing him as a great orator, for his circumstances did not admit of his being so. It is surely enough to say, and it is true, that though his diction was poor, and though his voice, which was good when he was calm, got sputtering and screechy when he became excited, he was, within the line of the forensic walk to which he confined himself, as good a speaker as that line requires in a man whose principal weapon is his wisdom. His true eloquence was in the dignity of his look and manner, and the weight of his reputation.

Nothing could be more characteristic than his progress. Beginning with the advantage of a respectable but not a high origin, he devoted himself quietly and steadily for rising, by merit alone, in the vocation he had chosen. He did rise at last, by legal force and good character, to the highest and best sort of practice; and having reached this eminence, he maintained it easily. No other counsel in my time has had a more universal or just reputation as a safe legal guide; nor does the life of any other barrister exhibit a more striking example of the value of character on the exertions of this profession. He might have had any promotion that he chose; but I have heard his friend the first Lord Melville say, that George the Third used to speak of him as the " man who would not go up." His noble indifference about office, and his abhorrence of the intrigues by which office is too frequently obtained, made him prefer the independence of his excellent practice, which he kept as if by right. While others were pushing and jostling for those things, which he was glad to be quit of, he held to his comfortable Solicitorship and to his own way so steadily, that there was a line along the floor of the Outer House where he generally walked, and which everybody else kept off when he was there, respecting it as his quarter-deck. His very superiors, both at the Bar and on the Bench, stood in awe of him. For example, in a criminal trial when the Lord Advocate is present, his Lordship, after having seen to the business part of it, generally leaves his representatives to hear the address to the jury of the prisoner's counsel, to endure the summing up, and to weary for the verdict. I doubt if Blair ever remained once. He withdrew, and left his chief and the case to their fate. His rising and moving off, which was done slowly and openly, always caused a smile; contrasted as it was with the visible desire of the colonel to go also, if he could only get the major to stay—a proposal, however, impossible to be made.

Yet, as I well know, he was most kind to young men; who, especially when they saw him at Avonton, his country place near Linlithgow, were always charmed with his attentions, and struck with his dignified but friendly style. His conversation, when he chose to indulge in it, was excellent, being intelligent, natural, and quiet. But he certainly had no objection to silence. Many were the jokes, even to himself, about his taciturnity. I have seen him play a long round game, with a dozen of people, without uttering a single word. But in this chattering world, one sensible man out of a million may well be allowed to be sometimes voluntarily dumb.

General politics he had never considered. His opinions were those of his party. Speculation indeed was not the habit of his mind; and innovation, besides being connected with outrage, disturbed his tranquillity, and excited him. But though devoid of political philosophy, and acting with a domineering party, his steady head, aided powerfully by a distaste of practical faction, saved his conduct from imputation, and his mind from harshness.

Robert Dundas of Arniston, the son of one Lord President, and the grandson of another, was, in public affairs, the most important person in this country. For he was Lord Advocate in the most alarming times, and at a period when extravagant and arbitrary powers were ascribed to that office. I knew him well; and lived many autumns with him, at Arniston, in my youth.

His abilities and acquirements were both moderate; and owing to the accident of his birth, which placed him above all risk of failure in life, he was never in a situation where he was compelled to improve either. Hence, with all the advantages of his position, all the favour of agents, and all the partiality of courts, he never commanded any independent private practice. His speaking, which was curiously bad, injured the effect of his better powers. For he had two qualifications which suited his position, and made him not merely the best Lord Advocate that his party could have supplied, but really a most excellent one. These consisted in his manner, and in his moderation. He was a little, alert, handsome, gentleman-like man,* with a countenance and air beaming with sprightliness and gaiety, and dignified by considerable fire; altogether inexpressibly pleasing. It was impossible not to like the owner of that look. No one could contemplate his animated and elegant briskness, or his lively benignity, without feeling that these were the reflections of an ardent and amiable heart. His want of intellectual depth and force seemed to make people like him the better. And his manner was worthy of his appearance. It was kind, polite, and gay; and if the fire did happen to break out, it was but a passing flash, and left nothing painful after it was gone.

Resistance of revolution, which he deemed his main public duty, implied the maintenance of his party, and of the Scotch supremacy of his family; and these accordingly were his direct objects, as the means of attaining the end. But though obliged to cultivate a very intemperate faction, he had the prudence to be less violent than his followers, and gained and deserved a character for moderation as the public accuser, which peculiarly fitted him for his place. It is true

* Mr Ferguson of Pitfour, M.P. for Aberdeenshire, is said to have complained in the House of Commons, when Dundas was Lord Advocate, that—"The Lord Advocate should always be a tall man. We Scotch members always vote with him, and we need, therefore, to be able to see him. I can see Pitt and Addington, but I can't see this new Lord Advocate."—G. W. T. Omond's *Arniston Memoirs*.

that it was on his motion that many of the iniquities
of the Court of Justiciary were committed; but then
he moved for nothing beyond what that Court held
him to be legally entitled to, or beyond what the public
approved of. I consider it as quite certain that he
might have got every political opponent transported
that he had chosen to indict. But the fewness of his
victims is the most honourable fact by which the
proceedings of any Lord Advocate could then be
distinguished. That he had Blair and Hume at hand
for aid in law, or that he was assisted or controlled
in his measures by his sagacious uncle, Lord Melville,
are no deductions from his merits. His being so coun-
selled was a proof of his sense. Nor can his success be
explained, as has been attempted, by the power of
his office, the devotion of the party he led, the
hereditary greatness, or the hereditary hospitality, of
the House of Arniston. These things might all have
concurred in a man of violence, and only made his
offensiveness the greater. They would have availed
nothing to Dundas, if he had been vindictive as public
prosecutor, or shabby in his conduct, or sour in his
looks.*

Charles Hope, who succeeded Dundas as Lord
Advocate in 1803, and was afterwards Justice-Clerk

* His statue, by Chantrey, though beautiful as a work of art, and
not unlike in its features, conveys no idea whatever of his healthy expression. If Chantrey ever saw him, it must have been when he was
dying, a state which lasted some years ; and accordingly the statue ex-
presses thoughtful languor, not amiable alacrity, which was the outward
character of the original.—H. C.

and Lord President, was the tongue of the party, and in the van of all its battles. He was tall and well set up, and had a most admirable voice—full, deep, and distinct, its very whisper heard along a line of a thousand men. Kind, friendly, and honourable, private life could neither enjoy nor desire a character more excellent. The vehemence of his politics, combined with his power of speaking, made him the usual organ of his political friends, in so much that, I believe, it was he who was put forward to move Henry Erskine's dismissal from the Deanship. Yet even this unfavourable position never alienated his heart from an adversary personally. He would have gone, and indeed did go, as far as anybody to tread down his opposites politically; but without ill-nature, or personal hostility, or even absence of candour. It is needless to say that the motion never cooled Erskine's affection for Hope, and neither did it Hope's for Erskine. No breast indeed could be more clear than Hope's of everything paltry or malevolent. And indirectness was so entirely foreign to his manly nature, that even in his plainest errors his adversaries had always whatever advantage was to be gained from an honest disclosure of his principles and objects. In short it is not easy to estimate his moral nature too highly.

The possession of considerable ability is implied in his extensive professional practice, and in the well-performed duties of his high judicial appointments. There is no peculiar faculty by which his intellect can be individualised. His were the ordinary powers of a well-educated gentleman, whose vocation was in

practical law. It was not by superiority of talent that
he was distinguished, but by his power of public
speaking, for which he had many of the qualifications
in a very remarkable degree. His language was full
and appropriate; his manner natural and commanding; and his voice was surpassed by that of the great
Mrs Siddons alone, which, drawn direct from heaven
and worthy to be heard there, was the noblest that
ever struck the human ear. Within the range of
luminous statement and manly sentiment he rarely
failed to be effective and pleasing.

His great defect, both as a speaker and as a public
man, consisted in a want of tact; and this arose from
the warmth, or rather the heat of his temperament.
It might have been supposed that one whose feelings
were so good, and who was so constantly evoking the
good feelings of others, could, under this star, scarcely
go off the right path. And he never would, had he not
been too often under the influence of a star of his
own. Declamation was his weapon, and it is one that
is seldom sheathed in correct wisdom. The very act of
declaiming inflamed him: this elevated him, need-
lessly, into the region of thunder; and then there was
generally a blaze, with which nobody could sympathise. This infirmity was apt sometimes to come
over him even in council. The result was that, though
possessed of superior abilities and every virtue, he
was often felt to be unsafe; and his vehemence made
him enemies who, hurt by his strong language,
represented him as harsh. He may have been occasionally overbearing and provoking; but I am certain that

this never proceeded from any bad passion, or even unkind feeling, but was solely the consequence of honest though erroneous emotion, and of over-animated mental nerves. Had he been acting in a higher sphere, and trained earlier under the discipline of a more formidable audience with the elements of eloquence which he so largely possessed, I cannot doubt that he would have proved a great speaker and a more sound adviser.

It is a pleasure to me to think of him. He was my first, I might almost say my only, professional patron, and used to take me with him on his circuits; and in spite of my obstinate and active Whiggery, has been kind to me through life. When his son, who was Solicitor-General in 1830, lost that office by the eleva-tion of the Reform Ministry, and I succeeded him, his father shook me warmly by the hand, and said, " Well, Harry, I wish you joy. Since my son was to lose it, I am glad that your father's son has got it." It was always so with him. Less enlightened than confident in his public opinions, his feelings towards his adversaries, even when ardently denouncing their principles, were liberalised by the native humanity and fairness of his dispositions.

The name of Charles Hope, the Lieutenant-Colonel of our First or Gentlemen Regiment of Volunteers, is associated with our recollections of these establish-ments. He entered into their business, as indeed into all his pursuits, with his whole heart, and persevered to the end. The judge's wig was by no means incom-patible, in his sight, with the colonel's cocked hat.

The occupation had strong attractions for him, and he was an excellent officer.

Two great legal works appeared about this time—the *Mercantile Commentaries* of Bell and the *Criminal Commentaries* of Hume; works that will ever hold their places in our system. Bell's is the greatest work on Scotch Jurisprudence that has appeared since the publication of Lord Stair's Institute. Its authority has helped to decide probably eighty out of every hundred mercantile questions that have been settled since it began to illuminate our courts; and it has done, and will do, more for the fame of the law of Scotland in foreign countries than has been done by all our other law books put together.

Hume's work was composed in a great measure for the purpose of vindicating the proceedings of the Criminal Court in the recent cases of sedition, and was therefore hailed with the loudest acclamations by the friends of those whose proceedings stood so much in need of defence. But we are far enough now from the passions of those days to enable us to appreciate its merits more candidly. And the judgment of the public is right in having decided that, for ordinary practice, it is a most useful work, the importance of which can scarcely be understood by those who have never had to grope their way amidst the darkness which he removed, and that there its merits end. But his admirers disdain this praise, and maintain it to be a great work of original thought, and the model of a criminal system, the supposed imperfections of which the author has shown not to exist. They will not allow his style to be heavy and affected, his delineation of principle superficial, his views on all matters of expediency or reason narrow, indeed monastic. The proceedings of the savage old Scotch Privy Council are held up by him as judicial precedents, even in political cases, at the end of the eighteenth century. The impeachable domineering of Braxfield in 1794 is just as commendable in his pages as if the times had been moderate, and the judge impartial. As an institutional writer, he certainly could not exclude either ancient or modern proceedings from his view; and he was perfectly entitled to put his own value on them. So was any mere chronicler of legal events. But before any one can deserve the praise of being an enlightened expounder of a system of law not previously explained or methodised, and of first delivering to the people the rules which they must obey, and ought to admire, the past actings of courts ought not to be merely stated, but to be criticised and appreciated, so that future tribunals may be guided, and the public instructed, on defects and remedies. On such matters there is no book that has worse stood the test of time. There is scarcely one of his favourite points that the legislature, with the cordial assent of the public and of lawyers, has not put down. [*Edinburgh Review*, No. 167, art. 7.]

There were no judicial reporters or " collectors of decisions " formerly, except two advocates, who were appointed and paid by the Faculty for doing this work. Right reporting was attended then with some risk. It had never been the practice to give any full and exact account of what passed on the Bench, but only results. The public, or at least the independent portion of the legal profession, had begun to require something more, and their Lordships were very jealous of this pretension. They considered it as a contempt; and the contempt was held to be aggravated by the accuracy of the report. Mr Robert Bell, afterwards lecturer on conveyancing to the Society of Writers to the Signet, was the first who adventured on independence in this matter; and he announced that he meant to report without any official appointment, and to give the opinions of the judges. This design was no sooner disclosed than he met with many threatening hints, and as much obstruction as could be given in an open court. The hated but excellent volume at last appeared; and though the judges were only denoted by letters, he was actually called into the robing room, and admonished to beware. Eskgrove's objection was " the fellow taks doon ma' very words "—a great injury to his Lordship, certainly. More than ten years passed before it was acknowledged by rational judges that the offensiveness of publishing each opinion was no inconsiderable proof of its utility. Fear lest the Faculty should assert its right generally disposed the court in favour of submissive and unambitious collectors; and this, it was thought, operated against Jeffrey, who, in 1801, dared to aspire to the office.*

* *See* Cockburn's *Life of Jeffrey.*

The party that would not let Jeffrey subside into a reporter were soon rewarded in a way they little thought of. His failure in this competition was one of the proximate causes of the appearance of the *Edinburgh Review*, of which the first number was published on. the 10th of October 1802. It elevated the public and the literary position of Edinburgh to an extent which no one not living intelligently then can be made to comprehend.

Mr Smith's account of the origin of the *Edinburgh Review* is this:—" One day we happened to meet in the eighth or ninth storey or flat, in Buccleuch Place, the elevated residence of the then Mr Jeffrey. I proposed that we should set up a Review; this was acceded to with acclamation. I was appointed editor, and remained long enough in Edinburgh to edit the first number of the *Edinburgh Review*."*—(Preface to Sydney Smith's Works.)

The merit of having first suggested the work is undoubtedly due to Mr Smith. He himself claims it in the preceding words, and to those acquainted with his character, this is sufficient. But Jeffrey admits it. His " *Contributions* " are dedicated to Mr Smith, expressly as " *The Original Projector of the* Edinburgh Review." And no other person has ever come forward to dispute the fact. Whatever credit, therefore, attaches to the first announced idea of the undertaking, it belongs to Mr Smith. But his statement might make it appear that the resolution to begin it was sudden and acci-

* See *Life and Times of Lord Brougham.*

dental, and as if it had occurred and been acted upon at once at that casual meeting. But probably all that is meant is, that it was then that the matter was brought to a practical conclusion. Because it is difficult to believe that such an undertaking could have been determined upon on the suggestion of a moment, and without previous calculation and arrangement. Accordingly, Jeffrey never ascribed more to this meeting than that it was there that they had their " *first serious consultations about it.*" It happened to be a tempestuous evening, and I have heard him say that they had some merriment at the greater storm they were about to raise. There were circumstances that tended so directly towards the production of some such work, that it seems now as if its appearance, in Edinburgh, and about this time, might almost have been foreseen. Of these it is sufficient to mention the irrepressible passion for discussion which succeeded the fall of old systems on the French Revolution; the strong feeling of resentment at our own party intolerance; the obviousness that it was only through the press that this intolerance could be abated, or our policy reformed; the dotage of all the existing journals; and the presence, in this place, of the able young men,* who have been mentioned, most of them in close alliance, and to whom concealed authorship was an irresistible vent.

* Their youth, though it was one of the established grounds of the pretended contempt of their opponents, was by no means excessive. Allen, in 1802, was thirty-two ; Smith, thirty-one ; Jeffrey, thirty ; Brown, twenty-four ; Horner, twenty-four ; Brougham, twenty-three. Excellent ages for such work. —H. C.

On looking back at those times, it is impossible not to be struck with the apparent absence of enlightened public views and capacities all over the community. I do not recollect a single Scotch work of any permanent, or almost of any respectable temporary value, which even the excitement of that age produced. When the *Edinburgh Review* appeared it received no published opposition, and no material aid on public questions, from any person at that time in public life. Even at the bar, which had always contained the best educated and the ablest of the middle and upper ranks, and been in advance of all other classes, Horner, Brougham, or Jeffrey, at the age of twenty-five, or perhaps of twenty-one, were better prepared to instruct and direct the public than all the other counsel, either Whig or Tory, in practice when they came forward. Indeed the suppression of independent talent or ambition was the tendency of the times. Every Tory principle being absorbed in the horror of innovation, and that party casting all its cares upon Henry Dundas, no one could, without renouncing all his hopes, commit the treason of dreaming an independent thought. There was little genuine attraction for real talent, knowledge, or eloquence on that side; because these qualities can seldom exist in combination with abject submission. And indeed there was not much attraction for them among the senior and dominant Whigs, among whom there was a corresponding loyalty to the Earl of Lauderdale. The adherents of both parties were saved the trouble of qualifying themselves for taking any charge of public

L

matters; the one by knowing that, in so far as their aid implied any independence, it would be offensive, and that, if they would only obey, their champion would be sure to carry them through; the other by despair of being either allowed to co-operate, or able to resist.

To Archibald Constable, the publisher of the *Edinburgh Review*, the literature of Scotland has been more indebted than to any other bookseller. Till he appeared, our publishing trade was at nearly the lowest ebb; partly because there was neither population nor independence to produce or to require a vigorous publisher; and partly because the publishers we had were too spiritless even for their position. Our principal booksellers were Bell and Bradfute, and Manner and Miller, in the Parliament Close; Elphinstone Balfour, Peter Hill, and William Creech, in the High Street; and William Laing in the Canongate. Laing was a good collector of good books, chiefly old ones, but did not publish much. Creech was connected with the publication of the works of Robertson and other respectable authors. All the rest were unimportant. Constable began as a lad in Hill's shop, and had hardly set up for himself when he reached the summit of his business. He rushed out, and took possession of the open field, as if he had been aware from the first of the existence of the latent spirits, which a skilful conjuror might call from the depths of the population to the service of literature. Abandoning the old timid and grudging system, he stood out as the general patron and payer of all promising publications, and confounded not merely his rivals in trade, but his very authors, by his unheard-of prices. Ten, even twenty, guineas a sheet for a review, £2000 or £3000 for a single poem, and £1000 each for two philosophical dissertations,* drew authors from dens where they would otherwise have starved, and made Edinburgh a literary mart, famous with strangers, and the pride of its own citizens.

Creech was one of the founders of the Speculative Society, and a person of some local celebrity. He owed a good deal to the position of his shop,† which formed the eastmost point of a long thin range of building that stood to the north of St Giles' Cathedral, its length running from west to east parallel to the Cathedral, and about twenty feet from it. Consequently the street north of the Cathedral was not one half of its present width. His windows looked down the High Street; so that his sign, " Creech," above his door was visible down to the head of the Canongate. The best thing he did was to make a curious and valuable collection illustrative of the modern changes of Edinburgh manners and habits. In spite of its absurd title, *Fugitive Pieces*, it is very interesting, and, in so far as one who knew only one end of the period can judge, generally correct. The position of

* By Stewart and Playfair—prefixed to a supplement of the *Encyclopædia Britannica.*—H. C.

† He also owed much to the fact that the business was founded on the old established one of MacEwan, who had premises under Allan Ramsay's Library. Kincaid was MacEwan's successor, and Creech joined Kincaid as his partner in 1771. Creech also had an intimate connection with the London houses of Strahan, King's Printer for England, and Andrew Miller, both of whom had been trained in Edinburgh. In a humorous letter on Scotch Booksellers John Leyden very happily hits off the foibles of the members of " the trade " of his day.

his shop, in the very tideway of all our business, made it the natural resort of lawyers, authors, and all sorts of literary idlers, who were always buzzing about the convenient hive. All who wished to see a poet or a stranger, or to hear the public news, the last joke by Erskine, or yesterday's occurrence in the Parliament House, or to get the publication of the day or news-papers—all congregated there; lawyers, doctors, clergymen, and authors. I attended the writing school of William Swanson, the great handspoiler of the time, whose crowded classroom was on the south side of the High Street, close by the Cross; and I always tried to get a seat next a window, that I might see the men I heard so much talked of moving into and out of this bower of the muses, or loitering about its entrance.

There was no class of the community so little thought of at this time as the mercantile. Their municipal councils, and chambers of commerce, and guilds, and all their public associations were recog-nised, because they had some power, however little. But individually, or merely as numbers of merchants, they were entirely disregarded. They had no direct political power; no votes; and were far too subservient to be feared. The lairds were not merely more deferred to, but were in the height of their influence. They returned thirty members to Parliament, and had themselves and their connections in all public posi-tions of honour or of pay. But our Scotch commerce was only dawning; and no merchants, great by the mere force of their wealth, had made either themselves or their calling formidable. Still less had they risen to importance as liberal patrons of liberal pursuits. This indeed is a character which has not arisen in Scotland even yet.* Academies have been founded by the aristocratic merchants of Italy, and galleries filled with art by the republican burgomasters of Holland, and colleges founded, or splendidly aided, by the munificence of traders in monarchical England; but nothing is so rare in Scotland as a merchant uniting wealth with liberal taste, and the patronage of art or science with the prosecution of private concerns. All Edinburgh attests that they have been profuse in the erection of charities that were to bear the names of the founders; and neither political nor ecclesiastical parties can justly charge them with shabbiness. But what have they done for learning, or art, or science? We are neither rich enough, nor old enough, for the rise of merchants princely in their tastes.

No part of the home scenery of Edinburgh was more beautiful than Bellevue, the villa of General Scott. It seemed to consist of nearly all the land between York Place and Canonmills—a space now almost covered by streets and houses. The mansion-house stood near the eastern side of the central enclosure of what is now Drummond Place; and a luxurious house it was. The whole place waved with wood, and was diversified

* Since Lord Cockburn's day, liberal patrons of the liberal arts have arisen and bequeathed to Edinburgh splendid memorials of their generosity in her New University Buildings and Hall, her National Portrait Gallery, her Public Library, and other institutions for the advancement of Art and Science.

by undulations of surface, and adorned by seats and bowers and summer houses. Queen Street, from which there was then an open prospect over the Firth to the north-western mountains, was the favourite Mall. Nothing certainly, within a town, could be more delightful than the sea of the Bellevue foliage gilded by the evening sun, or the tumult of blackbirds and thrushes sending their notes into all the adjoining houses in the blue of a summer morning. We clung long to the hope that, though the city might in time surround them, Bellevue at the east, and Drumsheugh (Lord Moray's place) at the west, end of Queen Street might be spared. But in 1802 Bellevue was sold. The magistrates, I believe, bought it; and the whole trees were instantly cut down. They could not all have been permanently spared; but many of them might, to the comfort and adornment of the future buildings. But the mere beauty of the town was no more thought of at that time by anybody than electric telegraphs and railways; and perpendicular trees, with leaves and branches, never find favour in the sight of any Scotch mason. But indeed in Scotland almost every one seems to be a " foe to the Dryads of the borough groves." It is partly owing to our climate, which rarely needs shade; but more to hereditary bad taste. Yet, though standing passive, I remember people shuddering when they heard the axes busy in the woods of Bellevue, and furious when they saw the bare ground. But the axes, as usual, triumphed; and all that art and nature had done to prepare the place for foliaged compartments of town architecture, if being built upon should prove inevitable, was carefully obliterated; so that at last the whole spot was made as bare and as dull as if the designer of the New Town himself had presided over the operation.

Gillespie's Hospital, for the shrouding of aged indigence, was commenced about this time, and completed in 1805. If I recollect right, this was the first of the public charities of this century by which Edinburgh has been blessed, or cursed. The founder was a snuff-seller, who brought up an excellent young man as his heir, and then left death to disclose that, for the vanity of being remembered by a thing called after himself, he had all the while had a deed executed by which this, his nearest, relation was disinherited. Another fact distinguished the rise of this institution. A very curious edifice stood on the very spot where the modern building is erected. It was called Wryttes-Houses,* and belonged anciently to a branch of the family of Napier.† It was a keep, presiding over a group of inferior buildings, most of it as old as the middle of the fourteenth century, all covered with heraldic and other devices, and all delightfully picturesque. Nothing could be more striking when seen against the evening sky. Many a feudal gathering

* "The popular derivation of the name is from the supposed fact of the wrights or carpenters having lived there while cutting down the trees on the Borough Muir in the reign of James IV."—Wilson's *Memorials of Edinburgh.*

† There is a good view of its position in one of Clerk of Eldin's sketches, printed for the Bannatyne Club ; and an excellent representation of its appearance, from a drawing by Charles Kirkpatrick Sharp, published in vol. ii. p. 208 of Wilson's *Memorials of Edinburgh in the Olden Time.*—H. C.

did that tower see on the Borough Moor; and many a time did the inventor of logarithms, whose castle of Merchiston was near, enter it. Yet was it brutishly obliterated, without one public murmur. A single individual whose name, were it known, ought to be honoured, but who chose to conceal himself under the signature of Cadmon, proclaimed and denounced the outrage, in a communication in July 1800 to the *Edinburgh Magazine ;* but the idiot public looked on in silence. How severely has Edinburgh suffered by similar proceedings, adventured upon by barbarians, knowing the apathetic nature, in these matters, of the people they have had to deal with. All our beauty might have been preserved, without the extinction of innumerable antiquities conferring interest and dignity. But reverence for mere antiquity, and even for modern beauty, *on their own account,* is scarcely a Scotch passion.

I had attended Dugald Stewart's first course of Political Economy, but not very steadily; and therefore I attended the second, which was given during the winter of 1801-1802. His hour was now three, but it was formerly seven in the evening, the lamps of which hour set off his bald sage-like head. The opening of these classes made a great sensation. The economical writings of Hume and Smith, though familiar with the liberal youth, had so little impregnated the public mind, that no ordinary audience could be collected to whom the elements and phraseology of the science were not matters of surprise. The mere term "Political

Economy " made most people start. They thought
that it included questions touching the constitution
of governments; and not a few hoped to catch Stewart
in dangerous propositions.* It was not unusual to see
a smile on the faces of some when they heard subjects
discoursed upon, seemingly beneath the dignity of the
Academical Chair. The word *Corn* sounded strangely
in the moral class, and *Drawbacks* seemed a profanation of Stewart's voice.

These lectures were distinguished by the acknowledged excellences, and the supposed defects, of his
ordinary course. Some called them superficial; a
worse imperfection in Political Economy, an exact
science, than in Moral Philosophy, a more diffuse one.
He certainly did not involve his hearers in its intri-
cacies; and there were dull heads to whom the absence
of arithmetical columns and statistical details was as
grievous a blank in the one class, as that of metaphysical subtleties was in the other. But adherence to
the exposition of general principles was equally
judicious in both. By chiefly exposing the edges of the
veins, and directing his pupils how to explore the
treasures of the mine, he at once heightened the
beauty of his discourses, and awakened the ambition of his students. The result, accordingly, was
the best evidence of the soundness of this plan. He
supplied both young and old with philosophical ideas
on what they had scarcely been accustomed to think
philosophical subjects, unfolded the elements and the

* It is plainly to this *disposition* of the times that Stewart alludes in
note D to his life of Smith.—H. C.

ends of that noble science, and so recommended it by the graces of his eloquence that even his idler hearers retained a permanent taste for it.

Edinburgh had never contained such a concentration of young men as now inspired it, of whose presence the *Review* was only one of the results. They formed a band of friends all attached to each other, all full of hope and ambition and gaiety, and all strengthened in their mutual connection by the politics of most of them separating the whole class from the ordinary society of the city. It was a most delightful brotherhood. But about the end of 1802 it began to be thinned by emigration, and this process went on till 1806. Within two years (1802-1803) Sydney Smith, Francis Horner, Thomas Campbell, John Allen, and John Leyden, all fell off.

Smith's reputation here then was the same as it has been throughout his life, that of a wise wit. Was there ever more sense combined with more hilarious jocularity? But he has been lost by being placed within the pale of holy orders. He has done his duty there decently well, and is an admirable preacher. But he ought to have been in some freer sphere; especially since wit and independence do not make bishops.

Allen was medical, but prosecuted medicine rather as a science than as a profession. He was the very first of our private lecturers; physiology being his favourite department. I have heard Doctor John Gordon, a judge on such a matter of the highest authority, say that Allen's single lecture on the circulation of the blood contained as much truth and view as could be extracted by an intelligent reader from all the books in Europe on that subject. Had not his political opinions made it prudent for him to despair of being ever allowed to adorn our College, he would probably have remained here, where he was much beloved by all who knew him, and had a great reputation. But, in his circumstances, an invitation to live with Lord Holland was irresistible. This alliance has shown him most of Europe well; and introduced him, confidentially, to the best society in England. The transition from this to the private political line was natural; and in this line there is no one man whose talent and learning is of so much use to his party. But all this latent importance, dignified luxury, and indirect usefulness was obtained (as it always has seemed to me) at far too high a price when it lost him the glory of being the first medical teacher in Europe.* His historical publications, chiefly though not entirely in the *Edinburgh Review*, especially those on the constitution and progress of England, are of the very highest value. Indeed it makes us almost regret the existence of a publication which enables such men to throw in their detached contributions to the treasury of knowledge, to think that if it had not been for such an opportunity, instead of evaporating in unconnected and anonymous discussions, they might have earned

---

* In 1811 John Allen became warden of Dulwich College, and master in 1820, which position he held till his death in 1843.

a more visible and permanent reputation by complete and original works.*

John Leyden has said of himself, " I often verge so nearly on absurdity, that I know it is perfectly easy to misconceive me, as well as misrepresent me." This was quite true; especially the vergency on absurdity. He cannot be understood till the peculiarities to which he alludes are cleared away, and the better man is made to appear. His conspicuous defect used to be called affectation, but in reality it was pretension. A pretension, however, of a very innocent kind, which, without derogating in the least from the claim of any other, merely exaggerated not his own merits, nor what he had done, but his capacity and ambition to do more.† Ever in a state of excitement, ever ardent, ever panting for things unattainable by ordinary mortals, and successful to an extent sufficient to rouse the hopes of a young man ignorant of life, there was nothing that he thought beyond his reach; and not knowing what insincerity was, he

* Horner says (Mem. i. 206) that "in point of candour and vigour of reasoning powers, I have never personally known a finer intellect than Jeffrey's, *unless I were to except Allen's.*" In point of candour they were both perfect, and in the mere power of deducting one thing from another, within a certain range, nobody could exceed Allen. But the difference of the ranges of the two men was immense. Allen's reasoning is always on minute objects. Whatever his logical eye might be capable of, it has never attempted the lofty and extensive regions which Jeffrey's reasonings comprehend. But Horner said this in 1802, when Jeffrey had scarcely begun to rise.—H. C.

† "To those who objected to the miscellaneous, or occasionally to the superficial nature of his studies he used to answer with his favourite interjection, 'Dash it, man, never mind ; if you have the scaffolding ready you can run up the masonry when you please.'"—*Scott's Miscellaneous Works.*

spoke of his powers and his visions as openly as if he had been expounding what might be expected of another person. According to himself, John Leyden could easily in a few months have been a great physician, or surpassed Sir William Jones in Oriental literature, or Milton in poetry. Yet at the very time he was thus exposing himself, he was not only simple, but generous and humble. He was a wild-looking, thin, Roxburghshire man, with sandy hair, a screech voice, and staring eyes—exactly as he came from his native village of Denholm; and not one of these not very attractive personal qualities would he have exchanged for all the graces of Apollo. By the time I knew him he had made himself one of our social shows, and could and did say whatever he chose. His delight lay in an argument about the Scotch Church, or Oriental literature, or Scotch poetry, or odd customs, or scenery, always conducted on his part in a high shrill voice, with great intensity, and an utter unconsciousness of the amazement, or even the aversion, of strangers. His daily extravagances, especially mixed up, as they always were, with exhibitions of his own ambition and confidence, made him be much laughed at even by his friends. Sir John Malcolm's account * of his Indian deportment agrees exactly with the accounts given by Scott of his Scotch one. Sir James Mackintosh calls him his " wild friend," and laughs at his professing to know " only seventy languages."

Notwithstanding these ridiculous or offensive habits, he had considerable talent and great excel-

* In Morton's *Memoirs of Leyden*.—H. C.

lences. There is no walk in life, depending on ability, where Leyden could not have shone. Unwearying industry was sustained and inspired by burning enthusiasm. Whatever he did, his whole soul was in it. His heart was warm and true. No distance, or interest, or novelty could make him forget an absent friend or his poor relations. His physical energy was as vigorous as his mental; so that it would not be easy to say whether he would have engaged with a new-found Eastern manuscript, or in battle, with the more cordial alacrity. His love of Scotland was delightful. It breathes through all his writings and all his pro-ceedings, and imparts to his poetry its most attractive charm. The affection borne him by many distinguished friends, and their deep sorrow for his early extinction, is the best evidence of his talent and worth. Indeed, his premature death was deplored by all who delight to observe the elevation of merit, by its own force and through personal defects, from obscurity to fame. He died in Batavia at the age of thirty-six. Had he been spared, he would have been a star in the East of the first magnitude.

John Richardson was the last of the association who was devoured by hungry London. This was in 1806. But he has been incorporated, privately and publicly, with all that is worthy in Edinburgh, and much that is worthy in London, throughout his whole life. No Scotchman in London ever stood higher in professional and personal character. The few verses he has published, like almost all he has written, are

in the style of simple and pensive elegance. His early
and steady addiction to literary subjects and men
would certainly have made literature his vocation,*
had he not foreseen its tortures and precariousness
when relied on for subsistence. But, though drudging
in the depths of the law, this toil has always been
graced by the cultivation of letters, and by the cordial
friendship of the most distinguished literary men of
the age.† He was the last of the old Edinburgh
emigrants. A cold cloud came over many a heart at
each of their departures; and happy and brilliant as
our society was afterwards, we never ceased to miss
them, to mark the vacant places, and to remember
that they were once of ourselves.

A stranger came among us while these men were
still here. This was Lord Webb Seymour, brother of
the Duke of Somerset. He had left his own country,
and renounced all the ordinary uses of rank and
fortune, for study; and never abandoned the place

* Richardson wrote a life of Scott and of Campbell, and was an
early contributor to *Blackwood's Magazine*. He undertook the office
of mediator between Leigh Hunt and William Blackwood when the
former threatened to bring an action against the publisher for the
article on the "Cockney School of Poetry" in No. 1 of *Maga*.

† His intimacy with Sir Walter Scott was particularly close and he
was one of the few entrusted with the secret of the authorship of
Waverley. Fishing the Tweed, on one of his visits to Abbotsford, with
Sir Walter as his companion, Richardson hooked a particularly large
trout, which, before it was landed, gave considerable trouble and broke
the rod. Tom Purdie, who had joined the party, admitted that "the like
of it had not been killed in the Tweed for twenty years." When Sir
Walter and Richardson had moved away they were highly amused to
observe Purdie giving the fish a kick, at the same time angrily ex-
claiming, "An tae be taen by the like o' him frae Lunnon."

he had selected for its prosecution, but continued
here during the rest of his life, with his books and
literary friends, universally respected and beloved.
Slow, thoughtful, reserved, and very gentle, he promoted the philosophical taste even of Horner, and
enjoyed quietly the jocularity of Smith, and tried
gravely to refute the argumentative levities of Jeffrey.
His special associate was Playfair. They used to be
called husband and wife; and in congeniality and
affection no union could be more complete. Geology
was their favourite pursuit. Before I got acquainted
with them, I used to envy their walks in the neighbourhood of Edinburgh, and their scientific excur-
sions to the recesses of the Highland glens, and to the
summits of the Highland mountains. Two men more
amiable, more philosophical, and more agreeable
there could not be.

Sir James Montgomery, the Lord Chief Baron,
resigned in 1801. This made Robert Dundas Lord
Chief Baron, Charles Hope Lord Advocate, and Blair
Dean of the Faculty in Dundas' stead.

Montgomery, the author of the Entail Act which
bears his name, was a most excellent and venerable
old gentleman. He lived in Queensberry House in the
Canongate, and I believe was the last gentleman who
resided in that historical mansion, which, though now
one of the asylums of destitution, was once the brilliant abode of rank and fashion and political intrigue.
I wish the Canongate could be refreshed again by the
habitual sight of the Lord Chief Baron's family and

company, and the gorgeous carriage, and the tall and
well-dressed figure, in the old style, of his Lordship
himself. He was much in our house, my father being
one of his Puisnes. Though a remarkably kind landlord, he thought it his duty to proceed sometimes with
apparent severity against poachers, smugglers, and
other rural corrupters; but as it generally ended in
his paying the fine himself, in order to save the family,
his benevolence was supposed to do more harm than
his justice did good. He died in 1803.

Not long after Hope's appointment he got into
difficulty. The occasion was one very likely to hit his
fiery fancy. A Banffshire farmer, named Morison,
chose to exercise his undoubted right of dismissing a
servant for·absenting himself without leave from
work, in order to attend a volunteer drill. In consequence of this offence, the Lord Advocate issued a
rescript to the Sheriff-Substitute of the county of
Banff, in which the farmer's conduct is said to have
been " atrocious," and " could only have arisen from
a secret spirit of disaffection and disloyalty "; and
therefore an official order is given to the Sheriff-
Substitute, that " on the first Frenchman landing in
Scotland, you do immediately apprehend and secure
Morison as a suspected person, and you will not
liberate him without communication with me; and
you may inform him of these my orders; and further,
that I shall do all I can to prevent him from receiving
any compensation for any part of his property which
may either be destroyed by the enemy, or by the
king's troops to prevent it from falling into the

M

enemy's hands." This was brought before the House of Commons by Mr Whitbread, on the 22nd of June 1804, on a motion for a vote of censure. The Lord Advocate's defence was more unfortunate than his original error, because it justified it. He maintained that, considering the situation of the country, what he had done was right; and that if wrong, it was an error of discretion in a matter as to which his official discretion was boundless. The Lord Advocate, he said, was vested with the whole powers, both civil and military, of the state, and of all its officers, most of which, as centring in himself, he specified.* Nevertheless, a motion for the previous question was carried; and its success stands as a striking example of the difference between a parliament of that time and any that could be assembled now. No one who knew him could impute cruelty or injustice to Charles Hope. This act was entirely owing to a hot temperament not cooled by a sound head. In spite of all his talent and all his worth, had he continued in the very delicate position of Lord Advocate, his infirmity might have again brought him into some similar trouble.

It was fortunate therefore that the gods, envying mortals the longer possession of Eskgrove, took him to themselves; and Hope reigned in his stead. He was made Lord Justice-Clerk in December 1804. It

---

* When he came home, his return was given in an English newspaper something in this way—" Arrived at Edinburgh the Lord High Chancellor of Scotland, the Lord Justice-General, the Lord Privy Seal, the Privy Council, and the Lord Advocate, all in one post-chaise, containing only a single person."—H. C.

has been often said, and often denied, that before taking this place to himself, he offered it to Henry Erskine, and urged Erskine to take it. There can be no doubt with me of his having made this very handsome proposal, because he told me himself that he had done so, and that Erskine after consulting his friends declined.

The only important legislative measure that Hope had an opportunity of officially promoting was the Schoolmasters' Act of 1803, which has been in force since that time. This is the statute which compels heritors to build what are there called *Houses* for the schoolmasters; but prescribes that the house need not contain more than two rooms *including the kitchen*. This shabbiness was abused at the time, and seems incredible now. But Hope told me that he had considerable difficulty in getting even the two rooms, and that a great majority of the lairds and Scotch members were indignant at being obliged to " erect palaces for dominies."

The armed truce—for it was rather this than peace —in 1802 made very little direct change in our habits or feelings. But, upon the whole, events were bringing people into better humour. Somewhat less was said about Jacobinism, though still too much; and sedition had gone out. Napoleon's obvious progress towards military despotism opened the eyes of those who used to see nothing but liberty in the French Revolution; and the threat of invasion, while it combined all parties in defence of the country, raised the confidence of the people in those who trusted them with arms, and gave them the pleasure of playing at soldiers. Instead of Jacobinism, Invasion became the word.

After the war broke out again in 1803, Edinburgh, like every other place, became a camp, and continued so till the peace in 1814. We were all soldiers, one way or other. Professors wheeled in the College area; the side arms and the uniform peeped from behind the gown at the bar, and even on the bench; and the parade and the review formed the staple of men's talk and thoughts. Hope, who had kept his Lieutenant-Colonelcy when he was Lord Advocate, adhered to it, and did all its duties after he became Lord Justice-Clerk. This was thought unconstitutional by some; but the spirit of the day applauded it. Brougham served the same gun in a company of artillery with Playfair. James Moncreiff, John Richardson, James Grahame (the Sabbath), Thomas Thomson, and Charles Bell were all in one company of riflemen. Francis Horner walked about the streets with a musket, being a private in the Gentlemen Regiment. Dr Gregory was a soldier, and Thomas Brown the moralist, Jeffrey, and many another since famous in more intellectual warfare. I, a gallant captain, commanded ninety-two of my fellow creatures from 1804 to 1814—the whole course of that war. Eighty private soldiers, two officers, four serjeants, four corporals, and a trumpeter, all trembled (or at least were bound to tremble) when I spoke. Mine was the left flank company of the " Western Battalion of Midlothian Volunteers." John

A. Murray's company was the right flank one; and as these two were both from the parish of St Cuthbert's, the rest being scattered over the county, we always drilled together. When we first began, being resolved that we townsmen should outshine the rustics, we actually drilled our two companies almost every night during the four winter months of 1804 and 1805, by torch light, in the ground flat of the George Street Assembly Rooms, which was then all one earthen-floored apartment. This was over and above our day proceedings in Heriot's Green and Bruntsfield Links, or with the collected regiment. The parades, the reviews, the four or six yearly inspections at Dalmahoy, the billettings for a fortnight or three weeks when on "permanent duty" at Leith or Haddington, the mock battles, the marches, the messes—what scenes they were! And similar scenes were familiar in every town and in every shire in the kingdom. The terror of the ballot for the regular militia which made those it hit soldiers during the war, filled the ranks; while duty, necessity, and especially the contagion of the times, supplied officers. The result was that we became a military population. Any able-bodied man, of whatever rank, who was *not* a volunteer, or a local militiaman, had to explain or apologise for his singularity.

Walter Scott's zeal in the cause was very curious. He was the soul of the Edinburgh troop of Midlothian Yeomanry Cavalry. It was not a duty with him, or a necessity, or a pastime, but an absolute passion, indulgence in which gratified his feudal taste for war and his jovial sociableness. He drilled, and drank, and made songs, with a hearty conscientious earnestness which inspired or shamed everybody within the attraction. I do not know if it is usual, but his troop used to practise, individually, with the sabre at a turnip, which was stuck on the top of a staff, to represent a Frenchman, in front of the line. Every other trooper, when he set forward in his turn, was far less concerned about the success of his aim at the turnip, than about how he was to tumble. But Walter pricked forward gallantly, saying to himself, " Cut them down, the villains, cut them down! " and made his blow, which from his lameness was often an awkward one, cordially, muttering curses all the while at the detested enemy.

Notwithstanding all our soldiering, the prevailing feeling about invasion was that of indifference. I do not think that people brought its realities home to their conception. The utter security of this island, ever since the blowing back of the Armada, made the population treat actual invasion as a thing not to be seriously contemplated. But thinking men were in a great and genuine fright, which increased in proportion as they thought. The apparent magic of Napoleon's Continental success confounded them: Ireland made them shudder; and they saw that a war in this thick set and complicated country, however short and triumphant for us it might be, must give a dreadful shock to our whole system.

The volunteers tended to unsettle the minds of those who belonged to them for ordinary business;

and hence they co-operated with the ballot in filling the ranks of the militia, which was the great nursery for the army. In this way the voluntary establishments were a very useful force; and if they had been called into active service, all the paid regiments, that is, all those composed of hardy ploughmen and artisans, would have soon become good practical soldiers. But for *immediate* service, for which it was intended they should be prepared, they were totally disqualified. They had no field equipage, and were scarcely ever trained to march beyond their parade ground. Certainly no volunteer regiment in Scotland ever passed twenty-four hours at a time, in the open air, upon its own resources. And even their drilling was universally vitiated by the essential and obvious defect of their not being moved in large masses. There was nothing done, beyond the performance of ordinary regimental business, for the creation of field officers. It was all single battalion drilling and useless shows; the work of each week being the same with that of the week before. Except as police the *Foot Gentlemen* were useless. The patrician blood is the best blood for soldiers, both for valour and for endurance; but it requires long and severe experience to subdue it to the details of the life of a private foot soldier.

We had hitherto been so innocent or so poor, and so long accustomed to undetected or irregularly detected crime, that the *City Guard*, composed of discharged soldiers, and whose youngest member was at the least threescore, was sufficient to keep us in what was then called order. But this drunken burgher force at last became too ludicrous; and its extinction (which, however, did not take place till 1817) was further recommended by its abridging the dark jurisdiction of the magistrates, and creating a new office. It was therefore resolved that the capital should have the honour of a civil police, which I think no other town in Scotland then had upon a regular system. Our first effort in this line forms rather a curious bit of local history. A person of harmless habits, correct principles, due poverty, and no head, was set up to show people what might be made of these institutions. In order to secure respect for his office he was invested with the double authority of Lord Advocate and Lord Justice-Clerk, being made both superintendent and Judge, and thus first accusing, and then trying those he accused. For this he got £500 a year; and lest the people should not be impressed with due reverence, his body was arrayed in a black gown garnished with knots of gold thread, and was marched in grand procession to his Lawnmarket Court, where Sir Harry Moncreiff was obliged to install him by prayer. The popular satisfaction at seeing the magistrates in some degree superseded was so general, that only a man dexterous in offence could have made the public doubt the wisdom of the new establishment. But he was not wise, and so ill-tempered officially that he soon raised a burgh rebellion, and nearly spoiled the whole experiment. Being prosecutor, his tendency was to suspect everybody; and being judge, his glory required that he should never decide against himself;

and the system being new, he was smitten with the usual weakness of absolute lawgivers, and introduced a code which at least was beautiful in his own sight. For example, it was his opinion that noisy mirth, especially at late hours, was a bad thing; and therefore when Mr George Thomson, the correspondent of Burns, gave a ball in his own house, the police officers, obeying their instructions for all such cases, having ascertained that the neighbours had neither been invited nor consulted, entered and dispersed the illegal assembly; and his Honour decided next day that this was all quite right. This tyranny was bad enough for the rich, but it was far worse for the poor, whom the accusing spirit and recording angel tortured without pity or control; not from cruelty, for personally he was good-natured, but from that love of vexatious petty regulation, and that impatience of check, which tempt weak heads. At last even our rulers admitted that he was intolerable; and this was the happiest event of his life, for he got £300 a year for getting out of the way. A better system was then introduced, and has in substance continued.

Nobody foresaw, and least of all its authors, the indirect consequences of this police establishment. So far as I am aware, *it was the first example of popular election in Scotland*. Aversion to be taxed was overcome by allowing the people to choose the Police Commissioners; a precedent always appealed to, till the Reform Act superseded the necessity of using it. The gradual extension of the police system over our towns trained the people to expect and to exercise

the elective privilege; and the effect of this in exciting
and organising public spirit was so great, that the
rise of the Edinburgh establishment is one of our
local eras. Dr John Thomson was not extravagant
when, in reference to our position, he used to call it a
Divine Institution.

The memorable case of Professor Leslie began early
in 1805, and though settled in the General Assembly
in May of that year, the public discussion was prolonged till far on in 1806. It made a deep and universal impression. The substance of the case is this:—
The promotion of John Playfair to the chair of
Natural Philosophy in the University of Edinburgh,
made a vacancy in Playfair's chair of Mathematics.
John Leslie, whose recent treatise on heat had placed
him high in science, was the only well qualified
candidate. He was patronised by Stewart, Playfair,
and all good judges who had only superiority of fitness
in view; and his subsequent eminence justified their
recommendation. But the Moderate clergy, who had
long encouraged pluralities, and wished to multiply
clerical professorships, allotted the place to one of
themselves. They probably cared little who the
individual should be, but it was understood, and
indeed never denied, that their favourite upon this
occasion was the Reverend Dr Thomas Macknight, the
son of the Harmonist; a most excellent man, by no
means devoid of science, but unheard of in the
scientific world, and not capable of being named
seriously as a worthy competitor of Leslie. However,

any clergyman would have done: but the first thing was to exclude the layman. The reverend faction therefore began by proposing to put the College Test to Leslie; but this was defeated by his at once agreeing to take it. Not one of the Presbytery of Edinburgh except Macknight had read, or could understand, the work on heat; but somebody told them that that treatise contained a note with these words—" Mr Hume is the first, as far as I know, who has treated of Causation in a truly philosophical manner. His *Essay on Necessary Connexion* seems a model of clear and accurate reasoning," etc. This supplied them with the very thing they wanted—a personal exception to the candidate whose science was unassailable. The cry of atheism was raised; a cry seldom raised in vain in this country, and to which the very name of David Hume gave particular force. It was proclaimed that these words, though only applied to physical science, involved the adoption by Mr Leslie of the whole of Hume's doctrine of Cause and Effect, and of all the moral consequences which that cunning sceptic deduced from it. The course therefore was now clear. The Presbytery of Edinburgh announced first, that, by the foundation of the University the Town Council could only elect " *cum avisamento eorum ministrorum*," which the clergy held to imply a *veto* in their favour; and then, that the note, being heretical, tainted the whole book, and the book the man; and lastly, that schools and colleges being subject to the presbytery of the bounds, it was both their right and their duty to have this philosopher excluded. The real value of this pretension was, that it would apply to every case in which the clergy could detect what they might think unsound doctrine; and therefore all the machinery, and all the rancour of the ecclesiastical courts was put into activity to aid it. No wonder that dispassionate men were alarmed by a conspiracy of which the object was to entitle the Church to control every patron in the election of every professor, and indeed to subject learning once more to priestcraft.

The weight of metaphysical authority was on the side of the note, and Thomas Brown's fine metaphysical spear shivered all the argumentative weapons by which, as applied to this point, it was assailed. Still the assailants may possibly have had truth on their side, though they fought their battle ill. But metaphysics had nothing to do with the matter. They were the pretence; while a claim of clerical domination over seats of learning was the real subject.

The Town Council, jealous of the attempt to supersede them, and encouraged by the support of liberal and pious men, stood firm and elected Leslie. The Presbytery, relying on ecclesiastical sympathy, stood firm also; but, after much manœuvring, it resolved to show its candour by only *Referring* the matter to the Synod for advice. It is honourable to the Presbytery that this course was only carried by fourteen against thirteen. The thirteen were for quashing the whole affair. The inquisitors formed a majority of the Synod, but this body also thought it safest to preserve the outward appearance of impartiality by *Referring* to the General Assembly. Sir Harry Moncreiff instantly entered a Complaint against this Reference—a sagacious move; for it made the Synod a party at the bar of the Assembly, and consequently excluded the votes of its members, and thus ultimately saved the case.

The prevailing public feeling was strongly against the persecution and its horrid principle. Toryism was rather in favour of the Church; Whiggism decidedly against it. The two proper Church parties were reversed. The Moderate clergy, more indifferent about scepticism than their opponents, yet liking power above all things, were nearly unanimous against Leslie. The Wild, cordial in their horror of heresy, almost all supported the supposed disciple of Hume. This singular position for them was not produced, as their enemies absurdly said, by their hating their ecclesiastical antagonists more than they hated infidelity, but by their honest incapacity, notwithstanding their jealousy of it, to discover any infidelity in the matter. There could not have been a stronger fact against the persecutors than that, on such a question, they were opposed by the whole evangelical clergy.

The debate in the Assembly wore out two long days. The result, in point of form, was, that the Complaint against the Reference was sustained; the meaning of which was, that the conduct of the Presbytery and the Synod was condemned, and the opposition stopped. The respective votes were ninety-six to eighty-four. It is frightful to think that such a result as was implied in the Reference was within twelve of receiving all the support that the ecclesiastical tribunal could give it. The Church could not settle the civil rights of the patrons or the presentee; but if the ecclesiastical decision had been that the presentee was a heretic, he would have been a bold man who would have answered for the Civil Court not giving effect to this decision in those days, when to oppose the Church was to oppose good order and the Government. It was a small house for such a question; but many of the Moderate stayed away from not liking the job, and some of the Wild from the words David Hume.

Some of the speeches, in this the most important Scotch debate I have ever known, were excellent. Sir Harry Moncreiff's, for practical effect, was the best. Avoiding the metaphysical slough into which it was the great object of the persecutors to lead their opponents, he was concise, vigorous, and contemptuous upon the common sense and truth of the case. It must have given the Lord President Campbell, who was a liberal man, some pain to quibble, and with little of his usual acuteness, in defence of a prosecution for which he could have no taste. He suffered severely for his imprudence from Lauderdale, whose appetite was evidently whetted by catching a judge rash enough to expose himself on equal terms in public debate. Adam Gillies and Henry Erskine were strong and useful on the just side; but neither of them equal to James Moncreiff, who on this occasion displayed, for the first time, the vigorous argumentative powers which made him afterwards the most habitually useful layman in the Assembly. Dr John Inglis, one of the deepest in the plot, was as good as ingenious metaphysics can ever be in a popular assembly. Principal Hill, the successor of Principal Robertson as the leader of the Church, was, as usual, plausible and elegant; and laid out his most dexterous and persuasive lures to fix every waverer, and to recall those who were inclined to forget their fidelity to the Moderate standard. Dugald Stewart closed the discussion by a speech which he meant to have been longer, but inexperience of such rough scenes made him too plain in his indignation, and he was called to order, and sat down; not, however, till he had delivered a few long-remembered sentences in a very fine spirit of scorn and eloquence.

A curious error was committed by the Reverend Dr Andrew Hunter, Professor of Divinity, a deeply religious gentleman, by whom the debate was opened in favour of the Complaint; an error very innocently fallen into, and very handsomely avowed, and which shows how much inaccuracy may sometimes pass undetected not merely in history, but in the discussions of living and intelligent men. Dr Henry Hunter of London, a Presbyterian minister of undoubted learning and piety, translated Euler's *Letters*, and this translation contains a note on Hume's doctrine of Causation, the same in substance as the note objected to in Leslie's book. Dr Andrew Hunter quoted this note by his namesake; and no authority that was produced had greater effect on the Assembly. But just after closing his speech, the worthy Professor, with his usual candour and simplicity, explained that he had been informed that the note in Euler was not by

Henry Hunter but by Condorcet. Of course, the detection that Leslie's doctrine was approved of, not by the Presbyterian divine, but by the French atheist, raised a hearty laugh on one side of the house against honest Andrew, and produced many a sneer at Leslie for his ally. This was so important that James Moncreiff was at the pains to take it up next day, and to demonstrate, as he thought, that after all the first statement was correct, and that the note was by Henry Hunter himself. But the truth, then only known to Mr Macvey Napier, was, that both statements were inaccurate, and that the note in Euler was written neither by Henry Hunter nor by Condorcet, but by John Leslie! He had assisted anonymously in a translation of one of Condorcet's works, and in doing so, composed and inserted this note, which Henry Hunter, finding it in the English Condorcet, and never doubting that it formed part of the original work, quoted as Condorcet's in his translation of Euler. All this used to be explained by Leslie afterwards. What an escape for him, and for his reverend champion in the Assembly, that no one there knew that he himself had been quoted as the strongest authority in his own support!

Hermand was in a glorious frenzy. Spurning all unfairness, a religious doubt, entangled with mystical metaphysics, and countenanced by his party, had great attractions for his excitable head and Presbyterian taste! What a figure! as he stood on the floor declaiming and screaming, amidst the divines—the tall man, with his thin powdered locks and long pig-tail, the long Court of Session cravat flaccid and streaming with the heat, and the obtrusive linen! The published report makes him declare that " the belief of the being and perfections of the Deity is the solace and delight of my life. It is a feeling which I sucked in with my mother's milk." But this would not have been half intense for Hermand; and accordingly his words were—" *Sir! I sucked in the being and attributes of God with my mother's milk!* "* His constant and affectionate reverence for his mother exceeded the devotion of any Indian for his idol; and under this feeling he amazed the House by maintaining (which was his real opinion) that there was no apology for infidelity, or even for religious doubt, because no good or sensible man had anything to do except to be of the religion of his mother; which, be it what it might, was always the best. " A sceptic, Sir, I hate! With my whole heart I detest him! *But, Moderator, I love a Turk!* "†

It was not without reason that the liberal, all over the country, rejoiced. Those in Edinburgh celebrated their victory by a dinner at which Sir Harry presided admirably. The defeated leaders of the clergy never entirely recovered their reputation. Many of them

* Lord Cockburn elsewhere tells the following story of Lord Hermand. Within a few hours of his end Mrs Ferguson was about to administer some spiritual comfort, when he told her, " You need say nothing of that, my dear ; I've made my peace with God *in my own way.*"

† The report, which was published about five months after the debate, is as bad as possible. It omits all that was striking, and smooths everything over with a dull surface of composed proprieties and generalities. No idea or feeling of this most interesting debate can be got from its vapidity.— H. C.

N

were excellent, and some of them able, men; but their accession to this plot could never be forgotten. The defeat undoubtedly helped to kill Dr Finlayson, who died in January 1808, without ever having resumed his habitual look of hard calm confidence. Though never exposing himself by a speech or a pamphlet, he was the underground soul of the dark confederacy. When sitting at the bar, pale with vexation, while they were taking the vote by calling the roll, and the issue became visible, Jeffrey, who was just behind, consoled him by saying in his sharp sarcastic style—" Take a little gingerbread, Doctor." The laugh did not relieve him. Giving the critic a slap in the face would. Finlayson's ecclesiastical life reminds one of Pascal's saying of the Jesuits—" Les plus habiles d'entre eux sont ceux qui intriguent beaucoup, qui parlent peu, et qui n'ecrivent point."

The controversy was distinguished by some publications of permanent value. Stewart contributed an *Explanation of Facts*, marked by his usual taste and judgment. Brown put forth the first draught of his inquiry into the nature of our idea of Causation; a work declared by Mackintosh to " entitle him to a place, very, very near the first among the living metaphysicians of Great Britain." Playfair published *A Letter to one of the Ministers of Edinburgh*—one of the best controversial pamphlets in the English language. Francis Horner gave an admirable exposition of the whole contest in an article in the *Edinburgh Review* [No. 13, art. 7]. Dr Inglis was the great writer and speaker on the other side. And he wrote and spoke well. So well that, until Brown appeared, he was thought to have the best of the metaphysical argument—the favourite bush into which he and his friends always pushed their heads. Chalmers came forward in his first publication, being *Observations on a Passage in Mr Playfair's Letter to the Lord Provost of Edinburgh, relative to the mathematical pretensions of the Scottish Clergy.* This was the famous pamphlet in which he stated, on the authority of his own experience, that, " after the satisfactory discharge of his parish duties, a minister may enjoy five days in the week of uninterrupted leisure for the prosecution of any science in which his taste may dispose him to engage." This was said before he became religious; and a noble explanation did he give, when it was quoted against him in the Assembly many years after the acquisition of his new nature.*

A genius now appeared, who has immortalised Edinburgh and will long delight the world. Walter

* It was during a discussion on pluralities in the Assembly of 1825 that the incident occurred to which Lord Cockburn refers. Dr Chalmers had condemned the practice when an opposition speaker quoted from an anonymous pamphlet—but one which it was well known had been written by Dr Chalmers many years before. The doctor at once accepted the responsibility, and thanking his opponent for giving him the opportunity, explained the position he had then taken up, and closed his defence with, " Alas ! sir, so I thought in my ignorance and pride. I have now no reserve in saying that the sentiment was wrong, and that in the utterance of it I penned what was most outrageously wrong. Strangely blinded that I was ! What, sir, is the object of mathematical science ? Magnitude and the proportions of magnitude. But *then*, sir, I had forgotten two magnitudes : I had thought not of the littleness of time—I had recklessly thought not of the greatness of eternity ! "— Hanna's *Life of Chalmers.*

Scott's vivacity and force had been felt since his boy-hood by his comrades, and he had disclosed his literary inclinations by some translations of German ballads, and a few slight pieces in the *Minstrelsy of the Scottish Border ;* but his power of great original conception and execution was unknown both to his friends and himself. In 1805 he revealed his true self by the publication of the *Lay of the Last Minstrel.* The subject, from the principle of which he rarely afterwards deviated, was, for the period, singularly happy. It recalled scenes and times and characters so near as almost to linger in the memories of the old, and yet so remote that their revival, under poetical embellishment, imparted the double pleasure of invention and of history. The instant completeness of his success showed him his region. The *Lay* was followed by a more impressive pause of wonder, and then by a louder shout of admiration, than even our previous Edinburgh poem—" The Pleasures of Hope." But nobody, not even Scott, anticipated what was to follow. Nobody imagined the career that was before him; that the fertility of his genius was to be its most wonderful distinction; that there was to be an unceasing recurrence of fresh delight, enhanced by surprise at his rapidity and richness. His advances were like the conquests of Napoleon: each new achievement overshadowing the last; till people half wearied of his very profusion. The quick succession of his original works, interspersed as they were with (for him rather unworthy) productions of a lower kind, threw a literary splendour over his native city, which had now the glory of being at once the seat of the most popular poetry, and the most powerful criticism of the age.

The society of Edinburgh has never been better, or indeed so good, since I knew it as it was about this time. It continued in a state of high animation till 1815, or perhaps till 1820. Its brilliancy was owing to a variety of peculiar circumstances which only operated during this period. The principal of these were— the survivance of several of the eminent men of the preceding age, and of curious old habits which the modern flood had not yet obliterated; the rise of a powerful community of young men of ability; the exclusion of the British from the Continent, which made this place, both for education and for residence, a favourite resort of strangers; the war, which maintained a constant excitement of military preparation, and of military idleness; the blaze of that popular literature which made this the second city in the empire for learning and science; and the extent, and the ease, with which literature and society embellished each other, without rivalry, and without pedantry. The first abstraction from this composition was by the deaths of our interesting old. Then London drew away several of our best young. There was a gap in the production of fresh excellence. Peace in 1815 opened the long closed floodgates, and gave to the Continent most of the strangers we used to get. A new race of peace-formed native youths came on the stage, but with little literature, and a comfortless intensity of political zeal; so that by about the year

1820 the old thing was much worn out, and there was no new thing, of the same piece, to continue or replace it. Much undoubtedly remained to make Edinburgh still, to those who knew how to use it, a city of Goshen, and to set us above all other British cities except one, and in some things above even that one. But the exact old thing was not.

CHAPTER IV

In 1806 the Whigs were surprised to find themselves in power. This was an unnatural result of mere accident; for there was no real foundation for the official rise of this party at that period, nor at any period during the life of George the Third. But it was a most salutary event for Scotland. It convinced the Tories that they were not positively immortal. It told the Whigs, and all the liberal population which was growing in silence, not to despair utterly. The tendencies of both parties, of the one towards hereditary insolence, and of the other towards confirmed despondency, were corrected in some degree by the mere fact of a change.

John Clerk was appointed Solicitor-General; Henry Erskine was replaced as Lord Advocate; and the Earl of Lauderdale became the real Scotch minister.* It was very unfortunate for the progress of sound opinions that Scotland was unavoidably put under the charge of persons not well qualified to turn the power thus given to them to the best advantage.

---

* The Earl of Lauderdale, although in 1792 one of the founders of the *Friends of the People*, and for some years recognised as the chief of the Whig party in Scotland, ultimately joined the Tories. In 1830 he opposed the Court of Session Bill in the House of Lords and was instrumental in securing the return of twelve of the sixteen Scottish representative Peers pledged to oppose reform in 1831.

Personally, Erskine was excellent; liberal, judicious and beloved. But he was married to Clerk, who personally was also excellent, but officially he was crotchety, positive, and wild; and domineered over the softer nature of Erskine. The younger Whigs, several of whom were far before these official persons, both in general knowledge and in present public affairs, were not taken into council at all. Even the spirit and wisdom of their Whig articles in the *Review* never made Jeffrey, Horner, or Brougham be consulted or considered. The truth is, that the senior Whigs had at this time considerable jealousy of the higher class of their juniors; especially after it became manifest that the younger men saw the imperfections of their leaders, and could not be relied upon as followers, except in so far as they were satisfied that the measures they were required to support were right.

Among the proceedings particularly affecting Scotland which occurred during this short administration, the provision made for Dugald Stewart is worthy of notice only because both it and he were much abused. In itself it is now utterly insignificant. A new office, called the Printer of the *Edinburgh Gazette*, was created, and given to Stewart, with a salary of (I believe) £300 and some emoluments arising from the sale of the paper. Because this was done by the Whigs, it was declaimed against by the opposition. And it was unquestionably wrong. It always is wrong to make a new office merely as a form for satisfying a just claim, especially if the office, publicly, is useless.

Stewart had done far more than enough to entitle him, a poor man, to be provided for directly as a distinguished moral teacher and a great philosophical writer. There were two occurrences more important— the impeachment of Lord Melville; and the proposed reform of the Court of Session.

Henry Dundas, the first Viscount Melville, was the Pharos of Scotland. Who steered upon him was safe; who disregarded his light was wrecked. It was to his nod that every man owed what he had got, and looked for what he wished. Always at the head of some great department of the public service, and with the indirect command of places in every other department; and the establishment of Scotland, instead of being pruned, multiplying; the judges, the sheriffs, the clergy, the professors, the town councillors, the members of parliament, and of every public board, including all the officers of the revenue and shoals of commissions in the military, the naval, and the Indian service, were all the breath of his nostril. This despotism was greatly strengthened by the personal character and manners of the man. Handsome, gentleman-like, frank, cheerful, and social, he was a favourite with most men, and with all women. Too much a man of the world not to live well with his opponents when they would let him, and, totally incapable of personal harshness or unkindness, it was not unnatural that his official favours should be confined to his own innumerable and insatiable partisans. With such means, so dispensed, no wonder that the monarchy was absolute. But no human omnipotence could be exercised with a smaller amount of just offence. It is not fair to hold him responsible for the insolence of all his followers. The miserable condition of our political institutions and habits made this country a noble field for a patriotic statesman, who had been allowed to improve it. But this being then impossible, for neither the government nor a majority of the people wished for it, there was no way of managing except by patronage. Its magistrates and representatives, and its other base and paltry materials, had to be kept in order by places; for which they did what they were bidden; and this was really all the government that the country then admitted of. Whoever had been the autocrat, his business consisted in laying forty-five Scotch members at the feet of the Government. To be at the head of such a system was a tempting and corrupting position for a weak, a selfish, or a tyrannical, man. But it enabled a man with a head and a temper like Dundas's, to be absolute, without making his subjects fancy that they ought to be offended. Very few men could have administered it without being hated. He was not merely worshipped by his many personal friends, and by the numerous idolaters whom the idol fed, but was respected by the reasonable of his opponents; who, though doomed to suffer by his power, liked the individual; against whom they had nothing to say, except that he was not on their side, and reserved his patronage for his supporters. They knew that, though ruling by a rigid exclusion of all unfriends who were too proud to be purchased, or too honest to be converted, he had no vindictive desire to persecute or to crush. He was the very man for Scotland at that time, and is a Scotchman of whom his country may be proud. Skilful in parliament, wise and liberal in council, and with an almost unrivalled power of administration, the usual reproach of his Scotch management is removed by the two facts, that he did not make the bad elements he had to work with and that he did not abuse them; which last is the greatest praise that his situation admits of.

The charges against Lord Melville were groundless, and were at last reduced to insignificancy. To those who knew the pecuniary indifference of the man, and who think of the comparative facility of peculation in those irregular days, the mere smallness of the sums which he was said to have improperly touched, is of itself almost sufficient evidence of his innocence.* If he had been disposed to peculate, it would not have been for farthings. Nevertheless, his impeachment did more to emancipate Scotland than even the exclusion of his party from power. His political omnipotence, which, without any illiberality on his part, implied, at that time, the suppression of all opposition, had lasted so long and so steadily, that in despair the discontented concurred in the general impression that,

* Horner, writing to J.A. Murray, says: "I consider his [Lord Melville's] acquittal as a foul stain upon the records of parliamentary justice ; bringing the mode of trial by impeachment into disgrace and subjecting the House of Lords to the distrust and contempt of the public. . . . I will say further that I consider that verdict to have been pronounced by a great proportion of those who acquitted him with a corrupt consciousness of its being contrary to evidence or a corrupt prostitution of the honour which they pledged without having considered the evidence."—Horner's *Memoir and Correspondence.*

happen what might, Harry the ninth would always be uppermost. When he was not only deprived of power, but subjected to trial, people could scarcely believe their senses. The triumphant anticipations of his enemies, many of whom exulted with premature and disgusting joy over the ruin of the man, were as absurd as the rage of his friends who railed, with vain malignity, at his accusers and the Constitution. Between the two, the progress of independence was materially advanced. A blow had been struck which, notwithstanding his acquittal, relaxed our local fetters. Our little great men felt the precariousness of their power; and even the mildest friends of improvement—those who, though opposed to him, deplored the fall of a distinguished countryman more than they valued any political benefit involved in his misfortune, were relieved by seeing that the main spring of the Scotch pro-consular system was weakened.

It was at a public dinner in honour of the acquittal (27th June 1806) that Scott produced, and his friend James Ballantyne sang, that unfortunate song so often brought against him afterwards, in which, Fox being then in his last illness, there is a line cheering " *Tally ho to the Fox !* " If, as was said, Scott really intended this as a shout of triumph over the expiring orator, it was an indecency which no fair license of party zeal can palliate. But I am inclined to believe that nothing was meant beyond one of the jocular, and not unnatural, exultations over the defeated leaders of the impeachment, of which the song is composed. There were some important persons, however, whose good opinion by this indiscretion was lost to Scott for ever.*

There was an illumination on the acquittal, which, in the absence of the Lord Advocate, gave John Clerk, the Solicitor-General, an opportunity of exhibiting his notion of the proper method of dealing with a city and his political opposites. Nothing could be more natural than for the friends of an acquitted man to rejoice, nor anything more unhandsome than for their opponents to mar their joy; especially as there was no symptom or probability of any disturbance. Yet Clerk was wrong-headed enough to obstruct the intended demonstration by writing officially to the Lord Provost that, if it took place, it would in his opinion lead to a popular outbreak, for which his Lordship and the Town-Council, who permitted the display, would be held responsible. This judicious epistle was instantly put to its proper use, by being sent through the town with tuck of drum, and read aloud by an officer who proclaimed that, in consequence of this objection, the magistrates trusted that the earnest and universal desire of the public to testify its delight at the late glorious event would be repressed. This probably did not save a single candle, but as the illumination was partial, its shabbiness was

* Lockhart's explanation (*Life of Scott*, chap 15) is, that Scott, having (apparently) just accepted of his Clerkship of Session from the Whigs, thought it necessary to show his independence by abusing them. It seems absurd to impute this to a sensible man. Besides, it does not hit the blot. It was not abuse of the Whigs that gave offence, but a supposed triumphant cheer over Fox's approaching death.—H. C.

See Sir Walter's *Journal*, and also Lady Rosslyn's letter on the subject quoted in the *Familiar Letters* of Scott.

ascribed, plausibly enough, to the illiberality of the Whigs.

The details of the scheme for reforming the Court of Session are to be found in the Parliamentary Proceedings, in the debates of the Faculty of Advocates, in an article by Jeffrey in the eighteenth number of the *Review*, and in clouds of pamphlets.

This was the first modern attempt to improve an ancient judicial establishment. Everything of the kind was so adverse to the spirit of the age that the idea of correcting judicial defects, on their own account, had no chance of being encouraged by any government, and indeed could only enter into very speculative private heads. But there were two collateral purposes to be served here: several new and high offices were to be created; and the troublesome flow of Scotch appeals into the House of Lords was expected to be dammed back, to the great comfort of the Lord Chancellor. But for these personal considerations, " The Auld Fifteen " would have gone on undisturbed for a long while.

What was proposed was—1st, to divide the existing single Court of fifteen judges into three separate Courts, each of five judges; 2d, to make at least one of these try causes by juries, which were not then employed in the decision of civil questions; 3d, to introduce an intermediate Court of Appeal between these and the House of Lords, with a sort of Scotch Chancellor at its head. These changes implied the creation of two new Heads and a Chancellor.

There were almost as many opinions as thinkers

upon every part of each of these proposals. The Court was fierce at the imagination of any change, especially of Whig conception. So were the country gentlemen, the absorbents of every prejudice. The towns interfered very little. They were crushed. The lawyers were divided into three parties. 1. Those who considered the matter only politically, and wishing chiefly to concur with the existing Government, defended the whole measure, in all its parts. The whole, or nearly the whole, senior Whigs, led by John Clerk and the other political office-holders, took this view. 2. Their political opponents, who were equally decided against all change. David Hume headed this section, and made a mournful oration over the death of any portion of the ancient system. So did even the practical Walter Scott, who after one of the Faculty meetings positively shed real tears over the threatened alteration of the old shape of the Court of Session. But in his case it was not the Court alone that moved him, but the probable decline of Scotch character and habits, of which this legal change was only a beginning. Properly applied, this was a sentiment with which I cordially sympathised. But it was misapplied by Scott, who was thinking of feudal poetry, not of modern business. 3. A class composed of the more moderate of all parties, who were neither sworn against the whole measure, nor in favour of it, but were for rejecting what in it they thought bad, and for adopting what they thought good. This section contained almost all the younger Whigs, and was headed by Jeffrey.

On the general merits of the measure the minds of good thinkers had come to nearly the result which, after more discussion and delay, was at last actually adopted by Parliament. 1. The erection of an intermediate Court of Review would have failed in its chief object of relieving the House of Lords, and would only have made the access to it more slow and expensive. It is very difficult for a small country, divided into strongly opposed parties, to administer law to itself, solely by native courts; especially after the people have been trained to expect purer justice from a higher and more distant tribunal. Much may be done for the protection of this tribunal by improving the native judicial system; but devices to obstruct the access to the great controlling power, though they may irritate, seldom satisfy. There are some who still think that a great error was committed in our not eagerly accepting the offer to revive our Lord Chancellor. All that I have seen convinces me that the rejection of this scheme was wise. We have no sufficient employment for such an officer; and no idle judge, or judge on whom unworthy work is thrown in order to give him an appearance of business, can ever be exhibited without disparagement to judicial respectability. The mere circumstance of his judgments not being final, would of itself have been inconsistent with the reverence necessary for the due weight of such a judge. 2. The separation of the Court into three chambers virtually took place, with general approbation, by its division into two, and the temporary erection of the Jury

Court. 3. Trial by jury has been actually established.

Some of the judges were ordered to attend the House of Lords to give explanations. Very sulky at being obliged to obey a mandate meant to promote their own reform, they were fretted into something like contempt by the rejection of a claim which they made to be allowed to sit within the bar. This decision was described as a piece of Whig insolence, and as intended to degrade judges. But the very same thing was done when the Scotch judges were ordered to attend the Peers about the Porteous Mob.* If a more honourable seat is given, as was asserted, in modern times to the English judges, the Scotch and Irish ought clearly to be treated in the same way. However, both the offended Lords and the Tories were unexpectedly relieved by the Whigs being suddenly dismissed from power in April 1807, before any scheme was carried.

The Whigs had only one opportunity of making a Scotch judge; and they made Charles Hay, a man famous for law, paunch, whist, claret, and worth. His judicial title was Newton, but in private life he was chiefly known as *The Mighty*. He was a bulky man with short legs, twinkling eyes, and a large purple visage; no speaker, but an excellent legal writer and adviser; deep and accurate in his law, in which he had had extensive employment. Honest, warm-hearted, and considerate, he was always true to his principles

* 2d May 1737. *Miscellany of the Maitland Club*, vol. ii. p. 68. —H. C.

O

and his friends. But these and other good qualities were all apt to be lost sight of in people's admiration of his drinking. His daily and flowing cups raised him far above the evil days of sobriety on which he had fallen, and made him worthy of having quaffed with the Scandinavian heroes. But there was no noise in his libations, no boisterousness, no wrangling, not even disputation. The kindly stillness of his ordinary manner, instead of being disturbed, was deepened by potation; and a cask so well seasoned was not liable to be inflamed by any thing so feeble as intoxication. His delight was to sit smiling, quiet, and listening; saying little, but that little always sensible—for he used to hold that conversation, at least when it was of the sort that excites admiration, spoiled good company; sated apparently with enjoyment, and only disturbed when he observed some unfortunate creature at table not taking as many or as full bumpers as himself.

He was the modern king of the *Ante Manum* Club —a jovial institution which contained, and helped to kill, most of the eminent topers of Edinburgh for about sixty years preceding the year 1818, when the degenerate temperance of the age at last destroyed it. When The Mighty died, the members dined, and did not fail to drown their sorrow in solemn mourning, each drinking a full glass to the memory of their departed chief, and bowing reverently to his portrait, which they had hung up in the tavern which had long been his field of fame. Jeffrey, Moncreiff, Keay, Murray. I and some other of the younger and less worthy spirits, joined this once famous association,* a few years before it expired, merely to have a glimpse of the last age. It was curious, but to us dull. Few of them had heads for talk, and none of us for much wine; we had to get the established jokes and other humours explained; and they were not quite at ease under our intrusion. There were no High Jinks, or sprightly sayings, or songs; but a good deal of kindly personal bantering, laughing at nothing or at very little, and steady quiet draughts of claret. But I believe there was a great deal of wild animation in the youth of the club, when its pulse was quicker. Hermand's star blazed in this hemisphere for at least half a century, when the meetings were every Friday for about six or seven months yearly. He used very often to go direct from the Club to the Court on the Saturday mornings. When some of us degenerate youths were once protesting against more wine, he exclaimed mournfully—" What shall we come to at last! I believe I shall be left alone on the face of the earth—drinking claret! "

Newton's potations and bulk made him slumberous both in society and in Court; and his management of this judicial inconvenience was very curious. In Court his head generally rested either on his heaving chest, or on his hands crossed on the bench, while, after getting a grip of the case, his eyes were locked in genuine sleep. Yet, from practice and a remarkably quick ear and intellect, nobody could say anything

---

* It was called the *Ante Manum* (as I have understood) because the original rule was that the bill should be paid *beforehand.*—H. C.

worth hearing without his instantly raising his huge eyelid, and keeping it open, and directing his powerful knowing eye, like a mortar, at the speaker, till he got what was necessary; after which, when the babbling began, down sunk the eyelid again, till lighted up by the next shot. The only way to waken him was to say something good, and this never failed. Accordingly no judge ever knew his cases better. Strangers wondered, but they seldom saw him rouse himself and deliver his opinion, which he was always ready to do on the spot, without being inclined, by his accuracy of statement and luminousness of view, to despise the judges whose eyes had been open all the while. I never heard this able, kind, and honest man mentioned by anybody but with respect and affection.

On the 13th of November 1806 a murder was committed in Edinburgh, which made a greater impression than any committed in our day, except the systematic murders of Burke. James Begbie, porter to the British Linen Company's Bank, was going down the close in which the bank then was,* on the south side of the Canongate, carrying a parcel of bank-notes of the value of four or five thousand pounds, when he was struck dead, by a single stab, given by a single person who had gone into the close after him, and who carried off the parcel. This was done in the heart of the city, about five in the evening, and within a few yards of a military sentinel who was always on guard

* Tweeddale Court. The premises are now the publishing offices of Oliver & Boyd, who have occupied them since the British Linen Bank removed to the New Town.

there, though not exactly at this spot, and at the
moment possibly not in view of it. Yet the murderer
was never heard of. The soldier saw and heard nothing.
All that was observed was by some boys who were
playing at hand ball in the close; and all that they
saw was that two men entered the close as if together,
the one behind the other, and that the front man fell,
and lay still; and they, ascribing this to his being
drunk, let him lie, and played on. It was only on the
entrance of another person that he was found to be
dead, with a knife in his heart, and a piece of paper,
through which it had been thrust, interposed between
the murderer's hand and the blood. The skill, boldness, and success of the deed produced deep and
universal horror. People trembled at the possibility
of such a murderer being in the midst of them, and
taking any life that he chose. But the wretch's own
terror may be inferred from the fact, that in a few
months the large notes, of which most of the booty
was composed, were found hidden in the grounds of
Bellevue. Some persons were suspected, but none on
any satisfactory ground; and, according to a strange
craze or ambition not unusual in such cases, several
charged themselves with the crime who, to an
absolute certainty, had nothing to do with it. About
twenty years after this a police officer, called Denovan,
an old High School fellow of mine and a clever man,
published the life of James Moffat or Maccoul, a
famous villain, who in 1820 was condemned to be
hanged for robbing a bank, but died in prison. In
this work the author tries to show that his hero was

Begbie's murderer. Many curious and plausible circumstances are gathered together in support of this
opinion; but the defect is that the reality of these
circumstances themselves is as uncertain as that of
the fact they are brought to establish. It is easy to
make almost any hypothesis have an appearance of
soundness when there is no contradictor. Moffat was
a very peculiar-looking scoundrel, both in face and
figure; and had certainly a very strong personal resemblance to the murderer as described by the boys;
but, if I recollect right, this circumstance is not much
founded on by Denovan.

When the Tories returned to power they made
Archibald Campbell of Clathick (who afterwards
became Colquhoun of Killermont) their Lord Advocate, and David Boyle (afterwards Lord Justice-
Clerk) their Solicitor-General. The Lord Advocate's
Deputes were William Erskine (Scott's friend, afterwards Lord Kinedder), Alexander Maconochie (afterwards Lord Meadowbank, the second), and myself!
I happened to be in London when, most unexpectedly,
the change of administration took place. I was sent
for by Lord Melville and his nephew, Robert Dundas
the Lord Chief Baron. On going to them, I was surprised to be offered one of the Advocate-Deputeships,
and objected to take it, on the ground that my
opinions were not those of the Government. To this it
was answered that the place was offered, and its
acceptance urged upon me, solely from family connection, and without the understanding of any

political tie; and this additional proof of the offer
proceeding from them, and not from the Lord
Advocate, was given. that Mr Campbell did not then
know of his own appointment. On saying this, the
Chief Baron pointed to a letter addressed to Campbell
that was lying on the table, and said, " There's his
own letter, not yet gone." I took a day to consider;
and consulted Francis Horner. He saw no good likely
to come of it; but no decent ground on which I could
quarrel with my kindred, since they gave the place on
such terms. After some more kindly expostulation, I
yielded; though in doing so, I had considerable misgiving as to the result.

The Scotch Tory party thought that the failure of
the effort to keep them out returned them to power
stronger than they had been before. Even they, however, did not dream of the twenty years of office that
followed; nor were they aware that time, instead of
consolidating their authority, was steadily though
silently undermining it. The country was getting
further removed every hour from the terror, or the
bugbear, of the French Revolution. The prescriptive
dominion of the old faction was interrupted. A generation not soured and darkened by the horrors which
had fixed, and seemed to justify, the intolerant prejudices of its predecessors was rising. And, above all,
the restored party returned with no reformation of
its feelings or objects. The Scotch managers were in
general excellent men personally. The rise of Robert
Dundas, Lord Melville's son, was an important event
for his party; for, without his father's force, or power

of debate, or commanding station, he had fully as
much good sense, excellent business habits, great
moderation, and as much candour as, I suppose, a
party leader can practise. The defect of the whole of
them was that they had no taste for good internal
measures, on their own account. So as their party
could have kept their places for ever, then for ever
there would have been no change of policy in this
country.

In May 1807 I pleaded my first case in the General
Assembly; and from that time I have been intimately
acquainted with, or rather personally concerned in,
all its judicial proceedings. The annual meeting of
this convocation was one of the most curious spectacles in Scotland.* It gave us the only local images of
royalty we had, and carried the imagination far back.
The old primitive raciness of the place had not been
much destroyed when I first knew it. The civilised
eloquence of Robertson had guided its councils, but
had left the manners and appearance of the great
majority of his brethren untouched; and the strict-
ness with which Lord Leven and Lord Napier, as His
Majesty's Commissioners, adhered, and made every
one who came within the royal circle adhere, to court
dress and etiquette, seemed like a hint to every fragment of the olden time to remain.

In 1807 Principal George Hill, of St Andrews, who

* The General Assembly met in those days, as it had done for about
two hundred years, in one of the aisles of St Giles Cathedral. Lord
Cockburn gives a graphic description of the scene it then presented in
his *Life of Lord Jeffrey*.

had succeeded Robertson as the leader of the General Assembly, was in the fulness of his sway. As he ruled the public proceedings of this ecclesiastical parliament for about thirty years, he must have been a person of considerable talent. But his influence depended on a single power—that of public speaking.* Though he was the spokesman of his party, he was not its oracle. Finlayson, with his silence, had a deeper brain, and was a more important man in the real management of the church. And even Hill's speaking was of rather a limited range. Elegant and luminous in exposition, he was very defective as a debater. The art of replying, indeed, was an art which he rarely even attempted. His almost invariable course was, either to speak first, when he professed to foresee no difficulty, and merely unfolded to his well-drilled followers what they ought to do; or to speak last, when, overlooking all the perplexities and personalities and obstacles of the discussion, he recalled his adherents to some simple general view, which he illustrated clearly, and then relieved them of all further anxiety, by bringing the matter to a distinct point, in a skilful motion. Thus, without force, elevation, or much argument, pleasing distinctness and persuasive evasiveness was his line; and whenever he ventured out of it into the warfare of true debate he was more easily unhorsed than any leader I ever saw. But within this line he was certainly

---

* Henry Mackenzie—"The Man of Feeling"—says that about 1763 "The General Assembly had then the boast of some of the best public speaking that was to be heard in Britain, the House of Commons scarcely excepted."—*Memoir of Horner*, prefixed to complete edition of Works, 4 vols.

a great artist. His voice was clear and agreeable, his gesture simple, and, though didactic, natural, and elegant; his visage dark; his eyes shaded by heavy black eye-brows; his whole manner and expression rather jesuitical.

The installed rulers of the Assembly after Hill were Dr Nicoll—a plain, good-natured man, with the appearance and manner of a jolly farmer, and an attractive air of candour and simplicity; and Dr John Inglis who, notwithstanding the sad blot of Leslie's persecution—his only stain, is a powerful and excellent man. He had two enemies to overcome in his look and his voice, both of which are unfortunate. It is an evidence of his intellectual power that he has triumphed over these obstacles. But a strong and acute understanding, general intelligence, deep and ready reasoning, clear diction, and the manners of a gentleman, make him a vigorous writer when he chooses to write, and always an admirable debater. No strong adversary ever measured mind against him without feeling his force. In point of power, he could at any moment have puffed Hill out, and crushed him beneath his feet. He is one of the many men who have been wasted and lowered by being cast on an unworthy scene. The powerful qualities which he has thrown away on the ignoble task of attempting to repress the popular spirit of our church, would have raised him high and on firm ground in any department of public life. Deducting eloquence and the graces, he is a first-rate preacher. The fanatical taste of the age, however, has gone on diminishing his hearers, till at last his church is nearly empty. Yet his almost bare walls hear as good, if not better, every-day sermons, than are preached in any church in Scotland except by Chalmers. Nor is it any slight mark of his judgment and worth, that though confined to one very limited set of objects, and to one way of dealing with them, his opinions have advanced in liberality and mildness with the advance of his years. His party has sometimes blamed him for intractableness; but when he and they differ I do not observe that he is always wrong. A leader generally sees further round him than his followers do, and seldom differs from them but on strong grounds.

Except Sir Harry Moncreiff, the Wild (as the Evangelical party is called) have never had an established head. Andrew Thomson and Chalmers have occasionally blazed for them; but the Moderate being the majority in every presbytery, college, and burgh, the Wild never have commanded fixed seats in the Assembly; and this single circumstance has dislocated their force, and prevented their being regularly represented and led publicly by their own chiefs. Thomson, moreover, is too self-willed, personal, and impetuous to have led his party long even though he had always been a member; and Chalmers, though he has ardently maintained its principles and objects, has been absorbed in achievements so much more splendid, that his exertions in the Assembly, however powerful, form but bright specks in his history: and he has scarcely troubled himself with the private management of the Church's little affairs.

But Sir Harry, throughout most of his life, was the oracle of the whole Church in matters not factious, and the steady champion of the popular side. In comparison with him every other Churchman who has appeared since I knew the world must withdraw. Nothing that I could say would express one-half of my affectionate and reverential admiration of this great man.

Sir Harry Moncreiff was not merely distinguished among his brethren of the Church of Scotland, all of whom leant upon him, but was in other respects one of the most remarkable and admirable men of his age. Small grey eyes, an aquiline nose, vigorous lips, a noble head, and the air of a plain hereditary gentleman, marked the outward man. The prominent qualities of his mind were, strong integrity and nervous sense. There never was a sounder understanding. Many men were more learned, many more cultivated, and some more able. But who could match him in sagacity and mental force? The opinions of Sir Harry Moncreiff might at any time have been adopted with perfect safety, without knowing more about them than that they were his. And he was so experienced in the conduct of affairs, that he had acquired a power of forming his views with what seemed to be instinctive acuteness, and with a decisiveness which raised them above being slightly questioned. Nor was it the unerring judgment alone that the public admired. It venerated the honourable heart still more. A thorough gentleman in his feelings, and immovably honest in his principles, his whole character was elevated into moral majesty. He was sometimes described as overbearing. And in one sense, to the amusement of his friends, perhaps he was so. Consulted by everybody, and of course provoked by many, and with very undisciplined followers to lead, his superiority gave him the usual confidence of an oracle; and this, operating on a little natural dogmatism, made him sometimes seem positive, and even hard; an impression strengthened by his manner. With a peremptory conclusiveness, a shrill defying voice, and a firm concentrated air, he appeared far more absolute than he really was, for he was ever candid and reasonable. But his real gentleness was often not seen; for if his first clear exposition did not convince, he was not unapt to take up a short disdainful refutation; which, however entertaining to the spectator, was not always comfortable to the adversary. But all this was mere manner. His opinions were uniformly liberal and charitable, and, when not under the actual excitement of indignation at wickedness or dangerous folly, his feelings were mild and benignant; and he liberalised his mind by that respectable intercourse with society which improves the good clergyman, and the rational man of the world.

I was once walking with him in Queen Street, within the last three years of his life. A person approached who had long been an illiberal opponent of his, and for whom I understood that he had no great regard. I expected them to pass without recognition on either side. But instead of this, Sir Harry, apparently to the man's own surprise, stopped, and took him by the hand, and spoke kindly to him. When they separated,

I said to Sir Harry that I thought he had not liked that person. " Oh! no. He's a foolish, intemperate creature. *But to tell you the truth, I dislike a man fewer every day that I live now.*" When the Whigs were in office, in 1806, one of his ecclesiastical adversaries, after having always opposed Catholic emancipation, wrote to him that if the subject should be renewed in the next assembly, he would now support it. It was renewed, but by that time the Whigs were displaced; and that very person opposed it, and, among other things, had the audacity to say that he could not comprehend how any Protestant clergyman could encourage Popery. Sir Harry was in great indignation, and told me himself that, when answering this, he put his hand into his pocket, and was on the very point of crushing his wavering friend by producing and reading his own letter, but that " *when I looked at ———'s face and saw his wretchedness, I had not the heart to do it.*" These were not the feelings of a hard man.

His great instrument of usefulness was his public speaking; the style of which may be inferred from that of his intellect and manner. In the pulpit, where he was elevated above worldly discord, he often rose into great views and powerful declamation; and he was the noblest deliverer of prayers at striking funerals. But though these professional exertions showed his powers, it was chiefly in the contests of men that his speaking was exerted, and was generally known. On such occasions it was so utterly devoid of ornament, that out of forty years of debate, it would be difficult to cull one sentence of rhetoric. And though very eloquent, he was never disturbed by the consciousness or the ambition of being so. It was never the eloquence of words, or of sentiments, conceived for effect, but of a high-minded practical man earnestly impressed with the importance of a practical subject; and who, thinking of his matter alone, dealt in luminous and powerful reasoning; his views clearly conceived, and stated with simplicity and assuredness. A fearful man to grapple with.*

Throughout nearly the whole of the seventeenth century the Church was the greatest field which our poor country contained for native talent and influence. The highest places in the state and in the law were open to its professional members; and it was our great asylum of learning. The success of Presbytery, and the consequent extinction of ecclesiastical dignities and wealth, would have soon sunk it in public importance had it been let alone. But it was persecuted; and persecution soon raised it to a greater and better height than it had ever attained in either its Episcopal or its Popish days. Under the Stuarts it combined the clergy and the laity into one brave and animated mass, where it was deemed an honour for the best of the gentry either to lead or to follow. The long and noble struggles of this party, which in truth formed the nation, its cruel sufferings, and its splendid triumph stamped a spirit and a reputation upon our clergy,

---

* There was really great justice in the remark of a little old north country minister, who, proud both of himself as a member, and of the Reverend Baronet who was predominating in the assembly, said to his neighbour, "Preserve me, sir! hoo that man Sir Harry does go on! *He puts me in mind o' Jupiter among the lesser gods.*"—H. C.

who had been the principal martyrs and heroes, which a century more could not efface. The Revolution composed these troubles, and clergymen were left to pursue their naturally peaceful callings, with no public interest or influence but what belonged to their obscure avocations. Without professional rank or political contention, or anything like wealth, and all the rest of the community rising rapidly around them, they kept a high position by being favourably associated in the public mind with the recollection of their history, by the respectability of their characters, and by the best of them always supporting the people in their fixed hatred of patronage. These circumstances sustained them throughout the fifty years or more that followed the Union. A minister was still reverenced in his parish, and was still welcome in all good society.

But the elevation of all other classes, which was the principal cause of the depression of this one fixed class, went on; and at length even patronage, which was the last struggle of popularity, was settled against them. From that day the clergy began to go down. Principal Robertson's ecclesiastical policy tended to divide our ministers into two classes; one, and by far the largest, of which had no principle superior to that of obsequious allegiance to patrons; the other, devoting itself entirely to the religion of the lower orders, had no taste or ambition for anything higher than what that religion required, or could, to ordinary minds, suggest. The old historical glory had faded; and, under the insignificance of repose, it was chiefly a lower description of men who were tempted to enlist in the ecclesiastical service. The humbleness of their livings, and even the well-meant cheapness of their education vulgarised them still more; so that learning and refinement, being scarcely attainable, ceased to be expected; and, with too few exceptions, vegetating in the manse, and the formal performance of the parochial duties, came to be the ultimate object of clerical ambition. A church that is poor, resident, and working is the best of all churches, both for the state and for the people: but it is not one that, in peaceable unpersecuting times, can sustain an elevated clergy.

Accordingly, the descent of the Scotch clergy throughout the last half of the eighteenth century was steady and marked. Not that there were no distinguished men among them; but there were not many, and they were always decreasing. Mouldering in their parishes was their general doom. And the descent proceeded with always increasing velocity. Take the case of Edinburgh, to which the best clergymen may be supposed to have been allured. About the year 1790 we had Blair, Henry the historian, Hardy the eloquent Professor of Church History, Principal Robertson, Dr Erskine, and Sir Harry Moncreiff; all literary and agreeable gentlemen, the delights of all society. But twenty years showed the change that was proceeding. Sir Harry alone remained, and not one other person had arisen to fill up the sad vacancies. I do not recollect a single work of any importance, which any one of our Established clergy during this time contributed to learning, or to science, or even

P

to theology; and in Edinburgh at least, but I believe everywhere, they had fallen almost entirely out of good lay society.

Had all this been compensated by higher professional eminence, it might have been said, that what this world had lost the other had gained. But at this period this could not be said with even a pretence of truth. It was the reverse. Until Chalmers and his consequences arose, the theological philosophy and eloquence of the Church seemed to be worn out. And no wonder. Nothing can inspire religious duty or animation but religion. Other causes may produce detached flashes, but nothing else can sustain general devotedness or enthusiasm. But a stern system of patronage, rendered more illiberal by its union with Toryism, tended to exclude all clergymen who were known to cherish a taste for the people and their piety and to reserve pulpits for those whose ambition ended in pleasing their political masters. This system, though it gave us *cauldrife* preachers, might have had perhaps a tendency to supply society with well-educated and agreeable gentlemen; but this consolatory tendency was defeated by the paltriness of the clerical position. A new presbyterian revolution was approaching, which brought out new men, and new dangers, and new popularity, with a necessary elevation of those who shone in it. But about this time the old thing was dead.

The first circumstance that afterwards tended to revive it was the poverty of town-councils. It was necessary to fill churches, for the sake of the seat

rents; and churches could only be filled by putting
in ministers for whom congregations would pay. This
business principle operated seriously in Edinburgh,
where the magistrates had laid out large sums in
building and repairing kirks. This brought Andrew
Thomson into this city; which was the opening of his
career. His Whig reputation was so odious, that it
rather seemed at one time as if civic beggary would
be preferred to it; and most vehemently was his
entrance into our untroubled fold opposed. But,
after as much plotting as if it had been for the Pope-
dom he got in, and in a few years rewarded his electors
by drawing about £1800 a-year for them; a fact
which, of itself, loosened all the city churches from
the dead sea in which they were standing.

Of our native presbyterian seceders, Struthers,
who died in 1807, was the only one in Edinburgh
who was entitled to the praise of eloquence. I know
no other person of the class who attracted people of
good taste, not of his community, to his church
merely for the pleasure of hearing him preach. His
last chapel was in College Street, but before it was
built he preached in the Circus, a place of theatrical
exhibition at the head of Leith Walk. It was strange
to see the pit, boxes, and galleries filled with devout
worshippers and to detect the edges of the scenes and
other vestiges of the Saturday night, while a pulpit
was brought forward to the front of the stage on
which there stood a tall, pale, well-dressed man,
earnestly but gently alluring the audience to religion by
elegant declamation. However, as my countrymen

have no superstition about the stone and lime of the temple, it did very well. Struthers was not of any superior talent or learning, but as a pleasing and elegant preacher he was far above any presbyterian dissenter then in Edinburgh.

The year 1808 saw the commencement of our new jail on the Calton Hill. It was a piece of undoubted bad taste to give so glorious an eminence to a prison. It was one of our noblest sites, and would have been given by Pericles to one of his finest edifices. But in modern towns, though we may abuse and bemoan, we must take what we can get. Princes Street was then closed at its east end by a line of mean houses running north and south. All to the east of these houses was a burial-ground, of which the southern portion still remains; and the way of reaching the Calton Hill was to go, by Leith Street, to its base (as may still be done), and then up the steep, narrow, stinking, spiral street which still remains, and was then the only approach. Scarcely any sacrifice could be too great that removed the houses from the end of Princes Street, and made a level road to the hill, or, in other words, produced Waterloo Bridge. The effect was like the drawing up of a curtain in a theatre. But the bridge would never have been where it is except for the jail. The lieges were taxed for the prison; and luckily few of them were aware that they were also taxed for the bridge as the prison's access. In all this magnificent improvement, which in truth gave us the hill and all its decoration, there was scarcely one particle of prospective taste. The houses alongside the bridge were made handsome by the speculators for their own interest; but the general effect of the new level opening into Princes Street, and its consequences, were planned or foreseen by nobody.

The completion of the new jail implied the removal of the old one; and accordingly in a few years after this " the Heart of Midlothian " ceased to beat. A most atrocious jail it was, the very breath of which almost struck down any stranger who entered its dismal door; and as ill placed as possible, without one inch of ground beyond its black and horrid walls. And these walls were very small; the entire hole being filled with little dark cells; heavy manacles the only security; airless, waterless, drainless; a living grave. One week of that dirty, fetid, cruel torture-house was a severer punishment than a year of our worst modern prison—more dreadful in its sufferings, more certain in its corruption, overwhelming the innocent with a more tremendous sense of despair, provoking the guilty to more audacious defiance. But yet I wish the building had been spared. It was of great age: it once held the parliament (though *how* it could, I can't conceive): it was incorporated with much curious history, and its outside was picturesque. Neither exposing St Giles, nor widening the street, nor any other such object, ought to have been allowed to extinguish so interesting a relic.

But by far the most gratifying occurrence that distinguished this period was one which proclaimed the dawn of modern Scottish Art. In 1808 our artists had a public exhibition of their works—being, so far as I am aware, the first display of the kind that had ever been made in Scotland. We had then a few respectable artists. Raeburn was great in portrait, greater than any Scotch painter of his day; the elder Nasmyth had cultivated landscape with some success, and for many years we had had an academy of instruction, not ill conducted, under the Board of Trustees. But still Edinburgh had not then emerged as a seat of art. There was no public taste for art, and, except for Raeburn's portraits, no market for its productions. Art was scarcely ever talked of. This Exhibition, however, showed that there were more pencils at work, though obscurely, than was supposed. It was a subterranean stir that had moved the surface. In general the works were below what would now be admitted into any Exhibition in Edinburgh. The best were those of Nasmyth, John Thomson, and Carse. The first two rose to great eminence afterwards, but Carse soon died. Some pretended to call him the Teniers of Scotland; a title by the help of which he excited attention, and some hope. But, though he certainly had humour, I doubt if he would ever have got the better of his coarseness and bad training, both in drawing and in colouring. However, this Exhibition did incalculable good. It drew such artists as we had out of their obscurity: it showed them their strength and their weakness: it excited public attention: it gave them importance.

Considering the rapid improvement which this experiment led to, we owe more than ought to be forgotten to a humble citizen called Core, who kept a stoneware shop in Nicolson Street. The admission money could not be depended upon to pay for the Exhibition room; the artists could not afford to make up the deficiency; and a public subscription would have been hopeless. In this situation Core, without communicating with any one, either hastily built, or hired, but I rather think built, a place afterwards called the Lyceum, behind the houses on the east side of Nicolson Street, and gave the use of it to the surprised artists. The Arts, thus brought into the light, advanced systematically; and there were more and better, and better paid, artists in Edinburgh in the next ten or fifteen years, than there had been in all Scotland during the preceding century.*

Though Lord Grenville's Court of Session scheme had fallen with the Whigs, public attention had been excited, and the subject was revived by the new administration. This produced a new deluge of pamphlets, meetings, and reports, which ended in the adoption of the great and decisive measure of cutting our single Court into two—that is of abolishing the old one. Accordingly, on the 11th of July 1808, that Court sat, as such, for the last time. Incorporated as it had been with the history of Scotland for about three centuries, it was a striking thing, to one who reflected, to see these fifteen judges rise that day,

* From 1809 to 1813 the Exhibition was held in Sir Henry Raeburn's house in York Place.

never to meet on the old footing again. Yet no monody was composed, no tear was shed, over its demise. I could not have conceived that anything so ancient could have gone out so quietly. It was the natural death of dotage. It disappeared, and was forgotten, as if nobody had known of its existence.

The old court had, I suppose, done very well for the old time. It had produced many great lawyers, and a most admirable system of law, the best indeed in Europe. But it was extinguished at last by defects which no modern tribunal could survive. Its radical defect was its numerousness. A bench of fifteen judges can only be " a learned crowd." Their number produced confusion, unseemly contention, prominence in the coarse, and shrinking by the gentle. These evils were greatly aggravated by the want of *permanent* Lords Ordinary. Except the Lord President, all the judges acted in separate Courts of their own, by a system so loose and complex that it left each to be nearly wherever he chose. There was always a judge, or several, wandering over the Outer House. One consequence of this was, that nobody could ever predict of whom *the Court* would be composed at any one moment. Hence it rarely happened that the successive parts of the same cause were decided by the same men. To force on his cause when he knew that certain judges would be out or in, was a great point with a cunning agent. Private consultation, public decorum, and a more deferential use of the President, though they could not have reconciled reason to such a Court, might have veiled its defects.

But Sir Ilay Campbell had too little of their confidence, and they were too many to confer harmoniously together, even if he had had more of it. Hence, when they assembled in public, they scarcely ever agreed. Each acting independently was tempted to stand up for every particle of his own notion; and a love of victory, display, and refutation was apt to supersede the calm feelings appropriate to the judgment seat. Plots and counterplots of management were occasionally irresistible; and this hubbub, jockeyship, and uncertainty had always to be settled by a vote; the putting and settling the result of which gave rise every hour to as keen conflicts as the original matter of the dispute. I cannot conceive that this system ever did well; but, at any rate, the growth of the population, the rise of an attentive public, and the increasing independence of counsel, made it no longer tolerable. Yet the ancient pile would have withstood even these blasts, at least for a time, had its demolition not been thought convenient for the House of Lords, which expected never to be troubled by another Scotch appeal.

General Vyse, an English officer who commanded the forces in Scotland, told the Lieutenancy of Midlothian, with whom he was dining, that in courts-martial the youngest member always gave his opinion first, but that he could not discover that there was any particular rule in the Court of Session. " Why, sir," said Hermand, " with us the *most impatient* speaks first, and you would observe that *I always begin.*"

President Campbell retired; and, to the delight of everybody, Blair was set to preside over the new scene. Mathew Ross, the king of doubters, succeeded him as Dean of Faculty.

Sir Ilay survived his retirement about fifteen years, having died in 1823, aged eighty-nine. He neither moped nor grumbled, nor got idle; but gave his assistance, in a very liberal spirit, to all the many schemes for the improvement of the law which then began to sprout. He was the most active of the Commissioners on the Fees in Scotch Courts, or rather was the whole Commission; whose elaborate and often learned reports were entirely his work. No sage's opinion was ever more anxiously asked, or more freely given, on new legal projects. And as if the guidance of Parliament and Government had not been enough for him, he performed all the duties of a Justice of the Peace, as patiently and zealously as if a cause was a novelty to him. The old gentleman combined this playing with judicial toys with the personal management of his estate of Garscube; and lived like a patriarch, in a house overflowing with company, beloved by troops of relations, and courted for his character and hospitality by many friends.

The Second Division of the Court sat for its first two years in what was then the Court of Exchequer. Its site does not exist, and cannot be easily explained now. But it was upstairs, and a hole was cut high in the east wall of the Outer House, through which the macer (or crier) called the causes and the counsel. This macer was an old, firm-set, hard, angular man, named Graham, who had long been in this vocation, and was the most official and picturesque person I have ever seen in it; large, square-faced, wooden-featured, grave, and formal; with an amazing voice—loud, distinct, and swinging. The murmur of the Outer House used to be stilled when this image stuck its awful head through the lofty orifice, and sent its slow articulate tones into every corner and every ear below, calling people up to their tasks and dooms. He could speak in no other way. I once saw him during the long vacation at a little place he had in Ayrshire, when he hoped I was well, and pointed out his shrubs, and addressed his family, all in his own loud, calm, crier style. He must have flirted in that voice. He was the monarch of macers, the only one I ever saw who was dignified and awful. No doubt Rhadamanthus has him.

Two sad privations clouded the close of the year 1809. The High School lost Dr Adam, and the College Dugald Stewart.

Adam died, after a few days' illness, in December. His ruling passion, for teaching, was strong in death. It was in his bedchamber, and in the forenoon, that he died. Finding that he could not see, he uttered a few words, which have been variously given, but all the accounts of which mean—" It is getting dark, boys; we must put off the rest till to-morrow." It was the darkness of death. He was followed to the grave (in the Chapel of Ease near Windmill Street)* by many eminent and grateful pupils. James Pillans,

* Now Buccleuch Parish Church.

his successor, has given a good short sketch of him in the *Encyclopædia Britannica*.

Mr Pillans had been educated at the High School, and was then a private tutor at Eton. His friend and schoolfellow Francis Horner advised him to stand for the Rectorship. It seemed hopeless; but he tried, and his character carried him through. His superiority to the other candidates was never doubted; but the black spot of Whiggism was upon him. This would certainly have been conclusive in the Town-Council, had not some of his friends there proposed a reference to a few of the judges, including President Blair, who quashed his brethren, and warmly recommended Pillans.* Nothing of the kind could be more important, or better timed, than this election. The modern improvements in education were just beginning to dawn, and it was very material to secure the services of a young man in whom their spirit was strong. Had a commonplace choice been made, we would probably have lost Pillans permanently, the earliest and the best of our reformed practical teachers, and who has been of incalculable use throughout the whole modern progress of Scotch education.

Stewart's health had made him nearly incapable of lecturing in the preceding session. Dr Thomas Brown supplied his place; and did it so admirably

---

* Horner was alarmed lest his patronage should hurt Pillans. "But if," said he, "the President takes the part which you expect, he will prove with great lustre the superiority of his character."—(Letter to Murray, 22d January 1810.—*Horner's Memoirs*, vol. ii. p. 23.)—H. C.

that, when Stewart withdrew finally in 1810, he was appointed his successor. Stewart's retirement made a deep and melancholy impression. We could scarcely bring ourselves to believe that that voice was to be heard no more. The going down of such a luminary cast a foreboding gloom over the friends of mental philosophy, and deprived the college it had so adorned of its purest light.

Brown, a profound metaphysician, an enthusiast in the science of mind, and, in a peculiar way, an eloquent lecturer, was perhaps the only man in the empire, except Mackintosh, who was worthy of coming after Stewart. Yet as his public principles, though so gentle as scarcely to be perceptible to his friends, were not decidedly Tory, he too was objected to on the ground of politics; and the warm recommendations of Stewart and Playfair would certainly have been disregarded, had he not been patronised by Dr Gregory, to whom he had for some time been secretary, and by Lord Meadowbank, who took metaphysics under his special charge.

Two still subsisting institutions arose in 1810—the Horticultural Society * and the Commercial Bank.

The Horticultural Society was chiefly the work of Patrick Neill, a printer; a useful citizen, a most intelligent florist, author of an excellent *Horticultural Tour in Flanders*, of the article, " Gardening," in the *Encyclopædia Brittannica*, and of various other

* The institution of the Royal Horticultural Society dates from 1809, as Lord Cockburn himself states on p. 386.

kindred works. The exotics in his little acre-garden at Canonmills * put many a grander establishment to the blush. He was also an archæologist, which made him one of the few defenders of our architectural relics. This Horticultural Society was one of the first buds of that extraordinary and delightful burst of floral taste which has since poured such botanical magnificence over our great places, and such varied and attainable beauty round our cottages. It is not in our public establishments, or in our great private collections, that its chief triumph is to be looked for; but in the moderate place, the villa, and especially in the poor man's garden; in the prevalence of little flower societies; its interest as a subject of common conversation; and the cheap, but beautiful and learned practical works that are to be found in the houses of the humblest of the people. I cannot doubt its proving a great civiliser. In innocence, purity, and simplicity, the florist—not the scientific botanist, but the florist of his own little borders, is the only rival of the angler. I wish we had a good Flowery Walton.

The rise of the Commercial Bank marks the growth of the public mind. It seems odd now that so slight an occurrence as the opening of a private association of money-changers could do so. But the principle on which this one was erected must be considered. No men were more devoid of public spirit, and even of the proper spirit of their trade, than our old Edinburgh bankers. Respectable men they were; but, without

* Patrick Neill's house still stands overlooking Scotland Street Station; the garden is now occupied by the printing office of the firm, Neill & Co., Ltd.

talent, general knowledge, or any liberal objects, they were the conspicuous sycophants of existing power.* What else could they have been? All the Whig business of the country would not have kept them going for a week; and Government dealt out its patronage in the reception and transmission of the public money only to its friends. So they all combined banking with politics. Not that they would discount a bad bill for a Tory, or refuse to discount a good one for a Whig; but their favours and their graciousness were all reserved for the right side. A demand for a bank founded on more liberal principles was the natural result of this state of things, as soon as these principles had worked their way into any considerable portion of the community. Hence the origin of the Commercial, professing to be the bank of the citizens. It was not meant, and has never acted, as a political engine; nor were all even of its founders, and still less of its proprietors, of the popular party. But simply because it was understood to be erected on the principle of excluding politics from its trade, and tended consequently to emancipate the people, its announcement was a clap of thunder; and efforts, of which the virulence attested the necessity of the establishment, were made to crush it. It prevailed over these unworthy attempts, and was at the time, and until the other banks were tamed, of incalculable benefit. Moderating the illiberality of the other establishments, by freeing the citizens from their absolute control, it deeply and

* An exception should surely be made of Sir William Forbes of Pitsligo, Bart.

silently improved the condition of our middle classes, on whose rise its effects have been far more real than apparent.

In July 1810 I had the honour of being dismissed by the Lord Advocate * from being one of his Deputes. The grounds of divorce were, that I had never been adequately of his party, and that I had voted against him at a Faculty meeting a few days before. I told him that I had long expected to be turned out, and reminded him of the terms on which I had unwillingly accepted the office, and which implied no fealty to him. He said he knew this, but that he, and the relatives to whom I had owed it, had deemed my scruples " a mere youthful fervour," which was expected to wear off. I might have told him truly that my fear that they might think so had only made the fervour warmer. I never felt more relieved than on getting rid of a connection which had all along been more than half compulsory, and never comfortable. A hearty shake of Sir Harry's hand, who called in a day or two to wish me joy of my liberation, was worth more than the three or four hundred pounds a-year of the office.

In March 1811 I married,† and set up my rural household gods at Bonaly, in the parish of Colinton, close by the northern base of the Pentland Hills; and, unless some avenging angel shall expel me, I shall never leave that paradise. I began by an annual lease

* *See* p. 214.   † *See* Introduction.

of a few square yards and a scarcely habitable farm-house. But, realising the profanations of Auburn, I have destroyed a village, and erected a tower, and reached the dignity of a twenty-acred laird. Every-thing except the two burns, the few old trees, and the mountains, are my own work, and to a great ex-tent the work of my own hands. Human nature is in-capable of enjoying more happiness than has been my lot here; where the glories of the prospects, and the luxury of the wild retirement, have been all en-hanced by the progress of my improvements, of my children, and of myself. I have been too happy, and often tremble in the anticipation that the cloud must come at last. Warburton says that there was not a bush in his garden on which he had not hung a specu-lation. There is not a recess in the valleys of the Pentlands, nor an eminence on their summits, that is not familiar to my solitude. One summer I read every word of *Tacitus* in the sheltered crevice of a rock (called " My Seat ") about 800 feet above the level of the sea, with the most magnificent of scenes stretched out before me.

As I was going along Maitland Street on the even-ing of the 20th of May 1811, I met Sir Harry Moncreiff, who asked me with great agitation if I had heard what had happened. He then told me that President Blair was dead. He had been in Court that day, apparently in good health, and had gone to take his usual walk from his house in George Square round by Bruntsfield Links and the Grange, where his solitary

Q

figure had long been a known and respected object, when he was struck with sudden illness, staggered home, and died.

It overwhelmed us all. Party made no division about Blair. All pleasure and all business were suspended. I saw Hermand that night. He despised Blair's abstinence from the pollution of small politics, and did not know that he could love a man who neither cared for claret nor for whist; but, at near seventy years of age, he was crying like a child. Next day the Court was silent, and adjourned. The Faculty of Advocates, hastily called together, resolved to attend him to his grave. Henry Erskine tried to say something, and because he could only try it, it was as good a speech as he ever made. The emotion, and the few and broken sentences, made this artless tribute, by the greatest surviving member of the profession to the greatest dead one, striking and beautiful.

The day before the funeral another unlooked-for occurrence deepened the solemnity. The first Lord Melville had retired to rest in his usual health, but was found dead in bed next morning. These two early, attached, and illustrious friends were thus lying, suddenly dead, with but a wall between them. Their houses, on the north-east side of George Square, were next each other.*

The remains of Blair were taken to the grave with all the civic pomp that Edinburgh could supply. But the most striking homage was paid in the solemn and impressive silence and respectfulness of the people.

* President Blair's house was No. 56. Lord Melville died at No. 57.

There were no soldiers, and scarcely a dozen of police officers. Yet the procession moved to the Greyfriars Churchyard through a mass of orderly populace, all as still as if they had been his family. When the sod was laid, his relations, as usual, took off their hats. So did the Judges who stood next: then the Magistrates: the Faculty and other legal bodies: the Clergy: and all the spectators in the churchyard; beyond whom it ran over the sky-lines of people ridged on all the buildings, and on the southern edge of the Castle-hill—all stood for a moment silent and uncovered.

His statue by Chantrey was obtained by public subscription. It is like, both in the features and the figure, and gives an idea of his calm repose. But the portrait by Raeburn is a much truer representation.

During the two years and a half this distinguished and excellent man was at the head of the Court he performed the duties of the place most admirably. His associates being greatly inferior to him judicially his eminence extinguished them all, and made himself the Court.* He heard them and the counsel with apparent tranquillity, and then roused himself and began. And his style was so uniform that it almost seemed as if it had been the result of a rule. He first stated the leading facts and the exact point of the case, formally and clearly, and then either worked out the deciding principle gradually, or, announcing it at once, proceeded to expound and apply it. The lumin-

* Lockhart, in *Peter's Letters to his Kinsfolk*, tells the story that on one occasion John Clerk, after having one of his sophistica arguments demolished by the Lord President, was heard to mutter, " My man ! God Almighty spared nae pains when he made your brains.

ousness of this system gave his judgments an air of greater superiority than they sometimes really had, merely because everybody understood him. He did not dive into the middle of a cause by a first plunge, nor was he contented by a mere intimation of his result, nor did he peck at its crumbs, nor rest upon allusions, but always set forth his grounds satisfactorily. This made the delivery of his opinion not merely a decision of the cause, but an explanation of it to the audience, and a lesson in law to the bar.

Lord Melville was buried privately at Lasswade. It has always been said, and never so far as I know contradicted, and I am inclined to believe it, that a letter written by him was found on his table or in a writing-case, giving a feeling account of his emotions at the President's funeral. It was a fancy piece, addressed to a member of Government, with a view to obtain some public provision for Blair's family; and the author had not reckoned on the possibility of his own demise before his friend's funeral took place. Such things are always awkward when detected; especially when done by a skilful politician. Nevertheless, an honest and a true man might do this. It is easy to anticipate one's feelings at a friend's burial; and putting the description into the form of having returned from it is mere rhetoric.

In its preservation of this powerful Scotchman, history is aided by a column and a statue, both in Edinburgh. The statue is perhaps Chantrey's worst. The column has received and deserves praise.*

* But it suffers severely from the want of the rail on the square pedestal at the top.—H. C.

A change was now so far advanced as to be publicly visible, which was of great consequence to Scotland.

I have mentioned that Whig opinions were dangerous accompaniments for success in life, especially to the young, whose fresh minds, however, presented the soil most favourable for their growth. The fate of the junior Whig lawyers, therefore, was looked to, for encouragement or for despair, by all those, but chiefly by the young, who were cherishing liberal principles. And I have stated that these lawyers, though strongly united among themselves, were not only suppressed as much as they could be by the opposite party, but were for some years not very cordially received even by the seniors on their own side. They had now, however, got their feet fairly on the greensward. Their talents had worked them up into obviously coming power in their profession. Their virtues, better understood, had extended their friendships, and opened society to them. The *Review*, with which many of them were connected, fixed upon them a large portion of the general fame of the work. Their seniors saw themselves surpassed both in literary and in social influence, and did not now grudge to acknowledge it. Through their Edinburgh comrades, who were rising into importance in England, a more lively and useful sympathy than had ever subsisted between the friends of reform was established in the two British capitals. The people of Scotland gave importance, and consequently power, to the rising lights whose guidance they now began to acknowledge.

Besides other valuable names, there was George

Cranstoun, firm in principle, and only too fastidious for practical work; John Archibald Murray, reared in the very hotbed of Toryism, but transplanted, by his own spirit, and his great friend Francis Horner's attraction, into the more congenial soil where through life he has flourished; Thomas Thomson, formidable in dignity and in antiquarian learning; George Joseph Bell, our greatest modern institutional writer; John Macfarlan, an apostle, and worthy of the best apostolic age; James Moncreiff, rivalling even his father in the energy of virtue; and James Grahame, a child in simple poetry and amiable piety,* and though shrinking from sensitiveness of nerve from all suffering, as ready for the flames, if his principles required it, as either Macfarlan or Moncreiff. These three, indeed, would have made the best martyrs I have ever known. Moncreiff would have gone to the stake refuting his persecutor's errors; Macfarlan smiling inwardly, and speculating on the oddity of the proceeding as a method of convincing; and Grahame, roused into indignation, proclaiming the atrocity of the tyrant. And, above all, and over all, there was Jeffrey, in brilliancy the star of the whole party.

George Cranstoun, with rather a featureless countenance, had a pleasing and classical profile. With a deadly paleness, a general delicacy of form, and gentlemanlike, though not easy, manners, the general air indicated elegance, thought, and restraint. His

* Author of *The Sabbath*, etc. He was admitted a member of the W.S. Society, but after a few years he became an advocate; finally he studied for the Church and was ordained by the Bishop of Norwich.

knowledge of law was profound, accurate, and extensive; superior perhaps, especially if due value be set on its variety, to that of every other person in his day. It embraced every branch of the science, feudal, mercantile, and Roman; constitutional and criminal; the system not of his own country alone but, in its more general principles, the jurisprudence of Europe. No great, though new, question could occur, on which he was not, or could not soon make himself, at home. His legal loins were always girt up; and his law was dignified by a respectable acquaintance with classical and continental literature, and a very considerable knowledge of the literature of Britain. Except two or three casual (and rather elaborate) levities, he wrote nothing but the legal arguments in which the Court was then so much addressed. His style in this line was so clear and elegant, that there can be no doubt that it would have sustained higher matter. His speaking was anxiously precise; while ingenious law, beautiful reasoning, and measured diction, gave every professional speech, however insignificant the subject, the appearance of a finished thing. It was not his way to escape from details by general views. He built up his own argument, and demolished that of his adversary, stone by stone. There are few in whose hands this system could have avoided being tedious. But he managed it with such brevity in each part, and such general neatness and dexterity, that of all faults tediousness was the one of which he was freest. He could not be forcible, and was too artificial to be moving, and therefore avoided the scenes where these qualities are convenient. His appropriate line was that of pure law, set off by elegance, reasoning, and learning. His taste was delicate, but not always sound, particularly on matters of humour, which his elaboration seldom gave fair play. He no doubt felt the humour of others, and had humorous conceptions of his own. But when he tried to give one of them to the public, the preamble and the point were so anxiously conned and polished that the principal pleasure of the audience, when they saw the joke on the stocks, consisted in their watching the ingenious care with which it was to be launched.

The defect of the whole composition was a want of nature. To a very few of the kernels of his friendships he was reported to be not incapable of relapsing into ease. But those less favoured, and his general acquaintance, were oppressed by his systematic ceremony. He shrunk so into himself, that those who did not understand the thing were apt to suppose him timid and indifferent to common distractions. But he was exactly the reverse. His opinions and feelings, both of persons and of matters, were decided and confident; in forming them he was entirely free from the errors that spring from undue admiration or enthusiasm; and behind a select screen they were sometimes freely disclosed. But the very next moment, if before the world, the habitual mask, which showed nothing but diffidence and fastidious retirement, was never off. He would have been far more powerful and popular could he have been but artless. His exposition of law was matchless; and he sometimes touched the right moral chord, but not always on the right key. The disposition to get into the region of exquisite art; to embellish by an apt quotation; to explain by an anecdote; to drop his distinctly uttered and polished words, one by one, like pearls, into the ear —adhered to him too inseparably.

Though a decided Whig, for which he suffered professional proscription for several years, it was chiefly by his character that he did good to his party. Retired habits and the unfortunate ambition of perfection excluded his practical usefulness. With no indecision of principle, and no public indifference, though with considerable distaste of popular vulgarity, it was beneath George Cranstoun ever to come forward but on a great occasion, and with a display of precise, unchallengeable excellence. This was not the man for plain public work, and accordingly he very rarely undertook it.

James Moncreiff, a son of Sir Harry, and worthy of the name, was more remarkable for the force, than for the variety, of his powers. His faculties, naturally, could have raised and sustained him in almost any practical sphere. But, from his very outset, he devoted himself to the law as the great object of his ambition. The politics of the Scotch Whig party, and the affairs of that Presbyterian Church which he revered, occupied much of his attention throughout life; but even these were subordinate to the main end of rising, by hard work, in his profession.

This restriction of his object had its necessary consequences. Though excellently educated at Edinburgh, Glasgow, and Oxford, he left himself little leisure for literary culture; and while grounded in the knowledge necessary for the profession of a liberal lawyer, he was not a well-read man. Without any of his father's dignified air, his outward appearance was rather insignificant; but his countenance was marked by a pair of firm, compressed lips, denoting great vigour and resolution. The peculiarity of his voice always attracted attention. In its ordinary state it was shrill and harsh; and casual listeners, who only heard it in that state, went away with the idea that it was never anything else. They never heard him admonish a prisoner, of whom there was still hope; or doom one to die; or spurn a base sentiment; or protest before a great audience on behalf of a sacred principle. The organ changed into striking impressiveness, whenever it had to convey the deep tones of that solemn earnestness which was his eloquence. Always simple, direct, and practical, he had little need of imagination; and one so engrossed by severe occupation and grave thought could not be expected to give much to general society by lively conversation. With his private friends he was always cheerful and innocently happy.

In the midst of these negative qualities, there were three positive ones which made him an admirable and very formidable person:—great power of reasoning,—unconquerable energy,—and the habitual and conscientious practice of all the respectable, and all the amiable virtues.

Though a good thinker, not quick, but sound, he
was a still better arguer. His reasoning powers,
especially as they were chiefly seen concentrated on
law, were of the very highest order. These, and his
great legal knowledge, made him the best working
counsel in court. The intensity of his energy arose
from that of his conscientiousness. Everything was
a matter of duty with him, and therefore he gave his
whole soul to it. Jeffrey called him the whole duty of
man. Simple, indifferent, and passive, when unyoked,
give him anything professional or public to perform,
and he fell upon it with a fervour which made his
adversaries tremble, and his friends doubt if it was
the same man. One of his cures for a headache was to
sit down and clear up a deep legal question. With
none, originally, of the facilities of speaking which
seem a part of some men's nature, zeal, practice, and
the constant possession of good matter, gave him all
the oratory that he required. He could in words un-
ravel any argument, however abstruse, or disentangle
any facts, however complicated, or impress any
audience with the simple and serious emotions with
which he dealt. And, for his purpose, his style both
written and spoken was excellent—plain, clear,
condensed, and nervous.

Thus, the defect lay in the narrowness of the
range; the merit in his force within it. Had it not been
for his known honesty, his inflexible constancy of
principle, and the impossibility of his doing anything
without stamping the act with the impression of his
own character, he would have been too professional

for public life. But zeal and purity are the best grounds of public influence; and accordingly, in Edinburgh, or wherever he was known, the mere presence of James Moncreiff satisfied people that all was right.

I am not aware how his moral nature could have been improved. A truer friend, a more upright judge, or a more affectionate man, could not be.

His love of the church was not solely hereditary. He himself had a strong Presbyterian taste, and accordingly both the Whiggism and the grave piety of what was called the *wild* side of the church, were entirely according to his heart. He was almost the only layman on that side, who used regularly to attend to the proceedings of the old General Assembly, and to influence them. It was a sad day for him when he thought it his duty to renounce that community, as he was certain that his father would have done, and to adhere to what he thought its ancient and genuine principles in the Free Church. He mourned over the necessity with the sorrow of a mother weeping for a dead child.

His attachment to his political principles was equally steady and pure. He owned them in his youth, and they clung to him through life. The public meeting in 1795, for attending which Henry Erskine was turned out of the deanship, was held in the Circus, which their inexperience at that time of such assemblages had made them neglect to take any means to light, and Erskine was obliged to begin his speech in the dark. A lad, however, struggled through the crowd with a dirty tallow candle in his hand, which he held up, during the rest of the address, before the orator's face. Many shouts honoured the unknown torch-bearer. This lad was James Moncreiff, then about sixteen. The next time that he recollected being in that place, which had changed its name, was when he presided at what is known here as the Pantheon Meeting in 1819. He died in the political faith in which he had lived; never selfish, or vindictive, or personal; never keeping back, but never pushing forward; and always honouring his party and his cause by the honesty and resolute moderation of all his sentiments.

Although these men were advancing into the front rank, there was no jealousy now on the part of those who were in that place. Erskine had retired. Gillies was scenting promotion. John Clerk was too self-willed and odd to act with anybody; but his strong party spirit and his respect for their talents made him favourable to his junior friends, who were not received with the less favour from the sociableness of their natures, and the impossibility of any competition interfering with his great practice. The pure and heroic Fletcher knew not what jealousy was, and would have cheered on a personal enemy if he had had one, provided he was going before him in the public cause. Malcolm Laing's literature had withdrawn him from the law, but not from a deep interest in the proceedings of the lawyers whose politics he approved of.

A very inadequate idea will be formed of the effect of the rise of these men, if it be confined to the

Parliament House. The rising or the sinking of a few professional lawyers, as such, is seldom of much public importance. But these lawyers represented *a class:* and this class consisted of all the younger men in Scotland to whom the prevailing intolerance was distasteful, but who were hourly warned that submission to it was essential for worldly success. The disenthralment of those who had liberated themselves from it in Edinburgh was like liberty proclaimed to all slaves. And, accordingly, besides the more numerous and daring in towns, there was scarcely a considerable village which did not contain some one who breathed more freely from what he had heard of the success of those in the metropolis, who had been in a similar state of depression with himself. There was an elevation of the whole liberal surface. So true was the remark of the quiet and observant Playfair, that it seemed to him that the whole cause of independence in Scotland hung upon the characters and the exertions of about half-a-dozen young men in the Parliament House.

The anti-revolutionary formation kept its old hardness and its old level; just as it does now. It has come in time to contain a smaller amount of human matter; but in its nature it is unchanged, and unchangeable. It still suppressed independence among its adherents as strongly as ever. And hence the otherwise incomprehensible fact of the still continuing deadness of all the classes which it could control. Individuals had emancipated themselves, but no masses. It is difficult to make a person accustomed to modern civic fermentations comprehend, or even believe, the utter political inanition which then silenced and awed our largest towns. The class called *citizens*—that is, the tradesmen, shopkeepers and merchants—even in Edinburgh, did not exist politically. They were ripening, for they soon produced fruit. But as yet they were so far back, that they were scarcely ever taken into account by the Whigs as political elements. To be sure, there were no political movements to excite them. Every public concern was superseded by volunteering and the war. But this was because the people were not then capable of being moved. If any of the measures, which twenty years afterwards agitated every political nerve in the kingdom, had been propounded, however attractively, they would have fallen to the ground cold. The total absence of public meetings exposes our whole condition.

Nor had the Whigs any particular hope, except the forlorn one of the Prince of Wales. Changes of ministry favourable to them were no more thought of while George the Third lived, than changes in the system of nature. They persevered, proclaiming their favourite objects; but merely that their colours might not be deemed struck. Even their Royal *friend* soon taught them the good sense of the advice which warns both Whigs and Tories not to put their trust in princes.

In 1811 our Edinburgh society still continued unchanged in its general character. Napoleon's con-

tinental padlock still sent us good English youths
and families: society and literature adorned each
other: the war sparkled us with military gaiety and
parade: London had not absorbed the whole of our
aristocracy either of wealth or of rank; and, notwithstanding several important emigrations, we still
retained far more native talent and reputation than
could be found in any other town in the empire,
except London.

No one who knew John Playfair can ever resist
basking in his remembrance. The enlargement of his
popularity after he began to verge towards age, was
the natural result of the beautiful process by which
that most delightful philosopher increased in moral
youthfulness as he declined in years. Admired by all
men, and beloved by all women, of whose virtues and
intellect he was always the champion,* society felt
itself the happier and the more respectable from his
presence. "Philandering at the Needles" was a
phrase by which Jeffrey denoted his devotedness to
ladies and to rocks.

Henry Mackenzie's excellent conversation, agreeable family, good evening parties, and the interest
attached to united age and reputation, made his
house one of the pleasantest. One of the Arbitri
Elegantiarum of old Edinburgh, he survived to
flourish in a new scene. But though he survived the
passing away of many a literary friend, and many a
revolution of manners, he accommodated himself to

* *See* his reviews of Donna Agnesi (*Edinburgh Review*, No. 6, Art.
13) and Corinne (*Edinburgh Review*, No. 21, Art. 12).—H. C.

unavoidable change with the cheerfulness of a man of sense, above the weakness of supposing that the world must have been in its prime only when he was in his. The title of " The Man of Feeling " adhered to him ever after the publication of that novel; and it was a good example of the difference there sometimes is between a man and his work. Strangers used to fancy that he must be a pensive sentimental Harley; whereas he was far better—a hard-headed practical man, as full of worldly wisdom as most of his fictitious characters are devoid of it; and this without in the least impairing the affectionate softness of his heart. In person, he was thin, shrivelled and yellow, kiln-dried, with something, when seen in profile, of the clever, wicked look of Voltaire.

Sir James Hall was a person of great intellectual vigour and considerable originality. In the then opening field of geology, and all its kindred subjects, he was profound; and whatever scientific object he took up he pursued with an energy before which obstacles that defied common minds disappeared. While the Neptunists were exulting over the Vulcanists on the supposed impossibility of such things as limestone and granite being igneous productions, and the Vulcanists were defending themselves by arguments, Sir James, after great forethought, set to work, and by fire, pressure, and perseverance actually made the stones. This was but an example of his way. His theory of Gothic architecture is, I suppose, not truer than many others; but no one equals him in the in-

R

genuity with which his fanciful principle is worked
out, or in the beauty of the book by which it is
illustrated. I regret that I never saw the little sylvan
cathedral in the garden at Dunglass by which he
showed his theory in its actual growth. He was held
in great admiration by all deep philosophers, and was
the most scientific of our country gentlemen.

His only misfortune was a bad manner; at least if
it be a misfortune for a clever man to be much laughed
at. Neither obtrusive, nor dull, nor coarse, but rather
kind, gentle, and cheerful, he said and did whatever
occurred to him; and as he had the always diverting
defect of absence of mind, there was seldom any saying what might occur to him. There was no inten-
tional disregard of the ordinary ceremonies of polite-
ness, but an unconsciousness of their existence. He
made one speech in Parliament; and I have heard
him say that he was not much discomposed by the
laughter of the whole members, but that he began to
suspect that he must be making a queer figure when
he saw the Speaker laugh too. It was a doubt in the
family, while he was a boy, whether he was to turn
out a man of genius or an idiot; and being in London,
he was taken to the top of St Paul's, where some one
on the hopeful side was certain he would disclose
himself by some grand burst of wonder. It was long
of coming; but at last he screamed with delight,
" Eh! there's a cuddie! " What better could a
sensible boy have observed? His large house in George
Street was distinguished by its hospitality both to
science and to fashion. And the interest of his many

evening parties was not lessened by the stories of
his oddities, which were sure to make the morning
laugh.

People used to be divided at this time as to the
superiority of Scott's poetry or his talk. His novels
had not yet begun to suggest another alternative.
Scarcely, however, even in his novels was he more
striking or delightful than in society; where the halt-
ing limb, the burr in the throat, the heavy cheeks,
the high Goldsmith-forehead, the unkempt locks, and
general plainness of appearance, with the Scotch
accent and stories and sayings, all graced by gaiety,
simplicity, and kindness, made a combination most
worthy of being enjoyed. Jeffrey, his twin star, made
a good contrast. He was sharp English; with few
anecdotes, and no stories, delighting in the inter-
change of minds, bright in moral speculation, wit,
and colloquial eloquence, and always beloved for the
constant transpiration of an affectionate and cheerful
heart.

For a small place, where literature sticks out,
Edinburgh has never been much encumbered by professed literary ladies; and most of those we have had
have been exotics. The two best about this time were
Mrs Elizabeth Hamilton, the authoress of the
Cottagers of Glenburnie, and Mrs Grant, widow of a
minister of Laggan, who had unfolded herself in the
Letters from the Mountains, an interesting treasury
of good solitary thoughts. They were excellent
women, and not too blue. Their sense covered the
colour. I think it was to Mrs Hamilton that Jeffrey

said, in allusion to the good taste of never losing the feminine in the literary character, that there was no objection to the blue stocking, provided the petticoat came low enough down. One wonders why Mrs Hamilton, with her good Scotch eye, did not put more Scotch among her cottagers than dirt, on which almost solely the book lives. Mrs Grant was a tall, dark woman, of very considerable intellect, great spirit, and the warmest benevolence. Her love of individual Whigs, particularly of Jeffrey, in spite of her amusing horror of their principles, was honourable to her heart. She was always under the influence of an affectionate and delightful enthusiasm, which, unquenched by time or sorrow, survived the wreck of many domestic attachments, and shed a glow over the close of a very protracted life. Both she and Mrs Hamilton were remarkable for the success of their literary conversational gatherings. Their evening parties had the greater merit from the smallness of their houses and of their means.

In November 1811 we all started, and none in such a fright as the Tories, at the first instance that had probably ever occurred of the promotion to a seat on the Bench of a person opposed in his opinions to the Government that appointed him. This miraculous exception took place in the case of Adam Gillies, a Whig, who was made a judge in the place of Lord Newton. The honour of effecting this marked deviation from the established practice was due to Charles Hope, the Lord President, who felt that his Court needed law, which it was expected that Gillies would supply.

Three useful associations—the Astronomical Institution, the Society for the Suppression of Public Begging, and the Lancastrian School—arose in 1812; each marking the advance of the place, and indeed of the age, and each followed by permanent effects. The Astronomical Institution, which now adorns the summit of the Calton Hill, was the work of Professor Playfair. He used to state, in order to show its necessity, that a foreign vessel had been lately compelled to take refuge in Leith, and that before setting sail again, the master wished to adjust his time-piece, but found that he had come to a large and learned metropolis, where nobody could tell him what o'clock it was.

The " Society for the Suppression of Public Begging " was the first modern systematic attempt that had been made in Scotland to check public mendicity, and to avert charity from supporting it. The disclosures made, and the attention excited, by this early step in the philosophy of pauperism, materially promoted the subsequent institutions of Houses of Industry, Houses of Refuge, Savings Banks, and many others for preventing, methodising, and relieving necessary destitution. We owed it to two causes—the dangerous extent to which public begging had reached, and the judicious benevolence of John Forbes, advocate, now Lord Medwyn. Let those who despair of eradicating mendicity from a spot on which it has fastened study the facts of this Edinburgh case, and be comforted. The swarm disappeared as soon as it was scared; and though it often returned, its settling or not settling just depended on the vigilance with which the flowers of bad charity it fed upon were crushed or fostered.

The Lancastrian School was a symptom and a cause of the advance of popular education, and was therefore a vital event, and a bold experiment at this time. It was the achievement of the Whigs and of the pious; and, though not openly opposed, was cordially hated by all true Tories, who for many years never ceased to sneer at and obstruct it. And when its success seemed certain, some of the established clergy disgraced themselves by trying to prevail on the Presbytery of Edinburgh to crush it indirectly; and in aid of this Presbyterian effort the Bishop of Meath, who happened to be residing here, was easily persuaded by the Episcopalian illiberals to preach an ignorant and insolent sermon against it. On this we discharged Sir Harry at him; who considerably improved the funds by a sermon which, as he spoke it, trampled on his lordship in a triumphant and contemptuous refutation. It was one of Sir Harry's greatest practical shouts. The original school was a long, low, wood and brick erection, stretched on the very top of the Calton Hill; where it was then the fashion to stow away everything that was too abominable to be tolerated elsewhere.

John Clerk of Eldin, the author of the work on

naval tactics, died in May 1812. An interesting and delightful old man; full of the peculiarities that distinguished the whole family—talent, caprice, obstinacy, worth, kindness, and oddity. His claim to the merit of having first suggested the idea of breaking the enemy's line in naval war is now disputed on grounds which are at least plausible and formidable. It is possible that the same thought may have occurred to different men at the same time; and my conviction of the honesty of Clerk is so complete, that I am certain he would have disdained to claim a discovery which he had not made. That conception, however, formed but a small part of his scientific merit; for though it is the matter with which his name happens to be chiefly connected in public talk, he was looked up to with deference by all the philosophers of his day, who were in the habit of constantly receiving hints and views from him, which they deemed of great value. He was a striking-looking old gentleman, with his grizzly hair, vigorous features, and Scotch speech. It would be difficult to say whether jokes or disputation pleased him most. I know no better account of the progress of a father and a son than what I once heard him give of himself and of his son John, in nearly these very words:—" I remember the time when people, seeing John limping on the street, used to ask, what lame lad that was? and the answer would be, That's the son of Clerk of Eldin. But now, when I myself am passing, I hear them saying, What auld grey-headed man is that? And the answer is, That's the father of John

Clerk." He was much prouder of the last remark than of the first.

Sir John Dalrymple, a Baron of our Exchequer, and author of the *Memoirs of Great Britain,* had died in 1810. He was succeeded in his estates by his son, then called Sir John [eighth Earl of Stair], whose energy and political independence have associated him with all the subsequent party struggles of Scotland. He began with the metropolitan county of Midlothian, which made as shameful an exhibition of itself as any parliamentary reformer could desire. It had immemorially been a mere appendage of the house of Arniston, as completely as Edinburgh, or one of the Arniston farms. Not that there were not some independent seeds; but they never got above ground. No formed opposition divided the shire: no rebellious whispers disturbed it. The new Sir John, a soldier and almost a stranger, had scarcely succeeded when he announced himself a candidate, and on Whig principles. It would be vain to attempt to make any modern man comprehend the indignation excited by this first interference with the hereditary monopoly. The Whig seeds sprang, and multiplied. However, they would have been shaded to death by the old branches, but that fidelity to his friends was ascribed to the Prince of Wales, and that he was about to become Regent without restrictions. This mistake drew traitors off from the colours they had sworn to stand by, and without their perfidy pure principle would after all have mustered but a slender host. There perhaps was not a single one of those deserters who had not asked, and probably obtained, and were then enjoying, favours from the Dundases solely on a pledge of political support. But they betrayed their patrons, as they would have sold their country. The result was that, at the election on the 26th of October 1812, Sir John was within ten votes of being returned; and if it had not been known by this time that the Regent was to be false, he would certainly have been made the member. They soon crouched into their old yoke again. But their momentary pretence of independence proved permanently useful. It laid the foundation of a regular county opposition. It showed the admirers of our representative system how little, without principle and without popularity, it could be depended upon, even for their ends. It shook the stability of all the shires, and directed their minorities to parliamentary reform as their only hope.

Alexander Fraser Tytler, Lord Woodhouselee, died in 1813. Though he continued Kames' *Dictionary of Decisions*, he was no lawyer, and indeed except as a judge was scarcely considered as of the profession. It was as Professor of History that he was chiefly distinguished. His lectures were not marked either by originality of matter or by spirit; but, though cold and general, they were elegant and judicious. Having long held the now abolished office of Judge-Advocate in Scotland, he was naturally led into his Treatise on Military Law, which is a clear and sensible exposition of the principles by which the absolute will of the sovereign over his army is supposed to be controlled and regulated. The Reverend Archibald Alison published a Life of his friend in the *Transactions of the Royal Society of Edinburgh* [volume viii.], a performance which owes no inconsiderable part of its pleasingness to the impression it imparts of the amiableness of the biographer. It is a dream of recollections, in which realities are softened by the illusions of the author's own tenderness. Tytler was unquestionably a person of correct taste, a cultivated mind, and literary habits, and very amiable; which excellences graced, and were graced by, the mountain retreat whose name he transferred to the bench. But there is no kindness in insinuating that he was a man of genius, and of public or even social influence, or in describing Woodhouselee as Tusculum.

Another amiable and celebrated person, Murray, commonly called the Orientalist, was withdrawn from us in 1813, very soon after reaching what to him was the great, and in the opinion of everybody else, the merited, elevation of the Chair of Oriental Literature in the College of Edinburgh. Sir Harry Moncreiff has published an account of him, by far the best part of which is Murray's own description of his early feelings and progress. Born a poor boy in the wilds of Galloway, an early thirst for knowledge, but particularly for languages, left him little rest by day or by night. I knew him at Dalzel's class, a little shivering creature, gentle, studious, timid, and reserved. His academical chair was the just and appropriate reward of his long

and silent enthusiasm, and was made the more honourable by the eminence of his competitors. But study
had worn out a weak constitution, and he survived
the attainment of his object only a few months. His
work on general philology, however able, is not such
high evidence of his depth in the philosophy of
language, as was furnished by his shorter essays, or
even by his conversatiòn. A good man, however, and
interesting from his mere studious recluseness, his
fate affected even those who only knew him by reputation, and sympathised with the story of his
meritorious rise and premature disappearance.

CHAPTER V

IN 1814 the Allies made their first conquest of Paris, and for a year Europe was without Napoleon. Hostilities were unexpectedly renewed in 1815, and then ceased, after the short and brilliant flash at Waterloo; but in 1814 a war which had lasted so long that war seemed our natural state was felt to be over.

This event separated the lives and the recollections of that generation into two great and marked parts. From this moment the appearance of everything was changed. Fear of invasion, contempt of economy, the glory of our arms, the propriety of suppressing every murmur at any home abuse, the utter absorption of every feeling in the duty of warlike union—these and other principles, which for twenty years had sunk the whole morality of patriotism in the single object of acknowledging no defect or grievance in our own system, in order that we might be more powerful abroad, became all inapplicable to existing things; and after a little time for settling into peace, the removal of the foreign pressure was followed by a rebound of internal improvement which will mark itself by its results on many ages of our history. Abuses and defects had, perhaps unavoidably, crowded into

every corner of our affairs. Had the party with the
absolute command of Parliament taken the gradual
reformation of these evils into their own hands, they
might have altered, and strengthened, the foundations of their power. But resistance of innovation
clung to them after it had become plainly absurd, and
was continued, fatally for themselves, as their test,
and their object. Meanwhile a generation was coming
into action so young that its mind had been awakened
by the excitement of the French revolution, and not
so old as to have been put under a chronic panic by
its atrocities, and which was cheered on by that
mistake of the adversary, which made the success of
every right measure a popular triumph. The force of
this new power was as yet unknown, even to those
among whom it was lodged, particularly in Scotland.
Nowhere in this part of the kingdom, except at Edinburgh, was there any distinct scheme, or rational
hope, of emancipation. But the mind of the lower, and
far more of the middle, classes had undergone, and
was still undergoing, a great, though as yet a silent
change, which the few who had been long cherishing
enlightened opinions lost few opportunities of promoting and directing.

The return of peace was distinguished by nothing
peculiar to Edinburgh. We got new things to speak
about; and the entire disappearance of drums, uniforms, and parades, changed our habits and appearance. We were charmed at the moment by a striking
sermon by Alison, and a beautiful review by Jeffrey,
on the cessation of the long struggle; the chief charm

of each being in the expression of the cordial and universal burst of joy that hailed the supposed restoration of liberty to Europe, and the downfall of the great soldier who was believed to be its only tyrant. Old men, but especially those in whose memories the American war ran into the French one, had only a dim recollection of what peace was, and middle-aged men knew it now for the first time. The change in all things, in all ideas, and conversation, and objects, was as complete as it is in a town that has at last been liberated from a strict and tedious siege.

In 1814 Scott published *Waverley*—the first of those admirable and original prose compositions which have nearly obliterated the recollection of his poetry. Except the first opening of the *Edinburgh Review,* no work that has appeared in my time made such an instant and universal impression. It is curious to remember it. The unexpected newness of the thing, the profusion of original characters, the Scotch language, Scotch scenery, Scotch men and women, the simplicity of the writing, and the graphic force of the descriptions, all struck us with an electric shock of delight. I wish I could again feel the sensations produced by the first year of these two Edinburgh works. If the concealment of the authorship of the novels was intended to make mystery heighten their effect, it completely succeeded. The speculations and conjectures, and nods and winks, and predictions and assertions were endless, and occupied every company,

and almost every two men who met and spoke in the
street. It was proved by a thousand indications, each
refuting the other, and all equally true in fact, that
they were written by old Henry Mackenzie, and by
George Cranstoun, and William Erskine, and Jeffrey,
and above all, by Thomas Scott, Walter's brother, a
regimental pay-master, then in Canada. But " the
great unknown," as the true author was then called,
always took good care, with all his concealment, to
supply evidence amply sufficient for the protection
of his property and his fame; in so much that the
suppression of the name was laughed at as a good
joke not merely by his select friends in his presence,
but by himself. The change of line, at his age, was a
striking proof of intellectual power and richness. But
the truth is, that these novels were rather the out-
pourings of old thoughts than new inventions.

A meeting against West Indian Slavery was held
in Edinburgh in July 1814. Sir Harry Moncreiff took
the lead in it, and a petition to Parliament was signed
by ten or twelve thousand persons. Except for
victories and charity, *this was the first assembling of
the people for a public object that had occurred here for
about twenty years ;* and if the termination of slavery
in our West Indian colonies had been a purely political matter, it could not have been held in Edinburgh
even in 1814. It was only made safe and respectable
by the attendance of the humane and the pious of
all politics; and even with this mitigation it excited
great alarm. The symptoms involved in the fact of

such a meeting, and of such a petition, were not unseen by any party. My excellent friend Thomas
Erskine [of Linlathen] was united with me in the
charge of a copy of the petition that lay for subscription in the Grassmarket; and we were both
surprised to find a piece of Calvinistic Whiggery,
which we thought had faded, still deeply seated.
Many who signed the petition to the Commons shrunk
back from the one to the Lords. They could not get
over the *Lords* SPIRITUAL. No reasoning could reconcile them to the title. " I would rather not homolo-
gate " was the general and conclusive answer.

The extension of the city gave rise in 1815 to the
New Town Dispensary. Any such institution seems
at least harmless; yet this one was assailed with a
degree of bitterness which is curious now. It was a
civic war. Two of its principles were, that medicines
and medical advice, including obstetrical aid, were
to be administered to patients *at their own homes*,
and that the office-bearers were to be elected *by the
subscribers :* which last, though not absolutely new,
was then rare in Edinburgh. All the existing establishments had the usual interest to suppress a rival. But
they disavowed this, which, however, was their true
motive, and raised the cry against these two peculiarities. A mob selecting a doctor! The Lying-in
Hospital was eloquent on the danger and the vice of
delivering poor women at their own houses. The Old
Town Dispensary, which did not then go to such
patients as could not come to it, demonstrated the

beauty of the sick poor being obliged to swallow their doses at a public office. Subscribers choose managers! Impracticable, and dangerously popular! However, common sense prevailed over even this political bugbear, and the hated institution rose and flourished, and has had all its defects imitated by its opponents.

These are small matters. But they show through what strange follies every effort leading, however indirectly and distantly, to independence had to struggle. After a certain time, the hackneyed objections to everything may, in all communities, be stereotyped, and thrown aside as soon as they are attempted to be made use of.

The most conspicuous opponent of this charity was Dr Andrew Duncan, senior, one of our professors and physicians, and the great patron of the Old Dispensary; one of the curious old Edinburgh characters. He was a kind-hearted and excellent man; but one of a class which seems to live and be happy, and get liked, by its mere absurdities. He was the promoter and the president of more innocent and foolish clubs and societies than perhaps any man in the world, and the author of pamphlets, jokes, poems, and epitaphs, sufficient to stock the nation; all amiable, all dull, and most of them very foolish. But they made the author happy; and he was so benevolent and so simple, that even those who were suffering under his interminable projects checked their impatience and submitted. Scientific ambition, charitable restlessness, and social cheerfulness made him thrust himself into everything

s

throughout a long life. Yet, though his patronage was generally dangerous, and his talk always wearisome, nobody could ever cease to esteem him. He was even the president of a bathing club; and once at least every year did this grave medical professor conduct as many of the members as he could collect to Leith, where the rule was that their respect for their chief was to be shown by always letting him plunge first from the machine into the water. He continued, till he was past eighty, a practice of mounting to the summit of Arthur's Seat on the first of May, and celebrating the feat by what he called a poem. He was very fond of gardening, and rather a good botanist. This made him president of the Horticultural Society, which he oppressed annually by a dull discourse. But in the last, or nearly the last, of them he relieved the members by his best epitaph, being one upon himself. After mentioning his great age, he intimated that the time must soon arrive, when, " In the words of our inimitable Shakespeare, you will all be saying, ' Duncan's in his grave.' "

Peace, with its other blessings, wrought no change more striking or more necessary in Edinburgh than the improvement of our architectural taste. This quality, for the indulgence of which Scotland has such advantages in its materials and its positions, had never been cultivated, or at least had never been acted upon, in modern times. There was a period during which feudal war created striking castles, and Popery glorious temples; but when the operation of these ceased, and internal defences became useless, and religious pomp odious, we sank into mere convenience, which we were too poor to associate with architectural beauty or grandeur. How many edifices can architecture justly boast of having produced in Scotland during the first hundred years after the Union? In towns the great modern object has uniformly been to extinguish all the picturesque relics and models of antiquity, and to reduce everything to the dullest and baldest uniformity. In addition to the varied forms exhibited by our forefathers, almost every city on the Continent supplied us with specimens of striking and cheap town architecture perfectly adapted to the purposes of ordinary life. Yet we went on as if these examples were ridiculous, and as if the common sense of building consisted solely in making it mean, and all mean in the same way. In Edinburgh, moreover, we were perpetually mistaking the accidental effect produced by situation, for that which can only be secured by design; and our escape from the old town gave us an unfortunate propensity to avoid whatever had distinguished the place we had fled from. Hence we were led into the blunder of long straight lines of street, divided to an inch, and all to the same number of inches, by rectangular intersections, every house being an exact duplicate of its neighbour, with a dexterous avoidance, as if from horror, of every ornament or excrescence by which the slightest break might vary the surface. What a site did nature give us for our New Town! Yet what insignificance in its plan! what poverty in all its

details! The creation of that abominable incumbrance, the " Earthen Mound," by which the valley
it abridges and deforms was sacrificed for a deposit
of rubbish, was not merely permitted without a
murmur to be slowly raised, but throughout all its
progress was applauded as a noble accumulation.
Our jealousy of variety, and our association of
magnificence with sameness, was really curious. If
a builder ever attempted (which, however, to do
them justice, they very seldom did) to deviate so far
from the established paltriness as to carry up the
front wall so as to hide the projecting slates, or to
break the roof by a Flemish storm window, or to turn
his gable to the street, there was an immediate outcry; and if the law allowed our burgh Edile, the Dean
of Guild, to interfere, he was sure to do so. Abercromby Place, though not begun till about 1809, was
the first instance in which the straight line was
voluntarily departed from. People used to go and
stare at the curved street. There were then probably
not six houses in George Street, or twenty in the
whole New Town, in which the unbroken surface of
vulgar slate did not project over the front wall. Yet
there has very rarely been so large, so well placed,
and so free a surface exposed at once to the taste of
any architect who had ever seen the Continent. But
every conception except of straight lines, cut rect-
angularly into equal spaces, and of every thirty front
feet being covered with the plainest and the cheapest
house, each exactly like its neighbour, seems to have
been excluded. It will take many years, and the cost

of building about a half of the original New Town over again, to lessen the baseness of the first ideas. We have now some pillars, balconies, porticos, and ornamental roughening; and money, travelling, and discussion will get us on.*

It was the return of peace that first excited our attention, and tended to open our eyes. Europe was immediately covered with travellers, not one of whom, whether from taste, or conceit, or mere chattering—but it all did good—failed to contrast the littleness of almost all that the people of Edinburgh had yet done, with the general picturesque grandeur and the unrivalled sites of their city. It was about this time that the foolish phrase, " The Modern Athens," began to be applied to the capital of Scotland; a sarcasm, or a piece of affected flattery, when used in a moral sense; but just enough if meant only as a comparison of the physical features of the two places. The opportunities of observing, and the practice of talking of foreign buildings in reference to our own, directed our attention to the works of internal taste, and roused our ambition.

It was fortunate that it was about this stage of our advancement that, independently of any object beyond mere access, all the old approaches to the city had to be abandoned, and new ones made. I wish that anybody had thought of preserving the lines of these old Appians in an intelligible map. They seemed

* We can now say (1909) it is accomplished in Princes Street, from which the original buildings have almost entirely disappeared, not in every case to advantage ; and George Street is rapidly having its long straight lines broken by some fine examples of modern architecture.

to have been planned, or rather used—for there was no planning about them—not so much for the convenience of the people, as with a view to keep enemies out. Narrowness, crookedness, and steepness, was the principle of them all. They luckily could not be improved, and therefore new approaches had to be made. This brought free ground to sale; and the result was the creation of admirable accesses, all connected with much very respectable building; the owners being always tempted to allure the spreading population by laying out their land attractively. Hence Newington, Leith Walk, the grounds of Inverleith, the road to Corstorphine, and to Queensferry, and indeed all the modern approaches, which lead in every direction through most comfortable suburbs.

A few years before this William Stark, the best modern architect that Scotland had produced, appeared. After he had established his reputation at Glasgow and other places, bad health compelled him to seek a retreat in Edinburgh, where however he only survived till October 1813. Thus he was too young to have done much; but he had excited attention and given good principles, particularly in reference to the composition of towns. The magistrates consulted him on the best way of laying out the ground on the east side of Leith Walk; and he explained his views in a very sensible, though too short, memorial. On the 20th of October 1813 Scott mentions his death to Miss Baillie in these terms, " This brings me to the loss of poor Stark, with whom more genius has died than is left behind among the collected universality of Scottish architects." His mantle, however, dropped on his pupil William Playfair, to whom Edinburgh has been more indebted since, than to the taste of all other modern architects it has produced or employed. The earliest evidence of his talent was in his attempt to retrieve the fatal errors that had nearly ruined our College; and the purity of his Grecian taste has since been attested wherever it has had an opportunity of displaying itself. It is now to be seen conspicuously in every quarter of the city. There are blots no doubt; but they have been made by his employers, not by him. For an architect is almost the only professional man who can never be rightly judged of by the works which he *executes*. His art is costly, and each part is fixed as soon as it is done. There is no rubbing out. This would be severe, even were he allowed to have his own way. But how often does it happen that he is thwarted by position, poverty, or obstinate ignorance. He must perpetually sacrifice his taste to suit the humours and the purses of his employers. Yet nothing is so common as to hear an architect condemned on the mere sight of a work against every defect of which he protested. Painters don't paint, nor do poets write on these terms.

The influence of these circumstances can only be appreciated by those who knew Edinburgh during the war. It is they alone who can see the beauty of the bravery which the Queen of the North has since been putting on. There were more schemes, and pamphlets, and discussions, and anxiety about the improvement of our edifices and prospects within ten years after the war ceased, than throughout the whole of the preceding one hundred and fifty years.

One lamentable error we certainly have committed, are committing, and, so far as appears, will ever commit. We massacre every town tree that comes in a mason's way; never sacrificing mortar to foliage. Stark raised his voice against this atrocity, but in vain. I do not know a single instance in which the square and the line have been compelled to accommodate themselves to stems and branches. To a considerable extent this is a consequence of our climate, which needs sun and not shade. But there are many situations, especially in a town, where shade is grateful, and many where, without interfering with comfort, foliage, besides its natural beauty, combines well with buildings. And there was no Scotch city more strikingly graced by individual trees and by groups of them than Edinburgh, since I knew it, used to be. How well the ridge of the old town was set off by a bank of elms that ran along the front of James's Court, and stretched eastward over the ground now partly occupied by the Bank of Scotland. Some very respectable trees might have been spared to grace the Episcopal Chapel of St Paul in York Place. There was one large tree near its east end which was so well placed that some people conjectured it was on its account that the Chapel was set down there. I was at a consultation in John Clerk's house, hard by, when that tree was cut. On hearing that it was actually down we ran out, and well did John curse the Huns. The old aristocratic gardens of the Canongate were crowded with trees, and with good ones. There were several on the Calton Hill: seven, not ill grown, on its very summit. And all Leith Walk and Lauriston, including the ground round Heriot's Hospital, was fully set with wood. A group was felled about the year 1826 which stood to the west of St John's Chapel on the opposite side of the Lothian Road, and formed a beautiful termination of all the streets which join near that point. One half of the trees, at the least, might have been spared, not only without injuring, but with the effect of greatly adorning, the buildings for which they have been sacrificed. Moray Place, in the same way, might have been richly decorated with old and respectable trees. But they were all murdered on the usual pretence of adjusting levels and removing obstructions. It was with the greatest difficulty that Sir Patrick Walker, the superior of the ground, succeeded in rescuing the row in front of Coates Crescent from the unhallowed axes of the very vassals. It cost him years of what was called obstinacy. I tried to save a very picturesque group, some of which waved over the wall at the west end of the jail on the Calton Hill. I succeeded with two trees; but in about four years they also disappeared. It only required a very little consideration and arrangement to have left the whole of these trees and many others standing without abating a single building. But the sad truth is that the extinction of foliage, and the unbroken display of their bright free-stone, is of itself a first

object with both our masons and their employers.
The wooded gardens that we have recently acquired
are not inconsistent with this statement. There was
no competition between them and building. It is our
horror of the direct combination of trees with
masonry, and our incapacity to effect it, that I complain of. No apology is thought necessary for murdering a tree; many for preserving it.

In 1815 Jeffrey set up his rustic household gods at
Craigcrook, where all his subsequent summers have
been passed. This was scarcely a merely private
arrangement. It has affected the happiness, and improved both the heads and the hearts of all the worthy
of this place. No unofficial house in Scotland has had
a greater influence on literary or political opinion.
Beautiful though the spot, as he has kept it, is, its
deepest interest arises from its being the residence of
such a man. Nothing can efface the days they have
passed there from the recollection of his friends.
Their rural festivities are dignified by his virtues and
talents, by all our Edinburgh eminence, and by almost
every interesting stranger. The Craigcrook Saturdays
during the summer session! Escape from the court and
the town, scenery, evergreens, bowls, talk, mirth,
friendship, and wine inspire better luxury than that
of the Castle of Indolence, without any of its dulness.

The first modern Musical Festival was held in
Scotland in 1815. It sprang more from charity than
from love of harmony. But the music, as I am told—
for though I heard some of it I did not comprehend

it—was good; and the outer House, where it was performed, was not ill calculated to give it effect. We have become an infinitely more harmonious nation since then. Indeed none of our advances is more decided than our musical one. But this is not for one with dead ears to speak of.

The beginning of the year 1816 was distinguished by one of the most important events in the progress of our law. " The Jury Court " was opened, and on the 22nd of January tried its first cause. We had long been verging towards the introduction of civil juries. The experiment was keenly resisted, chiefly by the older judges, and by the established obstructors of change. It is easy now to discover that in some respects the plan might have been mended; but on the whole, the introduction of so complicated and difficult a novelty was conducted with considerable wisdom. A separate court, a presiding judge trained to English practice, special issues, and no more extensive jurisdiction in matters of law than was indispensable for the trial of facts, were all necessary at first. For a while the idle public took great interest in the new tribunal; partly because the causes were intelligible, which the decisions of civil causes on printed evidence never can be to spectators, and partly because the counsel were expected to make play in every trial. Jeffrey and I were the chief delinquents in this line, because we had the largest share of the business, and every client thought his cause ill used, if it was not made a great cause of.

However, though this expectation is abated in litigants, and extinguished in the public, I suspect that the modern harangues are fully as animated and as long as ours.

William Adam, David Monypenny (Lord Pitmilly), and Allan Maconochie (Lord Meadowbank) were the first three judges. Adam had the misfortune to come into this new scene under exaggerated expectations of what he was to do.* He owed this to his Scotch nativity and education, the tastes and feelings of which forty years' general residence in England had only strengthened; to the kindliness of his manners; to his spirit in Parliament on several Scotch questions; and to his having been an associate of important public men on many great public occasions. Extravagant anticipations were formed of the person who had first fought Fox, and then been his friend; who had spoken in debate with Pitt; managed the affairs of Royal Dukes; been the standing counsel of such clients as the East India Company and the Bank of England, and in great practice in Parliamentary Committees. His appearance was good. It was that of a farming gentleman. He had a distinct rational voice, and an admirable, plain, well-bred manner. Though well read for a busy gentleman, he was not a person of either learning or general ability. His true merits resolved into industry, practical sense, agreeable deportment, and a conscientious ambition to secure the success of the Jury Court experiment.

* A Parliament House witticism of the period was: Why is the Jury Court like the garden of Eden? Because it was made for Adam.

His conspicuous defect was obscurity of judicial speech. It is very difficult to account for this; because on other matters he had a very clear head, and a very clear tongue. I cannot analyse the process by which one so versant in the practice, and in the explanation, of business, and so totally unencumbered by either diffidence or conceit, should have generally contrived to get mystical on the bench. It arose partly, I have no doubt, from his not being at home with the legal ideas and legal terms of the law of Scotland. Yet this will not account for it entirely. The acute and mathematical Lord Glenlee once described the thing very well. Adam was delivering an opinion, or explaining something, in the Court of Session, when Glenlee, after listening for a long time, without attaining any definite idea, to his well-sounding sentences marked by all the appearance of precision and all the reality of confusion, observed—" He speaks as if he were an Act of Parliament."

Yet no other man could have done his work. He had to guide a vessel over shoals and among rocks. This was his special duty, and he did it admirably. His experience of English practice enabled him to remove difficulties formidable to our awkwardness. He protected his court from prejudices which, if not subdued by his patience and dexterity, would have crushed it any week. He saw that the Scotch could scarcely be expected to fall into the old English idolatry of jury trial; but believing that, *when properly applied*, civil juries were nowhere more valuable than in Scotland, where the people were generally educated, and yet had no popular institutions, he had no pride and no pleasure so great as that of permanently securing them, in one shape or other, for his native country. Both on the bench and at chambers he gave us the best example of judicial urbanity that we had ever seen. Nothing could be more beautiful, and sometimes even affecting, than the anxiety of this old, and at last nearly blind, man to do his work, and the earnest patience and polite cheerfulness with which he gave himself to it. So far as we are to retain civil trial by jury in this country, we shall owe it to him personally. No one else could have either launched or piloted it. When in 1830 the Jury Court ceased to exist as a separate court his vocation was at an end; and he retired with the respect and the affection of the whole legal profession and of the public.

Nothing could exceed his delightfulness in society, and especially in domestic life. He was not a whit the worse of a hot temper. When it transpired, it only amused his friends. A day passed with the Chief Commissioner at Blair-Adam—his Eden, where his heart laughed in its boyhood—was a day of amiable virtue, always to be remembered with pleasure.

When I first saw Monypenny, I was a boy looking out of a window in the High Street of Edinburgh at the foot procession of the Lord High Commissioner to the General Assembly; and Monypenny was walking before his Grace the Earl of Leven, dressed like a mackaw, as the Commissioner's purse-bearer. Little did he, or anybody, then dream that the day was to come in which he was to have a seat on three supreme benches, and to become some one in his profession. Of good sense, but of moderate ability, with no legal learning beyond what an ordinary hand to mouth lawyer needs, and no power either of speaking or of writing beyond that of clear statement, his judicial powers were very considerable, far above his powers as a counsel. Slender, pure-eyed, clear-skinned, a beautifully composed manner, a distinct quiet voice, and an air of steady propriety in all he said or did, his outward style was excellent and striking, simple yet dignified, without feebleness, and patient, yet neither passive nor dull. This admirable and very peculiar manner left his judgment and industry to operate unobstructed; and they were concentrated on his profession, the exercise of which was his sole enjoyment. Amidst the vexatiousness of the most complicated case, aggravated by the strife of the bar, and the collisions of the bench, he sat so serenely, and got through his work with such composure, that it made one cool to look at him.

Meadowbank ought neither to have taken nor to have got a seat in this court. His health scarcely allowed him even to enter it; and he died soon after his appointment. For above a year before his death he was worn away by some painful disorders, which he bore up against with great energy. Though obliged to forego the court, the conflicts and the toils of which were his luxury, he read, and wrote, and discussed to the very last.

One great outcry against this court, at first, was excited by our being required to adopt the English *unanimity* of juries. We had been accustomed to it for above a century in the Exchequer, which was an English Court. But its sittings were solely in Edinburgh, and its verdicts were of a penal nature; so that the country at large knew little about its proceedings, and it had not to deal with the complexity of civil competitions. It therefore got on without much practical obstruction. But when it was proposed to carry the principle into all proofs, and all over the land, hosts of fiery objectors started up, who on grounds logical, political, metaphysical, and religious, denounced the scheme as justifying rebellion at the least. The religious objection, which resolved into the perjury (as it was called) of the minority, sacrificing its conscience to the conscience of the majority, was the one that made the deepest impression on the Scotch mind. Meadowbank wrote a good pamphlet explanatory of the true working of the principle of unanimity, which operates (as he said) by producing discussion and concession among jurors, and thus makes a verdict by even compulsory unanimity a truer extract of the average sense of the whole of them, than if all reasoning had been superseded by a vote. There is some ingenuity in this, which is all that can be said in defence of the venerable English habit. But if it was sound, it is odd that of all the tribes of mankind the habit has been tolerated in England alone. I believe it to be absurd; and that, whether a bare majority ought to be allowed to decide or not, always requiring unanimity is nonsense. Experience has not in the least diminished our Scotch aversion to it.

Another advance towards the habit of public meetings, and a far more important one than that of the preceding year in favour of slaves, took place in February 1816. A meeting was then held in the Merchants' Hall to petition Parliament against the continuance of the property and income-tax. This was the first respectable meeting held in Edinburgh, within the memory of man, for the avowed purpose of controlling Government on a political matter; and was justly considered by the prophetic as a striking indication of the tendency of the public mind; the more so that it was attended by a few Tories, who, though attached to ministers, were more attached to their money. Mr Menteath of Closeburn presided; Jeffrey moved resolutions, which Moncreiff seconded.

In this year we lost George Wilson, a person whose very name was unknown to the public, but whose character tinged the character of some of those whose names were never out of the public ear. He was the person who is spoken of with such reverence and affection by Romilly and Horner, and who stood so high in the confidence and love of all the really eminent in London; a Scotchman by birth and education, and an English lawyer by profession. Better fitted by calmness and simplicity for the Bench than for the jangling work of the Bar, no elevation

T

would have been above his merits or the reasonable hopes of his friends.* But all their and his views were blighted by a severe attack of paralysis, which compelled him to leave London. He withdrew to Edinburgh in 1810, and died there in June 1816. His life here was a rare and noble example of practical philosophy. Driven suddenly by ruined health from his accustomed scenes of ambition and enjoyment, he had to reconcile himself to a retired existence on a very low scale of vitality, in a place where, except to his old friends Dr Gregory and Henry Mackenzie, and two or three more, he was unknown. And he did it beautifully. His mildness and intelligence attracted the worthy; and good society temperately enjoyed, literature and benevolence, a deep interest in the friends he had left, and in all the public subjects that engaged them, and a growing affinity for those he had recently acquired, occupied him as fully as was safe; and he resigned himself with such a contented attachment to the new scene, that it almost seemed as if he was glad of a calamity that enabled him to indulge in so rational a retirement. He rarely missed the Friday Club,† where his serenity and excellent con-

* "His uncommon cleverness of expression, and the remarkable correctness of his understanding, qualified him in the most eminent degree to fill the office of judge ; and on that point there was but one opinion in the profession. If the office had been elective and the Bar had been the voters he would probably have been unanimously elected to it."—Sir Samuel Romilly's *Memoirs*.

† "The Friday Club, so called from the day on which it first used to meet. It was entirely of a literary and social character, and was open, without any practical limitation of numbers, to any person generally resident in Edinburgh who was supposed to combine a taste for learning

versation, over his glass of cold water, made us feel as if we ought to despise ourselves for our champagne. In writing to Gregory about his attack, after it occurred, he said, " we bachelors have a great advantage over you married men *in dying*." The Club always brightened at his appearance. It was sure of admirable talk and opinions, great knowledge of good books and good men, perfect candour, a gentle manner, and a soft voice. It is a pleasure to recollect him, and to preserve a character which, except in the memories of his friends, he has done nothing to perpetuate.

It was in 1816 also that we heard the first whisperings of what was termed " the National Monument of Scotland." The idea of commemorating the triumphs of the late war, and of exciting the heroisms of future conflicts, was first thrown out publicly at a county meeting; and the scheme was often discussed throughout some succeeding years. The original plan did not go beyond a pillar, or some such thing. But there were some who thought that the prevailing effervescence of military patriotism created a good opportunity for improving the public taste by the erection of a great architectural model. The Temple of Minerva, placed on the Calton Hill, struck their imaginations, and though they had no expectation of being able to

and science with agreeable manners ; and especially with perfect safety. ' The idea was Scott's,' Jeffrey says in a letter to Murray. At first meetings were held weekly ; there were no written laws, no motions, no disputes, no ballot, no fines, no business of any kind except what was managed by one of ourselves as secretary."—Lord Cockburn's *Life of Lord Jeffrey*.

realise the magnificent conception they resolved, by beginning, to bring it within the vision of a distant practicability. What, if any, age would finish it, they could not tell; but having got a site, a statute, and about £20,000, they had the honour of commencing it.

Two edifices were begun this year, of respectable beauty. Our Episcopalians used to be so few that their two principal congregations met, the one in a humble place at the west end of Rose Street, the other in a chapel which, though handsome and spacious when got at, was buried in an inaccessible close on the south side of the Canongate. Indeed it was only within a few years before that this sect had got some of the legal vexations which had clouded it removed. They now raised their heads; and growing in numbers and in aristocracy, erected their new chapels at the west end of Princes Street, and at the east end of York Place. The ambition of architecture has since begun to infect the Presbyterian seceders.

Archibald Alison, the author of the *Essays on Taste*, was then the most distinguished of the Episcopalian clergy of Edinburgh and, so far as I know, of Scotland. A most excellent and agreeable man; richly imbued with literature; a great associate of Dugald Stewart, Playfair, Dr Gregory, Jeffrey, Francis Horner, and all the eminent among us; delightful in society; and, in truth, without a single defect except the amiable one of too soft a manner. As a preacher he was a consummate artist, in his own peculiar line of feeling and impressive elegance. His voice was clear and sweet, his taste very refined, and his air and gesture very polite. It was the poetry of preaching. The prevailing defect was that it was all too exquisite. The composition, the sentiments, the articulation, and the look were in too uniform a strain of purity and feeling. To the hearer, cloyed by a system of studied perfection, artlessness, though leading to some carelessness or even coarseness, would have been a relief. Notwithstanding this deduction, however, from the effect of exertions which always derive their greatest charm from simplicity, it was impossible to hear Alison preach without being moved and delighted. Even at this distance of time, his discourses during the occasional fasts and thanksgivings throughout the war, the whole of which I heard, still thrill in my ear and my heart. He was almost the only preacher I have ever known who habitually made the appearances of external nature, and the kindred associations, subservient to the uses of the pulpit. This copious and skilful application of the finest, and most generally understood, elements of taste was one great cause of his peculiar success; and, managed with judgment, sensibility, and grace, it explained how those who sometimes entered his chapel determined to dislike his excess of art, rarely left it without being subdued by the beauty and impressiveness of his eloquence.

The year 1816 closed bitterly for the poor. There probably never were so many people destitute at one time in Edinburgh. The distress was less in severity than in 1797; but the population having increased, it was greater in extent. Some permanent good was obtained from the labour of the relieved. Bruntsfield Links were cleared of whins, and of old quarries; walks were made, for the first time, on the Calton Hill; and a path was cleared along the base of the perpendicular cliff of Salisbury Crags. Until then these two noble terraces were enjoyable only by the young and the active.

This walk along the Crags was the first thing that let the people see what we were in imminent danger of losing by the barbarous and wasteful demolition of the rock, which had been proceeding unchecked for nearly thirty years. When I first scrambled to that cliff, which must have been about 1788, the path along its base was certainly not six feet wide, and in some places there was no regular path at all. By 1816 the cliff had been so quarried away that what used to be the footpath was, in many places, at least 100 feet wide; and if this work had been allowed to go on for a few years more, the whole face of the rock would have disappeared. This would have implied the obliteration of some of the strata which all Edinburgh ought to have revered as Hutton's local evidence of the Theory of the Earth, and one of the most peculiar features of our scenery. The guilty would have been —first, the Hereditary *Keeper* of the Park, who made money of the devastation by selling the stones; secondly, the Town-Council and the Road Trustees, who bought them; thirdly, the Crown and its local

officers, who did not check the atrocity. Of these the
Crown was the least criminal. It did interfere at last;
and it was reserved for Henry Brougham, who had
often clambered among these glorious rocks as a boy,
to pronounce as Chancellor the judgment which
finally saved a remnant of them.

The change which was taking place in the character
of our population was now evinced by an occurrence
which was remarkable both as an effect and as a cause.
The first number of *The Scotsman* newspaper was
published in January 1817. The incalculable importance of this event can only be understood by those
who recollect that shortly before this the newspaper
press of Edinburgh, though not as much fettered as
in St Petersburg (as it has been said to have been),
was at least in as fettered a condition as any press
that is legally free could be.* Most candid men who
knew Scotland before the peace of 1814 will probably
agree, that if the most respectable and unprosecuted
London opposition newspaper had been published in
Edinburgh, the editor would have been better acquainted with the Court of Justiciary than he would
have found comfortable. The undisturbed continu-

* "The local press was utterly abject; no Edinburgh paper could be
found independent enough or courageous enough to expose almost any
sort of abuse, however flagrant, if in doing so there was the slightest
risk of giving offence in high quarters. It was an incident of this sort—
the refusal of the public prints in the city to publish a statement of the
mismanagement of the Royal Infirmary, prepared by Mr William Ritchie
at the request of some friends and clients—that drew the attention of
that gentleman and of Mr Maclaren to the great need of some free organ
of public opinion in Scotland."—*Select Writings, Political and Scientific,
with a Memoir of Charles Maclaren.*

ance of the *Edinburgh Review* would be inconsistent with this statement, were it not that there is no analogy between a work of which the politics are dignified by general literature, and which only appears quarterly, at the price of five shillings, and the provocations of a cheap and purely political and generally accusative publication, tormenting every week or every day. When Major Cartwright, the itinerant reformer, lectured here about 1812, he was attended by considerable audiences; yet because he preached the doctrines of universal suffrage, and annual parliaments, no editor of any Edinburgh newspaper, though offered to be paid as for an advertisement, and one of them a hearer of the discourses, had courage to allow any account whatever of the lectures to appear in his paper. The editor who attended them told me that, though he differed from the lecturer, what he said was a good and perfectly lawful defence of the doctrines, and that he would have liked to have published their substance, but that he could not ruin his paper. He felt, and explained, that the bare exposition of such reforms would hurt the mere reporter.

The appearance therefore of a respectable opposition newspaper was hailed and condemned according to people's tastes:* but they all saw in it a sign. Though only published once a week, and taking only literary advertisements, it soon attained a large circulation. It is now flourishing in a vigorous manhood,

---

* Many lawyers subscribed for it in the names of, and had it conveyed to them privately by, their clerks, in order to avoid giving possible offence to their clients.

immeasurably the best newspaper that exists, or has ever existed, in Scotland.* Its only defect has been heaviness; a defect, however, inseparable from provincial locality, particularly in Scotland, where the people are grave, and too far out of the world to acquire smartness and tact. The original projectors of this the first Scotch newspaper which combined independence with intelligence, and moderation with zeal, were Charles Maclaren, who has since distinguished himself in science,† William Ritchie, solicitor, and John Robertson, bookseller [musicseller]. Its earliest conductors were Ritchie and Maclaren, and John Ramsay Macculloch, now chiefly celebrated as a political economist, the principles of which science he has examined and disseminated with a talent and success that will make his career an era in its history. They were all able men, and honest in the public cause, the greatest virtue the conductors of a newspaper can possess. Ritchie was bold and zealous, and a very respectable legal practitioner. He died, after a tedious illness, a short time after the news of the first accession of the Whigs to real power in 1830 reached Edinburgh, when his last political act consisted in raising himself in bed on his elbow, and giving a feeble cheer.

* This can still be said of it. The heaviness complained of in the next sentence soon gave place to vigour and vivacity, and under the direction of Alexander Russel and Charles Cooper it has maintained the position Lord Cockburn assigned it from the start.

† Mr Maclaren's contributions to the *Encyclopædia Britannica* and other papers were published in two volumes in 1869 under the title of *Select Writings, Political and Scientific, with a Memoir of Charles Maclaren*.

Nobody was enjoying the progress of sound opinions in Scotland more than Francis Horner. But alas! our forebodings were realised; and the gaiety of the Outer House was stilled by our learning, one day this spring, that on the 8th of February 1817 he had died in Italy. Every virtuous heart was covered with mourning. We did not think so much of his loss to the empire as to Scotland and ourselves. Acquainted with all our circumstances, and ambitious of nothing so much as the elevation of his native country, he would have brought to the discussion of all the vital questions that were about to arise talents which, already great, were steadily improving, and a character that made him almost the representative of virtue itself. In this his native city, the sorrow for his family, to whom it was an honour to bear his name, and for the premature extinction of his own prospects, was deep and nearly universal. The last time I saw him was about the end of September 1816. It was at Dryden, near Roslin, where his father was then residing. Rutherfurd [afterwards Lord Rutherfurd] and I had gone to visit him. He was very ill, breathless and weak. Removing for the winter into milder air had been resolved on; but we both feared it was too late. He walked out a little with us. Never can I forget the fading avenue, and the autumnal day, in which we parted from him, as we foreboded never to meet again.

The valuable and peculiar light in which Horner stands out—the light in which his history is calculated to inspire every right-minded youth, is this.

He died at the age of thirty-eight; possessed of greater public influence than any other private man; and admired, beloved, trusted, and deplored by all except the heartless or the base. No greater homage was ever paid in Parliament to any deceased member. Now let every young man ask—how was this attained? By rank? He was the son of an Edinburgh merchant. By wealth? Neither he, nor any of his relations, ever had a superfluous sixpence. By office? He held but one, and only for a few years, of no influence and with very little pay. By talents? His were not splendid, and he had no genius. Cautious and slow, his only ambition was to be right. By eloquence? He spoke in calm good taste, without any of the oratory that either terrifies or seduces. By any fascination of manner? His was only correct and agreeable. By what then was it? Merely by sense, industry, good principles. and a good heart—qualities which no well-constituted mind need ever despair of attaining. It was the force of his character that raised him; and this character not impressed upon him by nature, but formed, out of no peculiarly fine elements, by himself. There were many in the House of Commons of far greater ability and eloquence. But no one surpassed him in the combination of an adequate portion of these with moral worth. Horner was born to show what moderate powers unaided by anything whatever except culture and goodness may achieve, even when these powers are displayed amidst the competition and jealousy of public life.*

* So attractive was his appearance when a youth, that it was remarked of him "That boy has the ten commandments written on his face."

Considering what *Blackwood's Magazine* soon became, it seems strange that a just memoir of Horner, and by Dr Gordon, should have been the first article of its first number. The rise of this publication forms another important mark in our local story.

Our only monthly periodical work was the dotard *Scots Magazine*, which now lived, or rather tried to live, upon its antiquity alone. Constable imprudently broke its last spell by changing its title and structure, which gave Mr William Blackwood, an active bookseller, an opening for a new adventure; though probably he had no anticipations beyond those of an ordinary magazine of ordinary success. But it soon became, in its politics, a work of violent personality; and it was to this, far more than even to its unquestionable talent and spirited writing, that its influence, at least for a long time, was owing.

There was a natural demand for libel at this period. The human mind had made a great advance, and the pressure of war being removed, new opinions were coming everywhere into collision with the old ones; so that there was a general shock between those who wished to perpetuate old systems, and those who wished to destroy or reform them. Even in Greece, Italy, Spain, South America, and various other parts of the world, a movement of intellect, or of discontent, produced open war between bigotry and liberality. In Britain, where open violence was checked by the strength of the law, it engendered fiercer conflicts of parties than had been known, except near revolutions. Now a war of opinion is a condition of which libel is one of the natural products.

Edinburgh was peculiarly ripe for the use of this weapon, because there was no place where the contrast between the new and the old internal systems was so strong. The whole official power of Government was on one side, nearly the whole talent and popularity on the other; and the principles espoused by each admitted of no reconciliation. The Tories could boast of some adherents of talent, and of many of great worth, but their political influence now depended almost entirely on office. With the exception of Scott, I cannot recollect almost a single individual taking at this time a charge of public opinion, and of personal weight, who was not a Whig. In opposition to this official authority, which in itself is seldom deeply seated, and is always disliked, there was arrayed almost the whole body of our local talent and independence cordially united. The Whigs, condemned no longer to cherish their principles in silence, finding public spirit revive, assumed the lead, and their standard was followed by a host consisting of all those who felt themselves raised into something like a region of freedom. They came forth from despised dissenting congregations, from half liberated corporations, from shops, from the law, and, which was a better sign of the current, even from medicine, and, which was the best symptom of all, from the aristocracy of the lower orders. All these, aided by the emancipated in the shires, soon became accustomed, as if it was a part of the necessary order of things, to see official power against them, and moral influence in their favour.

In this situation, when the popular cause had got *The Scotsman*, it was natural for the opposite cause to set up its magazine; and, in the circumstances, a certain degree of personality was only to be expected. The fault of the new organ lay in its excess; which was the more offensive from our being then so little accustomed to it, and the smallness of the society into which the firebrands were cast. This is alluded to in the " *Noctes Ambrosianæ* " in speaking of the *Beacon* Newspaper. " A *Beacon !* Gude pity us! etc. Though your *Antijacobins*, and *John Bulls*, and *Twopenny Post-bags*, and sae on, do very weel in the great Babel of Lunnun, the like o' thae things are quite heterogeneous in this small atmosphere of the Edinbro' meridian. The folk here canna thole't." [*Maga.*, vol. xv. p. 708]. Posterity can never be made to feel the surprise and just offence with which, till we were hardened to it, this work was received. The minute circumstances which impart freshness to slander soon evaporate; and the arrows that fester in living reputations and in beating hearts are pointless, or invisible, to the eyes of those who search for them afterwards as curiosities. The favourite calumny was founded on charges of irreligion. Such charges, however false, are always favourably received by a large portion of the public, even though proceeding from persons of whom laughter at religion, and clever parodies of Scripture, are notoriously the favourite pastimes.* No wonder, then, that divisions in our narrow society which all reasonable men had practically agreed to close were re-opened, and much of the ferocity of 1793 revived.

This vice of offensive personality, which was flagrant at first, is the more to be lamented, that in talent and originality this magazine has been, and is, the best that has been published in its day in Britain. It has been supported by a continued succession of able men, who have covered it with contributions of great and inventive power; and, avoiding the lethargy which seems the constitutional malady of prolonged magazines, its thinking and writing have always been spirited. Its literary compositions and criticisms have generally been excellent. But it was set up chiefly as a political work; and in this department it has adhered with respectable constancy to all the follies it was meant to defend. It is a great depository of

* "The bookseller and Pringle soon quarrelled; and the Magazine assuming, on the retirement of the latter, a high Tory character, Laidlaw's Whig feelings induced him to renounce its alliance; while Scott, having no kindness for Blackwood personally, and disapproving (though he chuckled over it) the reckless extravagance of juvenile satire which by-and-by distinguished this journal, appears to have easily acquiesced in the propriety of Laidlaw's determination" (Lockhart's *Life of Scott*, vol. iv. p. 65). A chuckle from Scott, in the blaze of his reputation, was all that young men needed to instigate them. In another passage Mr Lockhart describes these monthly attacks as "those grotesque *jeux d'esprit* by which, at this period, Blackwood's young Tory wags delighted to assail their elders and betters of the Whig persuasion" (vol. iv. p. 109). Deducting gloss, this means that respectable characters were wilfully and systematically slandered, but that it was funnily done; which was not always the case, for it was often with bitter gravity.—H. C.

Some interesting details of the relations between Scott and Blackwood at the launching of the magazine will be found in Mrs Oliphant's *William Blackwood and his Sons*, 2 vols.

exploded principles; and indeed it will soon be valuable as a museum of old errors.

It was long enlivened by the "*Noctes Ambrosianæ*," a series of scenes supposed to have occurred in a tavern in Register Street kept by one Ambrose. And no periodical publication that I know of can boast of so extraordinary a series of jovial dramatic fiction. Wilson [Christopher North], I believe, now professes to regret and condemn many things in these papers, and to deny his authorship of them; but substantially they are all his. I have not the slightest doubt that he wrote at least ninety per cent of them. I wish no man had anything worse to be timid about. There is not so curious and original a work in the English or Scotch languages. It is a most singular and delightful outpouring of criticism, politics, and descriptions of feeling, character, and scenery, of verse and prose, and maudlin eloquence, and especially of wild fun. It breathes the very essence of the Bacchanalian revel of clever men. And its Scotch is the best Scotch that has been written in modern times. I am really sorry for the poor one-tongued Englishman, by whom, because the Ettrick Shepherd uses the sweetest and most expressive of living languages, the homely humour, the sensibility, the descriptive power, the eloquence, and the strong joyous hilarity of that animated rustic can never be felt. The characters are all well drawn, and well sustained, except that of the Opium Eater, who is heavy and prosy: but this is perhaps natural to opium. Few efforts could be more difficult than to keep up the bounding spirit of fresh boyish gaiety which is constantly made to break out amidst the serious discussions of these tavern philosophers and patriots. After all just deductions, these *Noctes* are bright with genius.

It was a matter of course, that as soon as the country began to awaken, the great question of Burgh Reform should be revived. Those who were bent on this subject had the advantage of having to deal with a single and clear evil, capable of being removed only in one way. By the constitution of all the Royal Burghs in Scotland (above 60 in number) each town-council elected its successor; which in practice meant that they all elected themselves. The system of self-election was universal, and very jealously adhered to. The effect of this system in depressing the civic communities, and encouraging municipal abuse, could not be exaggerated. Hence it was one of the earliest of the constitutional vices which public-spirited men saw the necessity of attacking, when the era for political reform began to dawn. The subject had been keenly agitated, but with little hope of success and no general support, so far back as 1785. But as the town-councils were the only electors of our city representation in Parliament, and these bodies were easily kept in ministerial order by simple, direct, and scarcely concealed bribery, their unchanged continuance was defended as obstinately as the drawbridge of the castle. Yet I consider it as a fact that, with the burgh reformers, the improvement of our parliamentary representation, if

U

an object at all, was infinitely less so than the improvement of the system by which our municipal affairs were managed. When the struggle began, and for many years afterwards, the reformers would have been content with such a relaxation of the existing system, as would have kept the political power of the Tory party nearly as safe as it was under self-election. But concession was withheld till a triumph on the opposite side made it useless. Meanwhile the collateral effect of the contest, in provoking the citizens into a spirit of independence, was far more useful than the attainment of their merely burgh objects could have been. Government thought that the subject had been forgotten. But the hopelessness of prosecuting any civil struggle while the war lasted had only kept it in abeyance. The fire was not out. Its ashes lay smouldering; and protracted abuses only blew them up the more fiercely when they came to be stirred. The battle lasted several years after this, and its movements became complicated; but, generally, its progress was this:—

The election of the magistracy of Montrose became void from a failure to comply with the *Set*, or constitution, of the burgh. On this the Crown revived the magistracy by a *Poll warrant*—that is, a warrant to elect addressed to the burgesses at large. The effect was the creation of a town-council with a taste for some independence. Other burghs instantly saw that this was a precedent which might be followed wherever legal ingenuity could detect a flaw in the rather nice and technical mysteries of a town-council

election; and that an independent magistracy being
once formed, self-election might enable it to be perpetuated. Government, however, soon repudiated the
example which it had been misled to rear up, and
would grant no more poll warrants; but fell on the
scheme of repairing lapsed councils by warrants addressed to the members of the council who had been
last duly elected. It got well abused by the Whigs for
its retreat, but far better by the Tories for its advance.

In order to try whether the Crown would persist
in always restoring the old magistracies, several com-
plaints of undue election were brought into the Court
of Session. One of these, directed against the town-
council of Edinburgh, made a great noise. Only two
of them, from Aberdeen and Inverness, succeeded;
and in both cases the Crown adhered to its principle.
This raised a crop of new legal proceedings; first, by
burgesses, who challenged the Crown's right to grant
any other than poll warrants, and then by the Officers
of State, who challenged its right to grant these. It
is needless to trace the progress of this mass of litiga-
tion. It produced a good deal of legal learning and
investigation, great public excitement, and very
little legal result. The Court of Session was not supposed to have gained credit under the discussions.
Instead of applying a severer candour, and a more
strictly judicial calmness, to questions plainly in-
volving party passions and objects, it was allowed to
transpire too obviously, through the tone and manner
of most of the judges, that they were neither ignorant
of the objects of the litigants, nor indifferent about

the results. Judges cannot be made of ice or wood, and it is not their duty to extinguish, even if they could, all their public principles. Some allowance, therefore, ought to be made for disclosures of feeling which it is so difficult to resist, and the sensitive jealousy of suitors, and their professional champions, is always to be distrusted. Still, inflexible fairness being the most necessary of all the judicial duties, every incident that attests its absence is most properly watched and denounced. Public officers, who are trained and honoured for the practice of impartiality, have infinitely less excuse than other men for tolerating objects or passions within their breasts, which either are, or must be supposed to be, inconsistent with the power of holding the scales of justice steadily.

While these matters were agitating the courts, Lord Archibald Hamilton, one of the very few active and independent Scotch members, succeeded (by a miracle) in obtaining a committee on our burgh system. Loud were the rejoicings on the one side, and sad the dismay on the other, when the tidings of this scarcely credible vote reached Scotland. Edinburgh seemed to have wakened into a new existence, when its civic functionaries were obliged to repair to London, and to open the windows of the council chamber, and let in the light. The affairs of four burghs were investigated; and it was held to be clearly proved that these four were bankrupt, and that this had been the result of municipal mismanagement. In the case of Aberdeen this was publicly admitted by the magistrates in a formal act of abdication. These disclosures, instead of convincing Government of the absolute necessity of proceeding, in one way or other, through the whole burghs, unfortunately convinced it of the very reverse. The results were that the inquiry was suddenly quashed, that the legal proceedings died away, and that the people were thus compelled to return to their old bondage. But the evil day of reform was only put off, with a deeper accumulation of abuses, till the arrival of a more favourable hour.

No single folly ever opened so many Scotch eyes. The minister who had had the sense to do anything merely to check municipal expenditure, or to concede to corporations the valuable, but for remoter objects the perfectly insignificant, privilege of electing their own deacons in reality, and not in form only, might have retarded the regeneration of Scotland. But the course adopted first excited the hopes, and then the indignation of the people. It began by disclosing the trustlessness of town-councils, and ended by hardening them in their protected abuse of power. However, it worked to good. It reared a generation of intelligent and active citizens, who were trained by the struggle to political concert.

It is impossible to think of burgh reform without remembering Archibald Fletcher,* advocate, its stoutest and most indefatigable champion. He gave his whole energies to it in the dawn of its agitation; and its revival after a thirty years' slumber, though

* Lord Cockburn's appreciation of Archibald Fletcher's efforts on behalf of Burgh Reform is given in his *Life of Lord Jeffrey*.

it found his body old and infirm, found no abatement of his spirit. Even in the extremity of old age he compiled a volume of tracts in furtherance of his favourite cause, the renewal of which, in spite of what appeared to others to be its unavoidable dulness of detail, he declared " had revived his youth."

About this period the first preachers of sedition, who had openly practised their calling since 1793-4, ventured to begin business again; not in Scotland, where transportation was still the law, but in England, which they greatly disturbed. It is usual to ascribe all that followed to the harangues of these crazy orators. But demagogues are almost always effects; very rarely causes. They are the froth that rises and bubbles on the surface, when the mass of the people ferments. The sedition of opinion moreover was promoted by the sedition of the stomach. The country was in deep distress; and natural dearth was aggravated by the artificial arrangements of trade and manufactures, which operated like what miners call *troubles*, in the transition from war to peace.

It was in these circumstances that certain judicial proceedings were taken in Scotland against several persons accused of sedition,* and of having taken

* The first adventure was with Baird and Maclaren, who were tried for sedition on the 5th of March 1817. Jeffrey and I were counsel for one prisoner; John Clerk and James Campbell of Craigie for the other. And there occurred an excellent piece of Clerkism. Campbell called on Clerk on the morning of the trial. He found him dressing, and in a frenzy at the anticipated iniquities of the judges; against whom, collectively and individually, there was much slow dogged vituperation throughout the process of shaving. He had on a rather dingy-looking

and administered unlawful oaths. These proceedings created an intense interest both in Parliament and in the country, and are well worthy of being studied in all their details. The general story of the unlawful oaths case is this:—

There was a weaver in Glasgow called Alexander Richmond. Jeffrey and I had got acquainted with him in 1812, from having been his counsel when he was accused of accession to the most extensive and peaceful combination of workmen that had ever appeared in this part of the kingdom; the organisation and management of which was better evidence of his talent and influence than many men of high political station could have produced. Knowing the temper of the Court in these matters, we advised him to submit to outlawry; whereby he escaped the outrageous sentence which doomed some of his companions to eighteen months' imprisonment. When the irritation was over he reappeared and pleaded guilty; and after proving that he was in very bad health, and getting a great character, even from his former masters, he was only imprisoned about a month. His gentleness and air of melancholy thoughtfulness made us believe him to be a heart-broken contem-

night shirt ; but a nice pure shirt was airing before the fire. When the toilet reached the point at which it was necessary to decide upon the shirt, instead of at once taking up the clean one, he stopped and grumphed, and looked at the one and then at the other, always turning with aversion from the dirty one ; and then he approached the other resolutely, as if his mind was made up ; but at last he turned away from it, saying fiercely, " No ! I'll be d——d if I put on a clean sark *for them.*" Accordingly he insulted their Lordships by going to Court with the foul one. Not like Falkland.—H. C.

plative man, who had formed the association, and then let himself be its victim, solely from devotion to what he held to be the rights of his comrades. We felt so interested in him that we gave, and got for, him a little money to set up in business, and then we lost sight of him for some years; when to our amazement we heard him charged with having been recently acting as a Government spy.

In 1824 he published a curious " *Narrative* " of his connection with the authorities, and with the troubles, in Glasgow, chiefly with a view to vindicate his character. This was rather a delicate effort, partly because it implied his disclosing communications which he must have known were confidential; and partly because he had to meet the inconvenient fact of his having received considerable sums, and more considerable promises, from Government—not for his spyship, which both he and his employers denied, but as a compensation for his being thrown out of work, by being obliged to leave Glasgow. His " Narrative " may not be vitiated by purposed falsehood; but though there is a general foundation of truth in it, the details of no such statement can ever be relied upon when they depend entirely on the authority of the narrator. His being implicated and paid for what looked too like spy's work, greatly shook our faith in him; but still the peculiar circumstances in which he had let himself be placed in that position, and our conviction of his benevolence, prevented us casting him off.

The way he was drawn in, according to his own

account, was this. Government, or its Glasgow representatives, suspecting that illegal oaths were
administered there, resorted to Richmond as a person
who could best ascertain whether this was the fact.
His statement has uniformly been that his love of
his old associates made him anxious, on their account,
and to save them from deeper guilt, to find out what
they were really doing; but that as he was aware
that his appearance among them might make them
think such oaths safe, his employers came under a
positive engagement with him, that no one should be
prosecuted who might administer or take an oath in
his presence on the only occasion on which he meant
to go among them. This engagement was denied;
and though there are facts which make its having
been entered into not improbable, the presumption
is certainly against him, chiefly from the apparent
absurdity and illegality of the bargain. However,
he soon ascertained that the crime had been committed, and reported accordingly; but whether the
exact words of the unlawful oath were brought away
I do not know.

A copy of what was supposed to be the oath having
been obtained, it seems to have been impossible to
resist the temptation of producing an impression by
reading it in the House of Commons. And doubts
being expressed of the accuracy of the information,
the Lord Advocate was cheered by his party into the
rashness of pledging himself to prove its accuracy by
speedy convictions. Accordingly, several persons
were apprehended on warrants charging them with

high treason; which, as the law was then generally understood, had the effect of depriving them of the benefit of the Act 1701. The prisoners, instead of being committed to an ordinary jail, were taken to the Castle of Edinburgh, where access to them was made nearly impossible. All the while, however, there was no serious intention of trying them for high treason; and hence, though this charge was always kept up in the warrants, it never entered any of the many indictments.

As it was certain that there would be a series of trials if one should succeed, and the whole affair, whatever the guilt might be, was thought to be conducted with far too high a hand, the counsel employed for the different prisoners acted in concert at all the material moves. This made an array of counsel not usual in Scotland, consisting of Clerk, Cranstoun, Thomas Thomson, Jeffrey, John Peter Grant,* Moncreiff, Murray, and myself. Many were the sneers by the prosecutors, and even by some of the judges, at this confederacy. Hermand often snorted with open contempt at what he called " the combination of learned gentlemen." To all which the combiners used to say that they trusted that the Bar of Scotland would always supply any force that the defence of political prisoners, with the Crown against them, might require.

When the first prisoner, William Edgar, was placed at the bar [9th April 1817], the prosecutor seemed to

* Afterwards Sir John Peter Grant and one of the supreme judges at Calcutta.—H. C.

expect an easy conviction that very day. But the advisers of the prisoners, believing Time to be the surest composer of violence, resolved to procrastinate as much as they could; and their opponents supplied them with ample materials for preliminary discussion and delay. This produced a long and memorable struggle, in which the prosecutor was so often baffled, that Mr Finlay, the member for Glasgow, a ministerialist, and who was in the heart of the whole affair, made a direct charge of incapacity against the Crown counsel in the House of Commons [20th June 1817]. At last, after above three months had been wasted in changing and mending indictments, and in verbal and printed argumentation, one prisoner, Andrew M'Kinlay, was actually brought to trial on the facts [19th July 1817].

But the trial had scarcely begun when something more extraordinary transpired. The first witness, John Campbell, on being asked the absurd initial question then put to every witness in criminal trials —whether he had received or been promised anything for giving evidence, said that he had. On being asked by whom? he answered, " By that gentleman "— pointing to the Advocate-depute. The audience seemed to start at this statement, and were then anxiously silent. The judges frowned on the man as if they would have eaten him on the spot. His statement was taken down in writing, and is to be found in the Reports of the trial.*

* *State Trials*, vol. xxxiii. p. 584, etc. But no report can convey any idea of the living scene, which was one of the most striking I ever witnessed in a court of justice.—H. C.

If the witness is to be believed, it is difficult to avoid the conclusion that there had been an attempt to corrupt. For the substance of his statement is, that besides merely protecting a witness on the unpopular side from personal harm, a reward was promised, or held out, provided he would give evidence of a particular tendency; and the real meaning of what was proposed was such, that the sheriff, who was there as a magistrate bound to see justice done, would not allow it to be set down in *writing.* No witness ever gave his testimony in a manner more entitled to credit. Calm, clear, and unexaggerating, he went into all the details with precision and apparent probability, and often suggested minute but material corrections to the presiding judge, as he was dictating to the clerk of Court; and I am not aware that there ever was a surmise against his general character.

When the deposition was adjusted, everybody looked as if thinking—" What's to come next? " Hermand at once cut the knot by suggesting that, if what had been sworn was true, the witness was inadmissible, an attempt having been made to corrupt him; and if it was false, then he was inadmissible from being perjured; so he was inadmissible either way. This conclusion was evidently not warranted by law; because not having been *convicted* of perjury, his mis-statements only went to impeach his credit; and if he was trying to disqualify himself,* the prosecutor was entitled to disprove what he had said.

* This is the theory put by Hume into the second edition of his Commentaries, vol. ii. p. 364.—H. C.

But the Court at once adopted a view which closed a very painful scene. So the witness was allowed to walk away.

If the accusation had depended solely on Campbell, it might have been fairly said that his single testimony was insufficient to criminate high public officers. But it did not depend on him alone. The gentlemen accused did, or allowed to be done for them, three things which it was difficult to reconcile with the idea of their being conscious of innocence. One was, their not *strenuously* resisting the Court in excluding further inquiry. The prisoner put on record an offer to corroborate the witness. The prosecutor put on record an answer professing his anxiety that this matter should be gone into. But though this looks very well in the report, it was seen, and felt, and understood at the time that the saving process of the Court, instead of being heartily opposed, was virtually acceded to.* Another, and a far more material, blunder was, that when a motion was made in Parliament (10th February 1818) for a committee to inquire into the truth of Campbell's statement, it was resisted, and by the aid of Government thrown out.

---

* I myself do not well see—though this was not the ground taken—how the examination could have been gone into *on the spot ;* because the names of those to be examined were in no list of witnesses; and according to our still subsisting and absurd rule, no persons not in the list can be called by the prosecutor, even though this is necessary not only to rebut matter not naturally connected with the case, and introduced by surprise. But though the inquiry could not have been gone into *as a part of the current trial*, the matter, like any other alleged obstruction of justice, might have been investigated by a separate proceeding as soon as the trial was over.—H. C.

The only ground on which this insane course (innocence being assumed) was explained, rested on the assertion that Campbell, who must have been the chief witness, was perjured already. Yet they completed their folly by a third apparent inconsistency with conscious rectitude. Campbell's perjury was their main point; yet he was never indicted for this offence, although they were goaded to bring him to trial. If he had been put to the bar, his evidence would have been excluded, while that of the Solicitor-General, the Advocate-depute, the Sheriff of Edinburgh, and the Procurator-fiscal, who were the persons mentioned by Campbell, might have been received.* But no indictment was ever adventured upon. They may have been innocent. But if they were, they were surely not wise. And if they only meant to *protect* the witness, which is sometimes necessary, this, as usual, ought to have been done openly, and both the prisoner and the Court ought to have been told of it.

Richmond in his " Narrative " assumes that the prisoner's counsel knew what Campbell was going to say, and compliments them for acting surprise well. There was no acting in the matter. Campbell had been locked up, inaccessibly, in the Castle; and seeing an acquaintance passing threw a bit of tobacco to him from his window. His friend picked this up; and finding that it contained a piece of dirty paper with something written on it, took the paper to Mr David Ramsay, a most respectable writer to the

* *See* Romilly's *Memoirs*, vol. iii. p. 329.—H. C.

Signet, who had all along been agent for most of these prisoners. The bit of paper merely stated the general fact that Campbell had been tampered with by the authorities, without mentioning how, or by whom. Mr Ramsay of course informed his counsel of this; but they, having no means of questioning the witness, who was sealed up, and distrusting the statement, resolved to do nothing, but to let things take their own course.*

Campbell being disposed of, the trial proceeded; and it was very soon established that illegal oaths had been administered, and, in all human probability, by the prisoner. But the truth of the *particular charge* was by no means so clear. This depended on the exact words used. A very slight change of expression could easily soften the character of the oath into mere rashness, or doubt, or even innocence, or aggravate it into worse guilt than that charged. Jeffrey and Thomas Brown, our moral professor—two of the acutest of men, used to amuse themselves by trying how many different constructions they could put on the words, and by how few and how slender variations of expression they could make it all harmless. Now, when the prosecutor examined the witnesses he chiefly relied on for the precise terms, it came out that they had seen an oath in the newspapers which was said to have been quoted in the House of Commons, that

* Hence amidst many other errors, and a complete vapid deadness, there is a material mistake in the Edinburgh Report of the Trial, which has been copied into the *State Trials*. Jeffrey, when Campbell began, is made to say, "I am *enabled* to ask pointed questions of the witness." *Enabled* should be *unable* (*State Trials*, vol. iii. p. 585). The Edinburgh Report was about a year too late of appearing, and nobody then cared about its blunders or omissions.—H. C.

this was like the one they had been privy to, but that they could not separate their recollection of what they had seen from their recollection of what they had heard; so that they could not tell whether, in giving evidence, they were doing more than reciting from the newspaper. On this the prosecutor struck.

The prison and castle gates were instantly opened, and all the kindred prisoners walked forth. And so ended this long, tough, and important conflict. The trial was over about nine in the evening of a bright summer Saturday. I instantly walked out to Bonaly, with a light step, and in an agitation of triumph. This was partly the produce of professional vanity; a passion stronger in the law than in the army or navy, or even in medicine or the church, and inferior only to that of verse, art, and the theatre. But there was also some feeling of justice in it. We were not satisfied of the prisoner's guilt in the precise matter charged, and were certain that his guilt had not been established; and there had been strange circumstances in the conduct of the prosecution, which was connected with the general system of a justly unpopular Government.

Shortly after this we were thrown into an uproar by a point of Calvinistic orthodoxy. Moved by the sad and unexpected death of the Princess Charlotte, which had melted all hearts, every clergyman in Edinburgh, except one, following the universal example, had religious service in his church on the 19th of November 1817, the day of her funeral, which was what we call a *week-day*—that is, not a Sunday. This, in Scotland, was not in obedience to the Royal proclamation, which we sons of Calvin always despise, but solely from natural decency and piety. Addressing their flocks on such an occasion, of course they all introduced the poor Princess, her virtues and her fate; and this in most cases probably amounted to a funeral sermon. But the Reverend Andrew Thomson maintained that all such sermons are repugnant to the Presbyterian system, and dangerous in themselves from their tendency to degenerate into sycophantish eulogy: and perhaps he was right in this. But most clearly he was wrong in bringing discredit on his party, by being the only minister who shocked the universal feeling by acting on this principle on this occasion. Several of his brethren entreated him to yield. Sir Harry in particular remonstrated and implored. But a useless personal battle, in which his will was on one side and all the world on the other, had always irresistible charms to Thomson. So he stood out; and while crowds rolled into every other church, the gates of his were closed, and he himself was made happy by being universally abused. On the following Sunday he preached on death, and alluded to the recent calamity, in a manner that disarmed those that heard him; and for the edification of those who did not, he published a pamphlet, demonstrating that everybody was wrong except himself. Possibly they were: but it seems odd how notices of striking deaths, which is so common on Sundays, and was so even in Thomson's own practice, should be so bad on every other day.

x

CHAPTER VI

In 1817 our streets were deprived of one of their most peculiar objects. The City Guard,* of which Scott has given so good an account in his *Heart of Midlothian*, after subsisting since about the year 1696, was abolished in November 1817. The police had made them useless; but I wish they had been perpetuated, though it had been only as curiosities. Their number was liable to be increased or diminished according to circumstances. At this period they amounted, I conjecture, to about 200, regimented like ordinary soldiers. They were all old, hard-featured, red-nosed veterans; whose general history was, that after being mauled in the wars, commonly in a Highland regiment, they brought their broken iron bodies home, and thought themselves fortunate if they got into this fragment of our old burgher militia, where the pay was better than nothing, and the discipline not quite inconsistent with whisky, while the service was limited to keeping the peace within the city. Naturally disliked by the people, they were always asserting their dignity by testy impatient anger. This excited the mischief and the hostility of the boys, by whom their small remains of temper were intolerably tried; and between the two

* Always called by the people "The Toon Rottens."—H. C.

there never ceased to be a cordial and diverting war. Their uniform was a red coat turned up with blue, a red waistcoat, red breeches, long black gaiters, white belts, and large cocked hats bound with white worsted ribbon. They had muskets and bayonets, but rarely used them; for their peculiar weapon was the old genuine Lochaber axe—a delightful implement. One saw Bannockburn in it. One of these stern half-dotard warriors used to sit at each side of the prisoners at the bar of the Court of Justiciary as guard; with his huge hat on his old battered head, and his drawn bayonet in his large gnarled hand. They sat so immovably, and looked so severe, with their rugged weather-beaten visages, and hard muscular trunks, that they were no unfit emblems of the janitors of the region to which those they guarded were so often consigned. The disappearance of these picturesque old fellows was a great loss.

After their extinction the Justiciary prisoners were put under the charge of police officers, a change which most of the judges lamented. The Court of Justiciary had long a very bad taste for military force, which is not eradicated yet. The Circuit processions to Court were always escorted by soldiers when they could be got, even in quiet country towns.

Some of the features of our ancient Circuits which time has effaced were curious. On looking back, the shades of many old lords, famous barristers, notorious provosts, sonorous macers, formal clerks, odd culprits and queer witnesses appear. Those who are born to modern travelling can scarcely be made to understand how the previous age got on. The state of the roads may be judged of from two or three facts. There was no bridge over the Tay at Dunkeld, or over the Spey at Fochabers, or over the Findhorn at Forres. Nothing but wretched pierless ferries, let to poor cottars, who rowed, or hauled, or pushed a crazy boat across, or more commonly got their wives to do it. There was no mail-coach north of Aberdeen till, I think, after the battle of Waterloo. What it must have been a few years before my time may be judged of from Bozzy's *Letter to Lord Braxfield*, published in 1780. He thinks that besides a carriage and his own carriage-horses, every judge ought to have his sumpter-horse, and ought not to travel faster than the waggon which carried " the baggage of the Circuit."* I understood

---

* I do not know the history of this pamphlet. It is a declaration against the vices of the criminal judges ; but as Boswell's father, to whom Braxfield succeeded, had been one of them, I doubt if he meant to attack them all. And as the letter is addressed to Braxfield, *on his promotion* to the criminal bench, he could have given no ground for it. The defects or habits, for which they are abused, are levity, carelessness, partiality, indecorum, pecuniary shabbiness, etc.

Speaking of the waggon, which I have nowhere else ever heard of, he says (p. 25), "The Lords of Justiciary should not contract their travelling equipage into that of a couple of private gentlemen on a jaunt of pleasure, but should remember that it is the train of a court composed of different members. Formerly every one of the judges had his led horse—his sumpter, in the procession. The disuse of that piece of pageantry may be forgiven, though not applauded. But the abolishing of a covered waggon for the baggage of the Circuit, though a paltry saving, is a great grievance. How shall the official clothes of the trumpeters ; nay, how shall the record of the Court, and the essential papers, be carried ? Not to mention the gowns and clothes of others who ought to be decently dressed. Without it, there must be such shifts and such pinching, as is to be found only in a company of strolling players. Shall the mace, the badge of authority, be crammed into the boot of a coach,

from Hope that after 1784, when he came to the bar,
he and Braxfield *rode* a whole north Circuit; and that
from the Findhorn being in flood they were obliged
to go up its banks for about twenty-eight miles, to
the bridge of Dulsie, before they could cross. I myself
rode circuits when I was Advocate-Depute between
1807 and 1810. The fashion of every depute carrying
his own shell on his back, in the form of his own
carriage, is a piece of very modern dignity.

There is nothing in which the old Circuits differed
more from the modern than in the excess of their
politics. Little as the business generally is now, it is
at least five-fold what it was formerly. To be sure,
being in no want of time, they wasted it freely. I have
heard Jeffrey say that if there was only one cause in
the world it would never be finished at all. It is only
necessity that produces judicial expedition. The old
debates on relevancy on every indictment, the
technical objections to witnesses, the long harangues
to juries in every case, the written verdicts—the
parents of endless additional objections and discussions; these, and much other useless and teasing
weft with which the woof of our old practice was
crossed, made every trial, however clear and insignifi-

amongst black-ball, shoe-brushes, and curry-combs? The trumpeters
be forced to ride in their official clothes, and look shabby? The embroidered G. R. upon the breast of their coats be turned out to the rain
and the tempest as poor Lear was turned out by his own daughters? The
record of the Court, the indictments, the criminal letters, precognitions,
etc., must be at the mercy of the weather. The four pleas of the Crown
may be blown about by the four winds of heaven," etc.

There is some more sense in the pamphlet than this, however, but
not much.—H. C.

cant, a matter of keenness, pertinacity, eloquence, and sweat. That fifteen cases may be disposed of in eight hours, and that an Advocate-Depute may do his duty well, and yet not address a jury once in fifty trials, and that prisoners' counsel may decline addressing in the great majority of cases—these facts with which we are now familiar, would certainly be discredited if they were told to Braxfield in Elysium. To make up for want of business, our predecessors exerted themselves powerfully as political trumpets. What harangues! about innovation, Jacobinism, and the peculiar excellence of every abuse. No judge could preserve his character, and scarcely his place for a month, who was to indulge in such exhibitions now. But that time applauded them.

The best modern practice is for the judge to go to and from the Court-house as quietly as possible. But the fashion, till lately, was never to move but in procession, always fully tailed; and on foot, that the tail might be seen the better. There was a foot procession to and from every meeting and rising of the Court even in Glasgow, where, whatever sneers it produced, it could create no village awe. Yet twice every day did they walk, horn-blown, about a mile, through that contemning mob; and with torches if it was at night.

At Edinburgh, the old judges had a practice at which even their barbaric age used to shake its head. They had always wine and biscuits *on the bench*, when the business was clearly to be protracted beyond the usual dinner hour. The modern judges—those I mean

who were made after 1800, never gave in to this;
but with those of the preceding generation, some of
whom lasted several years after 1800, it was quite
common. Black bottles of strong port were set down
beside them on the bench, with glasses, caraffes of
water, tumblers, and biscuits; and this without the
slightest attempt at concealment. The refreshment
was generally allowed to stand untouched, and as if
despised, for a short time, during which their Lordships seemed to be intent only on their notes. But in
a little, some water was poured into the tumbler, and
sipped quietly as if merely to sustain nature. Then
a few drops of wine were ventured upon, but only
with the water: till at last patience could endure no
longer, and a full bumper of the pure black element
was tossed over; after which the thing went on regularly, and there was a comfortable munching and
quaffing, to the great envy of the parched throats in
the gallery. The strong-headed stood it tolerably
well, but it told, plainly enough, upon the feeble. Not
that the ermine was absolutely intoxicated, but it was
certainly sometimes affected. This however was so
ordinary with these sages, that it really made little
apparent change upon them. It was not very perceptible at a distance; and they all acquired the habit
of sitting and looking judicial enough, even when
their bottles had reached the lowest ebb. This open-
court refection did not prevail, so far as I ever saw,
at Circuits. It took a different form there. The temptation of the inn frequently produced a total stoppage
of business; during which all concerned—judges and

counsel, clerks, jurymen, and provosts, had a jolly dinner; after which they returned again to the transportations and hangings. I have seen this done often. It was a common remark that the step of the evening procession was far less true to the music than that of the morning.

The new street along the southern side of the Calton Hill disclosed some glorious prospects, or at least exhibited them from new points. One of these was the view westward, over the North Bridge. But we had only begun to perceive its importance, when its interception by what are now called the North Bridge Buildings raised our indignation; and we thought that the magistrates, who allowed them to be set agoing in silence, had betrayed us. We were therefore very angry, and had recourse to another of these new things called public meetings, which we were beginning to feel the power of. It was held on the 2nd of December 1817. Professor Playfair presided; this being, I suppose, the only time in his life on which that unobtrusive and gentle philosopher permitted himself to be placed in such a position. James Stuart of Dunearn explained the matter in a clear and sensible speech. Old Henry Mackenzie made his first appearance at such a meeting, saying that, though no speaker, it was impossible to submit in silence to the destruction of the town, and that " *facit indignatio versum.*" Resolutions were passed, a subscription opened, and we went to law, where we got an ornate speech, from Cranstoun, who recited

" my own romantic town " to the Court. But this
was all we got. For while the judges were looking
rather favourable, our funds ebbed, and of course
our ardour cooled. Then persons of taste began to
hint that we were all wrong, and that the position
of the buildings was beautiful; and at last another
meeting was held in May 1818, when we struck our
colours. So we lost about £1000; the magistrates got
a fright; and the buildings stand. But much good was
done by the clamour. Attention was called nearly
for the first time, to the duty of maintaining the
beauty of Edinburgh. A respectable and organised
resistance of municipal power was new here, and the
example was not last, though the immediate object
of the battle was.

A Royal Commission had been issued in 1794
authorising certain persons to enter the jewel room
in the Castle of Edinburgh, and by breaking the door
if necessary, in order to ascertain whether the historical conjecture was true that the Crown of Scotland
and its pertinents were there. But that attempt to
discover them had failed; because, after breaking
the lock of the door, a punctilious commissioner
doubted whether their warrant sanctioned their also
using force against a chest that they found within.
This obstacle was suggested, I have heard, by Blair
the Solicitor-General; and it being thought formidable, the chest was left untouched, the outer door was
re-locked, and the Commissioners retired. After
another pause of twenty-four years, the experiment

was renewed by a better instructed Commission, and on the 4th of February 1818 the Commissioners proceeded, with due pomp, to their work. They unlocked the door and broke open the chest. And there, as Thomas Thomson had told them, they found the Regalia sleeping beneath the dust that had been gathering round them ever since the Union. It was a hazy evening, about four o'clock, when a shot from the Castle and a cheer from a regiment drawn up on the Castle Hill announced to the people, that the Crown of their old kings was discovered. Loyalty, antiquarianism, and the interest of finding something that had been long lost, created a good deal of anxiety, but less than I expected. This was owing chiefly to there having been very little said about it beforehand; and silence was prudent, while the discovery was uncertain. But there was no want of popular interest afterwards. John Kemble asked Scott if the Crown was not splendid? " The last time that I saw you as Macbeth you had a much grander one."

We this year lost a person of mature eminence— Malcolm Laing the historian. He was at the bar, and his speech in 1794 for Gerald, charged with sedition, was the best that was made for any of the political prisoners of that period. But his heart was little in a profession for which he was not well qualified, and from which he was allured by the more congenial pursuits of literature and history. Feeble health withdrew him from Edinburgh about 1808, when he returned to what to him was the paradise of his native

Orkney, which he never again abandoned. Depth, truth, and independence as a historian were the least of his merits, for he was a firm, warm-hearted, honest man, whose instructive and agreeable companionship was only made the more interesting by a hard peremptory Celtic manner and accent. He sent a copy of his *History of Scotland* to Dr Parr, who returned it, or at least one of the volumes of it, with numerous corrections of the style. There are few better lessons on English terms and idioms than what is given by a comparison of the original with the proposed emendations of the friendly and judicious critic.*

The natural tendency of the folly of Government in the Burgh Reform question appeared this year in certain civic proceedings, which, though of no importance in themselves now, are curious historically,

* The history was originally published in two volumes. It seems to have been the second volume only that Dr Parr thus returned to Mr Laing. The author in his second edition adopted to a very large extent the suggestions of his critic.

Bound up with this volume is the following autograph letter :—" Dr Mr Laing

"You know my esteem, my regard, my great respect for you, and my anxiety for the success of your History.

" You will therefore excuse my freedom in objecting, in criticising, in censuring, and in altering.

" Farewell. Remember me in terms of the highest, the very highest respect to Professor Stewart, and believe me

" Most sincerely yr friend,

" S. P.

" *Good Friday*, 1803.

" Mr Fox is a great admirer of your book, and he is, also,

" Puri sermonis amator.

I wish you were acquainted. As a critic he is quite as captious and fastidious in protecting English idiom from Scottish invasion, as I am. Farewell."

This interesting volume passed into the hands of Mr Thomas Thomson and later into the possession of Sir James Gibson-Craig.—H. C.

and as marking the gradual, but rapid, rise of popular opinion.

The Merchant Company of Edinburgh, instituted in 1681, was the only respectable mercantile body this unmercantile place possessed. And it had considerable influence; because while it could overawe the humble traders below, it could prostrate its head to the powers above. It was exactly such a body as could be produced by the condition of the country. Having not much trade to manage, it was little else than a small aristocracy of merchants, used for political purposes. They probably sometimes pleased themselves with the imagination that their title—The Merchant Company—made the ignorant equal them to the burgher communities of Holland, or the princely trading associations of Venice. But, in truth, whatever they were meant to be originally, they had become a mere political instrument, and of the paltriest description. Individually, its magnates were very good men, but publicly its " Master " and his " Twelve Assistants " were a king and a house of lords, without the commons. The people, however, had their Peter Wentworths, who now began to show that they were no longer to be frightened by hard words. In August 1818 the great men of the last generation were confounded by hearing it seriously proposed to give £100 of the funds in aid of the Burgh Reform, which the opponents of this measure now treated as merely a Whig and Tory question. The revolutionary motion was rejected, but only by a small majority. The victory of its authors was, however, complete when, on the same

day, they were within two votes of annihilating the
system altogether, on a motion denying the Master's
privilege of appointing the other office-bearers, and
claiming this power for the Company at large. On this
the old school withdrew; and the Society has since
managed its own affairs, and obtained due public
weight.

It was in the same spirit that the Guildry renewed
efforts, which had often been made before, to liberate
itself from the control of the Town-Council. Being a
more numerous and a more rebellious body than the
merchants, its pretensions had always been resisted
sternly. Its old and long silenced claims, particularly
that of electing its own Dean, were now revived. Of
course they were repelled; and it is very probable
that, in law, most of them were untenable. But it is
certain that they were resisted merely because the independence of the Guildry would have been inconvenient to the party in power. It was a political collision. Hence the importance of the struggle. Hence the
value of the spirit which the conflict generated, not
merely here, but over all Scotland.

Another loosening from the Town-Council occurred
about this period. It was one of the earliest of the
practical alienations, on matters of mere business,
which attested how unworthy of trust our municipal
system was believed to have become. Though standing in a rainy country, Edinburgh has always been
thirsty and unwashed. At this time the condition of
the city, in reference to water, was positively frightful. Our supply depended on a wretched tank of about

ten or twelve shallow acres on the north side of the Pentland Hills, which had been considered as far too small when it was made a long time before, but had now become absurd, even if it had been always full, instead of being often and long nearly empty. The Town-Council, on which our supply of this necessary of life depended, could or would do nothing. A joint stock company was formed, and a plan for bringing in the Crawley spring from the south side of the Pentlands was obtained. The danger of leaving a city at the mercy, for anything it cannot do without, of a single private company was foreseen, and has to a great extent been realised. But anything was thought better than the Town-Council; in so much that so long as the absolute exclusion of our civic rulers was doubtful scarcely any one would risk a shilling in the concern. But they being excluded, the company proceeded, and we occasionally got some water.

One consequence of this was, that as the supply was steadier than it used to be, it became worth while to put water-pipes into houses. And another consequence of this innovation was, that we were speedily deprived of a set of people fully as peculiar as the City Guard—the Water Carriers, of whom in a very few years there was not one extant. They were a very curious tribe, consisting of both men and women, but the former were perhaps the more numerous. Their business was to carry water into houses; and therefore their days were passed in climbing up lofty stairs, in order to get into flats. The water was borne in little casks, and was got from the public wells, which were then pretty thickly planted in the principal streets; and as there were far more candidates than spouts, there was a group of impatient and wrangling claimants, who, when not eloquent, sat on their kegs. These encampments of drawers of water had a striking appearance. The barrels, when filled, were slung upon their backs, suspended by a leather strap, which was held in front by the hand. Their carriage was made easier by leaning forward, which threw the back outward; and hence stooping was the natural attitude of these sons and daughters of the well. They were known by this peculiarity even when off work. Their backs, which would otherwise have never been dry, were protected by thick layers of hard black leather, on which the barrels lay; and the leather had a slight curl up at its lower edge, which, acting as a lip, threw the droppings, by which they could always be tracked, off to the sides. Still, however, what with filling, and trickling, and emptying, it was a moist business. They were all rather old, and seemed little; but this last might be owing to their stooping. The men very generally had old red jackets, probably the remnants of the Highland Watch or of the City Guard; and the women were always covered with thick duffle greatcoats, and wore black hats like the men. They very seldom required to be called; for every house had its favourite " Water Caddie," who knew the habits and wants of the family, and the capacity of the single cistern, which he kept always replenishing at his own discretion, at the fee (I believe) of a penny for each barrel. Their intercourse

with families civilised them a little: so that, in spite of
their splashy lives and public-well discussions, they
were rather civil, and very cracky creatures. What
fretted them most was being obstructed in going up
a stair; and their occasionally tottering legs testified
that they had no bigotry against qualifying the water
with a little whisky. They never plied between Saturday night and Monday morning; that is, their employers had bad hot water all Sunday. These bodies
were such favourites, that the extinction of their trade
was urged seriously as a reason against water being
allowed to get into our houses in its own way.*

The next spring opened by a public dinner in
honour of Burns (22nd February 1819). There were
about two or three hundred present. John A. Murray
was in the chair. By far the most interesting part of
the proceedings were the few words spoken by
Henry Mackenzie, who had been kind to the poet on
his first visit to Edinburgh about thirty years before,
and who was often rewarded by witnessing the glory
of the genius which he had so early discerned and
cherished. This was long remembered as the first
public dinner at which any of the Whigs of Edinburgh
had spoken. It was the first that showed them the use
to which such meetings could be turned, and was the

* I see—many years after the above was written—that they still
subsist in Madrid. " Hail ! ye Aguadores of Asturia ! who, in your dress
of coarse duffle, and leathern skull-caps, are seen seated in hundreds by
the fountain sides, upon your empty water casks, or staggering with
them filled to the topmost storeys of lofty houses."—Borrow's *Bible in
Spain*, Chapter 12.—H. C.

immediate cause of the political dinners that soon after made such an impression.

The Arts, of which I have mentioned the dawn, went on improving. " The Royal Institution for the promotion of the Fine Arts," though it got its charter only in 1827, was established in 1819; and it introduced itself to the public by the best exhibition of ancient pictures that had ever been brought together in this country; all supplied from the private collections of its members and friends. But here ended the use of the institution. Begun under great names, it had one defect, and one vice. The defect was that it did, and was calculated to do, little or nothing for art except by such exhibitions, which could not possibly be kept up long, for the supply of pictures was soon exhausted. A rooted jealousy of our living artists as a body (not individually) by the few persons who led the Institution was its vice. These persons were fond of art no doubt, but fonder of power, and tried indirectly to crush all living art, and its professors, that ventured to flourish except under their sunshine. The result was that in a few years they had not a living artist connected with them. Their tyranny produced the Academy; and then, having disgusted the only persons on whose living merit they could depend, the Institution itself sank into obscurity and uselessness.

On the 19th of April 1819 Lord Webb Seymour, after a long decline, sank as gently as a languid flower. The long voluntary residence of this stranger

Y

among us excited a deeper sympathy with his fate, and seemed to impart more virtues to his character. Hallam's account of him is perfect.* None of his peculiarities amused his friends more, or was a more frequent subject of joking to himself than the slowness and the vastness of his preparations.† He was perfectly aware of this conscientious and modest infirmity. " I in retirement am endeavouring to work out the distant good of mankind. Leave me exempt from the casualties of human life, and I am almost secure of my object."‡ No—you would not. An exemption from the casualties of life is a considerable postulate for a philosopher. But its having been granted would not have brought the cautious Seymour to a practical result. Immortality would only have lengthened his preparation.

Playfair, though ill, and the day bad, followed poor Seymour to his grave at Holyrood. But those who saw him there shook their heads; and in about three months he joined his friend. This was an irreparable loss both to the science and to the society of Edinburgh. Taking the whole man—his science, his heart, his manner, and his taste, I do not see how Playfair could have been improved. Profound, yet cheerful; social, yet always respectable; strong in his feelings, but uniformly gentle; a universal favourite, yet never moved from his simplicity; in humble circumstances, but contented and charitable—he realised our ideas

---

* App. to *Horner's Memoirs*, vol. i. p. 473. —H. C.
† Horner's letter to Murray, 16th July 1814. Horner's *Memoirs*, vol. ii. p. 175.—H. C.
‡ Letter to Allen, 30th September 1805.—H. C.

of an amiable philosopher. And is he not the best philosophical writer in the English language?* I have been told that when racked on his death-bed with pain a relation wished to amuse him by reading one of Scott's novels, of which he was very fond, but that he said he would rather try the *Principia*. Nothing can be more just than the application made to him, by Stewart, of Marmontel's description of D'Alembert [*Elements of Philosophy*]. His friends subscribed for a bust of him, and a monument. The bust has been most happily executed by Chantrey. The monument, designed by his nephew, has been placed on the Calton Hill, in connection with the Observatory, which owes its existence and its early reputation to Playfair. The deaths of Horner, Dr John Gordon,† Seymour, and Playfair, all within a very short time, clouded our city. Their true monuments were in the hearts of their surviving friends, who to this hour solve any doubt about science, or life, by recollecting what these men would have thought of it.

Another Edinburgh character, of a different sort, ceased in 1819 to be gazed at by men. This was Adam

* His countryman, Hugh Miller, has since displayed a power of scientific description which, in some respects, even Playfair could not have surpassed, if equalled ; but in the correct and simple beauty of calm thought, even Miller falls short of Playfair.—H. C.

Hugh Miller, author of *The Old Red Sandstone, Footprints of the Creator*, etc., edited *The Witness* newspaper, and died in 1856.

† Dr Gordon died in June 1818. " In flore primo, tantae indolis juvenis extinctus est, summa consecuturus, si virtutes ejus maturuissent. Quo ille studiorum amore flagrabat ! Quantum legit ! Quantum etiam scripsit ! Quæ nunc omnia cum ipso sine fructu posteritatis aruerunt." (Plin. Epist.—Lib. 5, epist. 9.)—H. C.

Rolland, advocate; sometimes said to have sat to
Scott for his picture of Pleydell; a worthy, but
fantastic personage. His professional practice had
been very extensive, but only as a consulting and a
writing counsel; for he never spoke, nor honoured the
public by doing anything in its presence. Divested of
buckram, he was a learned and sound lawyer, and a
good man, much respected by his few friends. But
there are many men to whom the buckram is everything, and he was one of them. It was by his outside
that he was known to the world. He was old at last;
but his youth was marked by the same external
absurdity that adhered to him through life, and I
presume followed him into his coffin.

His dresses, which were changed at least twice
every day, were always of the same old beau cut; the
vicissitudes of fashion being contemptible in the sight
of a person who had made up his own mind as to the
perfection of a gentleman's outward covering. The
favourite hues were black and mulberry: the stuffs
velvet, fine kerseymere, and satin. When all got up, no
artificial rose could be brighter or stiffer. He was like
one of the creatures come to life again in a collection
of dried butterflies. I think I see him. There he
moves, a few yards backwards and forwards in front
of his house in Queen Street; crisp in his mulberry-
coloured kerseymere coat, single-breasted; a waistcoat
of the same with large old-fashioned pockets; black satin
breeches with blue steel buttons; bright morocco shoes
with silver or blue steel buckles; white or quaker-grey
silk stockings; a copious frill and ruffles; a dark brown,

gold-headed, slim cane, or a slender green silk umbrella: every thing pure and uncreased. The countenance befitted the garb: for the blue eyes were nearly motionless, and the cheeks, especially when slightly touched by vermilion, as clear and as ruddy as a wax doll's; and they were neatly flanked by two delicately pomatumed and powdered side curls, from behind which there flowed, or rather stuck out, a thin pigtail in a shining black ribbon. And there he moves, slowly and nicely, picking his steps as if a stain would kill him, and looking timidly, but somewhat slyly, from side to side, as if conscious that he was an object, and smiling in self-satisfaction. The whole figure and manner suggested the idea of a costly brittle toy, new out of its box. It trembled in company, and shuddered at the vicinity of a petticoat. But when well set, as I often saw him, with not above two or three old friends, he could be correctly merry, and had no objection whatever to a quiet bottle of good claret. But a stranger, or a word out of joint, made him dumb and wretched.

It is difficult to account for his practice; for though industrious, honourable, kind, and timidly judicious, he had slender talents, and no force, and the age in which he acted was one in which I should have thought that neither bar nor bench would have had any patience with gilded filigree. I wonder Braxfield did not murder him by a single grunt. However, I suppose that there must have been something more in him than I am aware of, else he could not have been the oracle that some people held him. When I was about to begin my legal studies, I was reckoned a

singularly fortunate youth, because he had conde-
scended to intimate that he would advise me how to
conduct them. I was therefore ordered to wait upon
him. I did so, and after being eased of some of my awe
by a kind reception, and a few very simple jokes, the
lesson commenced. It consisted entirely of a short
discourse by the sage, for I sat nearly dumb; and its
result was more than once summed and repeated, as
if to make me recollect the very words. These I do
not now remember; but surprise has prevented my
ever forgetting their tone and import, which were
exactly to this effect—" In short, my young friend,
philosophy is the vice of the age. Take my advice, and
read nothing whatever but Scotch and civil law,
except the first volume of Blackstone, the introduction to Robertson's *Charles the Fifth*, Hume's *History
of the Stewarts*, and De Lolme; never have a pen out of
your hand, and keep a commonplace book on Locke's
plan "—a volume of which, kept by himself, he showed
me as a specimen. In so far as kindness and pedantry
went, he may be supposed to have had some resemblance to Pleydell; but nobody who knew, or indeed
ever saw, Rolland can imagine his descending to
High Jinks, especially in a tavern.

The year 1819 closed, and the new one opened,
amidst the popular disturbances called, gravely by
some, and jocularly by others, " The Radical War."
The whole island was suffering under great agricul-
tural and manufacturing distress. This was taken the
usual advantage of by demagogues; and consequently

there was considerable political excitement. Quite
enough to require caution, and even to justify alarm.
Its amount in Scotland was contemptible. But it was
first exaggerated, and then exhibited as evidence of a
revolutionary spirit, which nothing but Toryism and
Castlereagh could check. It was determined therefore
that the folly and violence of our western weavers
should be considered as a civil war, and be dealt with
accordingly. Edinburgh was as quiet as the grave, or
even as Peebles; yet matters were so managed, that
we were obliged to pass about a month as if an enemy
had been drawing his lines round our very walls.
The only curiosity in the affair now is the facility of
spreading panic.

The Mid-Lothian Yeomanry Cavalry was marched,
in the middle of a winter night, to Glasgow; remained
in that district a few days; did nothing, having nothing
to do; and returned, as proud and as praised, as if
fresh from Waterloo. The survivors of the Old Edinburgh Gentlemen Volunteers were called together
again, and disengaged a few soldiers by taking charge
of the Castle, under their former and still unquenched
Lieutenant-Colonel, Charles Hope, Lord President of
the Court of Session. New offers of voluntary service
were made, and accepted; and as the Whigs could not
keep back, without seeming to encourage the enemy,
once more did I prepare to gird on my sword as a
captain in a thing called " The Armed Association; "
which was meant to be something more military than
constables, and less military than soldiers. But this
gallant battalion never assembled. In about a fort-

night every sane eye saw that the whole affair was
nonsense; and our Tory Colonel, Sir James Fergusson
of Kilkerran, was too much ashamed of it to call us
together even to be disbanded.

Some people, however, were clear that a great blow
would be struck by the Radical army—an army much
talked of but never seen, on the last night of the year.
The perfect facility with which a party of forty or
fifty thousand weavers could march from Glasgow,
and seize upon the Banks and the Castle of Edinburgh, without ever being heard of till they appeared
in our streets, was demonstrated. Our magistrates
therefore invited all loyal citizens to congregate, with
such arms as they had, at various assigned posts. I
repaired to the Assembly Rooms in George Street,
with a stick, about eight in the evening. The streets
were as quiet as on an ordinary Sunday; but their
silence was only held by the excited to forebode the
coming storm. There seemed to be nobody abroad
except those who, like myself, were repairing to their
forlorn hopes. On entering the large room, I found at
least 400 or 500 grown gentlemen, pacing about,
dressed coarsely, as if for work, and armed, according
to taste or convenience, with bludgeons, fowling
pieces, dirks, cane-swords, or other implements. A
zealous banker laboured under two small swivels set
on stocks, one under each arm. Frivolity, though
much provoked, and a good deal indulged in in
corners, was reproved as unbecoming the crisis. At
last, about ten P.M. the horn of the coach from
Glasgow was heard, and the Lord Provost sent us

word from the council chamber that we might retire for the night. We never met again.

Next summer a Commission of Oyer and Terminer was sent down for the trial of the rebels, with an English serjeant as prosecutor to keep us all right on the law of treason. The commissioners visited Stirling, Glasgow, Paisley, Ayr, and Dumbarton; and the result was, that several persons were convicted, and that three or four were executed. They were all guilty of high treason, no doubt; as any old woman is who chooses to charge a regiment of cavalry. But to make such a parade about such treason did no good either to the law or to the people. The whole affair was composed of three nearly equal parts—popular discontent, Government exaggeration, and public craze.*

The long reign of George the Third was brought to a close on the 29th of January 1820. The chief interest of the people in this event seemed to consist in its depriving them of their sixty years holiday on the 4th of June. On the following Sunday Sir Harry Moncreiff, not satisfied with merely praying for the new Sovereign generally, said in plain terms, giving the very date, that there might be no mistake about it, " And, O Lord, stablish his heart in righteousness, and in the

---

* Lockhart has published a letter from Scott (*Life of Scott*, vol. iv. p. 335), which shows the incomprehensible excitement of him and his party. The bard was ardent for actual and instant war, and seems to have really believed that there were " upwards of 50,000 blackguards ready to rise between Tyne and Wear ! " Even his biographer calls this "a ridiculous exaggerated report." But the heads of seven-eighths of his party were stuffed with similar nonsense.—H. C.

principles of the glorious revolution of sixteen hunder
and echty echt."

After an absence of nearly half-a-century, Lord
Erskine revisited his native country early in 1820,
and remained in Edinburgh for about two months.
His old friend William Adam was living here, and
showed him off excellently; and every one received
him kindly. The Whigs gave him a public dinner on
the 21st of February, at which about 300 attended—
the largest convocation of the sect that had yet taken
place. Maxwell of Carriden was in the chair. Erskine,
though old and feeble, spoke several times, always
elegantly, gently, and with liveliness, and once or
twice disclosed gleams of his better days. He showed
also that his strange old superstitiousness still survived. He repeated the story of having seen and
talked with his mother's gardener or his ghost after
he was dead, and said, not merely with gravity but
with intense sincerity, that since he had come to
Edinburgh, he had stood on the very spot in the High
Street where the interview took place.

Dr Thomas Brown, the successor of Dugald
Stewart in the Moral Chair, died in April 1820; a
person of great and peculiar powers; acute, original,
rich in views, of very considerable though not always
correct eloquence, and of an affectionate, generous,
and honourable nature. Whatever differences of
opinion there may be among deep and nice judges as
to some of his metaphysical doctrines, even on this

branch of his subject he was a professor of the highest order; and the public was unanimous in its admira_ tion of his moral and practical expositions. There are few more delightful books in the English language than his lectures, which have been published since his death, with unexampled success for such a work. His more judicious friends were disturbed by his verse; which might have passed if he had done nothing better, but which, though neither devoid of thought nor feeling, was unworthy of his superior powers. Obscurity was the common objection to it; but clearness would not have improved it. His friend Dr Gregory described his poetry as too philosophical, and his philosophy as too poetical. His great defect was in his manner. It was so strongly marked by what seemed to be affectation—the affectation of nice discrimination, fine feeling, and pensive reflection, that it required the recollection of his worth and genius to avoid undervaluing him in society. Nobody indeed could appreciate him who had never heard him lecture. Mackintosh alludes to this misfortune with his usual gentleness,—" Some of these delightful qualities were perhaps hidden from the casual observer in general society, by the want of that perfect simp..city of manner, which is doubtless their natural representative." (Preliminary Dissertation, *voce* Brown.)*

* In his *Elements* (vol. iii. p. 501) Stewart has the most contemptuous passage that is to be found in his whole works against Brown's philosophical character and habits. I cannot resist the belief that Stewart, angry at Brown's rejection of the *Common Sense* of Reid and of himself, wrote this Note in a state of personal irritation ; for it is quite unlike

The friends of philosophy, recollecting what this
class had so long been, suggested Sir James Mackintosh as Brown's proper successor. His political
opinions were objected to openly, and the more fatal
objection of infidelity was whispered. The last was
answered by his character, by the warm attestation
of his early companion, the reverend Dr Macknight,
and by a reference from Mr Macvey Napier to an
article in the *Monthly Review* by Sir James on his
friend Robert Hill's sermons. A majority of the Town-
Council offered him the chair: but his London friends
would not let him leave them, and he declined it. An
unfortunate decision for himself and for science. An
effort was then made for Macvey Napier himself, who,
in point of philosophy, was well qualified for the

his dignified caution. To be sure, he skilfully founds his scorn on statements made by Dr Welsh, the learned and excellent biographer of
Brown ; and if it be assumed that Welsh is correct, then unquestionably
so is Stewart. But Welsh is plainly wrong ; and, as usual with friendly
biographers, makes his hero absurd. He not only makes Brown a proud
convert to Phrenology, in his approximation to the doctrines of which
without the phrenological instrument, is to be found "his greatest
merit," but describes him as having composed nearly his whole course
of lectures in a single year ; and this so perfectly that he never afterwards
required either to add or to retrench ! Nay, the very "subjects of many
of his lectures he had never reflected upon till he took up the pen, and
many of his theories occurred to him during the period of composition."
It is really astonishing how a sensible man like Welsh could expect this
inspiration, as Stewart calls it, to be credited ; or could fancy that its
being ascribed to Brown was complimentary. Brown's early consideration of metaphysical subjects was attested by his having written his
Zoonomia when only about eighteen. And instead of never feeling it
necessary to meditate his lectures, his thoughts were occupied with the
subjects of them every hour of his life. Stewart could not have written
so sneeringly of Brown, except through the casual folly of his biographer.—H. C.

place, and had the honour of being warmly patronised by Dugald Stewart. But by this time the Town-Council had relapsed into its true self. Its invitation to Mackintosh had excited great alarm, and it was soon made plain that that dangerous experiment would not be repeated, and that no Whig need be hopeful. So Napier gave it up. And Sir William Hamilton, a great scholar and a profound logician, but also a Whig, was beaten off too.

The great—indeed the vital improvement of enclosing, draining, and ornamenting the valley to the west of the Mound (a part of the North Loch), for which a statute had been obtained in 1816, was completed in the autumn of 1820. Its value, or rather its glaring and indispensable necessity can only be understood by those who knew, and who remember, what had become the dreadful, and apparently hopeless, condition of the ground. The place had just been sufficiently drained to prevent its ever again being a loch. But it was a nearly impassable fetid marsh, a stinking swamp, open on all sides, the receptacle of many sewers, and seemingly of all the worried cats, drowned dogs, and blackguardism of the city. Its abomination made it so solitary that the Volunteers used to practise ball-firing across it. The men stood on its north side, and the targets were set up along the lower edge of the Castle hill or rock. The only difficulty was in getting across the swamp to place and examine the targets, which could be done only in very dry weather and at one or two places.

Exclusive of our house-planted squares, it was the first piece of ground that was ornamented within the city. There was a feeble murmur against the ejection of what the few murmurers termed " The Public." But did the public offer to be taxed? Besides, what portion of the public was it that was ejected?

The proceedings of George the Fourth against his Queen threw Edinburgh, as they did every other place, into great agitation. But the uniformity of the excitement was varied in Scotland by a bit of Scotch Church law. The King put forth an order forbidding people to pray for Her Majesty. Being the head of the English Church, he might take that liberty in England. But the Presbyterians, who own no earthly head, kicked. Our whole seceders, and a great many of the established clergy, including of course Andrew Thomson, to whom the blunder was delightful, disdained this mandate, and prayed for her the more fervently that her husband's ministry declared that she was wicked. Thomson, however, had the rare prudence to name her only so gently, as to show that it was merely the supposed right of the crown to put words into the mouths of praying Presbyterians that he meant to resist. Notwithstanding this, those loyalists who backed the Monarch in his attack through the Queen upon the monarchy, instantly gratified Thomson by a violent outcry against himself. He, as might have been foreseen; took the bull by the horns by a direct motion in next General Assembly against the (supposed) royal claim. Most people agreed with him by this time; but it was thought decent to avoid the subject by a vague amendment, which was carried, that the rights of our church were already sufficiently fenced.

While this was disturbing the establishment, the seceders were strengthening themselves by a judicious union of Burghers with Anti-Burghers, who held their first meeting as the " United Associate Synod " here in September 1820. Their spiritual junction was celebrated by a corporeal feast. They were the first people who dined in the large room of the Waterloo Hotel. I wish I had seen the jollity of three or four hundred of the great-grandsons of Ebenezer Erskine.

Jeffrey surprised us this year, almost as much as he was surprised himself, by his elevation to the Lord Rectorship of the College of Glasgow. It was the first official honour he had received. And its proceeding from the students was a fact that concurred with many others in showing the ebbing of the old shallow tide. The reign of the professors and the adjoining lairds had plainly received a shock. Since 1787, when Adam Smith was elected, no person had been appointed solely from literary or scientific merit. The collegians, ashamed of the habitual abasement, took the election into their own hands, and have kept it, and justified their use of their power ever since. Thomson, Moncreiff, Murray, George Joseph Bell, Robert Graham, James Campbell, Pillans, Keay, Rutherfurd, and I accompanied Jeffrey to his installation on the 28th of December 1820. The horror of

most of the professors, at the sight of such a crew of
Whigs, was not diminished by the sound, still ringing
in their ears, of an assemblage of this party, called the
Pantheon Meeting, which had taken place in Edinburgh only a few days before. It seemed delightful,
however, to the students, to whom the Rector made
a beautiful speech. His ceremonious banquet with the
college authorities was succeeded by a night-long
supper at the hotel with his friends. The honour done
to Jeffrey, the triumph of the students, and the change
of times, inspired the party into the best joyous conviviality it has ever been my good fortune to partake of.

The proceedings against the Queen, though now
abandoned, had thrown the whole nation into a ferment. That Her Majesty was really innocent was the
belief of many: that there was at least no legal evidence of her guilt was the belief of a majority of the
nation: that even though she had been guilty, and her
guilt had been legally established, its exposure was so
dangerous that, as Mackintosh says, no republicans,
wishing to bring monarchy into disrepute, could have
done worse, was the opinion of almost all judicious
loyalists. These persons therefore concurred in condemning the whole proceeding; which, they thought,
showed that we were ruled by a ministry so servile to
the King that, in order to please him, they would not
scruple to endanger royalty. These sentiments may all
have been erroneous; but they were the sentiments of a
large portion of the nation, and fixed on the Government a more intense feeling of hostility than is usually

produced by ordinary party differences. It was almost
a personal hostility. Justly or unjustly, no public
man could be more hated than Lord Castlereagh
was.

It was in this state of the public mind that, in
December 1820, a requisition was presented to the
Lord Provost of Edinburgh, requesting him to call a
public meeting of the inhabitants, with a view to
petition the King to dismiss his ministers. The requisition was signed by about one hundred householders, who represented a considerable part of the
wealth, and by far the greater part of the talent and
public character, of the city. The Lord Provost refused, on which it was announced that the meeting
would be held on a call by the requisitionists. Efforts
were instantly made to obstruct it; and the leaders
in the movement were assailed by scurrilous libels.
One of Lord Castlereagh's six acts made an assembly
in the open air illegal; and, on this being ascertained,
every covered place under the influence of the Town-
Council or the Lord Advocate was refused. But that
universal receptacle the Circus, then termed the
Pantheon, opened its doors; and on Saturday the 16th
of December the meeting was held.

The place, though large and crammed, admitted
but a small portion of those who wished to get in.
They seemed to be mostly of the middle class of
citizens. My coat was said to be the worst there.
Moncreiff presided, seated on the stage—the very
place where, about twenty-five years before, he held
up the candle to Henry Erskine while he was making

z

the speech which cost him his Deanship. He opened the business by explaining the object of the meeting, and cautioning those present to disappoint their opponents by abstaining from all intemperance of language. Jeffrey then rose, and sealed the character of the meeting by an admirable address. When the meeting was over, John Clerk on retiring was accosted by a little, old, dark man, who came up to him, winking and rubbing his hands with delight, and said, "Weel, Sir! ou're at the auld wark again." He was found to be a respectable shopkeeper, and one of the spirits of 1793, who, without being known to Clerk, had acted with him in those fearful times.

This meeting was distinguished from the one in 1814 on the slave trade, the one in 1816 on the property tax, and the one in 1817 on the North Bridge Buildings, by its being purely political, and in direct and avowed opposition to the hereditary Toryism of Government. It was the first modern occasion on which a great body of respectable persons had met, publicly and peaceably, in Edinburgh, to assail this fortress.

No petition can be made secure against trick or mistake. But, after every precaution and deduction, the signatures to the petition proceeding from this meeting were as follows. Only males, above twenty-one, were allowed to sign, that is, all under that age, if detected, were debarred. If Edinburgh then contained about 100,000 inhabitants, including its immediate neighbourhood, which is about the truth, the male adults could not exceed 20,000. The ministerial party had an opposite petition, and strained every effort for subscriptions. The result was, that theirs got about 1600 or 1700 names, ours about 17,000. So that the unexampled spectacle was exhibited of a large Scotch community proclaiming itself, as in nearly unanimous hostility not merely to the existing power, but to the power which had seemingly established itself in prescriptive omnipotence.

The influence of all this can scarcely be overstated. Old Edinburgh was no more. A new day dawned on the official seat of Scotch intolerance. It was plain that a state of things had arisen in which that strange hard hatred of the people, though it might make its own victims miserable, could scarcely recall the time in which a local aristocracy could settle everything, for its own behoof, in its own way. The meeting had been held here, but the eyes of all Scotland were upon it, and all Scotland felt the result. The Tories alone would not read the sign. It required ten more years to open their eyes. A drop of water let in might bring down the whole embankment, no doubt; and if resisting every change could have stemmed the inundation, they were right, for their purposes, to resist. Their error, on this and on many other occasions, consisted in not seeing that the drop was already through; and that their true policy lay in regulating a flood which they could not prevent.

Fox's birthday had long been kept by a few of our more daring spirits in a quiet and obscure way. But the success of the Burns and Erskine dinners made it evident that a strong impression might be produced by now keeping it more openly. Leonard Horner, the brother of Francis, the most active and enlightened of our citizens, and with a singular talent for organisation, having consented to take the principal share in the arrangements, a gathering was announced. With the exception perhaps of the recent one to Lord Erskine, this, so far as I can recollect, was *the first public political dinner held by the Whigs in Edinburgh.* The birthday was the 24th of January. But as some members of Parliament could not wait so long, the meeting was fixed for the 12th. On this, the opposite party resolved that whatever we might do with the rabble, they would contrast us with their gentry; and that on whatever day we met, they should meet also, although this implied an anticipation of the nativity of their Saint by about four months. So both parties assembled in their respective fields, on the 12th of January 1821. The Pittites were the more numerous. As they never would publish any authoritative account of what took place, their superiority of number is all that I can attest. The Foxites mustered very nearly 500. The Earl of Rosslyn was in the chair, and spoke well, though as usual with him, better in spirit than in matter. The lawyers' addresses—by Cranstoun, Jeffrey, Moncreiff, Kennedy of Dunure, Murray, myself and others, were of less consequence than those of an order of men, who till about this period had shrunk from exposure—the ordinary trading citizens. Some of them spoke excellently; and the rise of booksellers and haberdashers in this line was very symptomatic.*

It would be more agreeable to forget past irritations; but everything is worth preserving which explains the state of people's minds on important changes. Instead of being taught liberality by events, the Tory party was exasperated into insanity. It was under the influence of this malady that they set up a newspaper which they called *The Beacon*. This famous publication first appeared, I think, in January 1821. Its funds and its machinery were concealed. All that was exposed was that a Mr Duncan Stevenson printed it, and a person called Nimmo was its ostensible editor. But its regular contributors were believed to be persons of a higher order; and articles were occasionally supplied by some it is very painful to think of as so employed. If I were to look at this paper now, after years have blunted its edge, and evaporated its allusions, and accustomed us to freer political personality, it is possible that I might be surprised at the offence it once gave. But the guilt of libel must be judged of as on the day it was committed, when the insinuations were understood, and the mis-statements not cleared up, the insolence fresh, and the victim quivering. The judgment of fair men, living at the time and on the spot, is always conclusive on such a question. Almost anything is libellous which such men think a libel. Tried by such a standard this

* This great and morally powerful assembly is thus described by Scott in one of those letters which have been published—"The Foxites had also a very numerous meeting, 500 at least, *but sad scamps*." (Lockhart's *Life of Scott*, chap. 50).—H. C.

publication was all a libel. It was the outlet for all the anonymous slander that the retainers of a once powerful, but now half defeated, party chose to pour out on their rising opponents. And the abuse was neither atoned for by talent, nor veiled by wit. Yet, strange to say, it was patronised even by the respectable portion of the party it disgraced, though there were a few honourable exceptions. Scott chuckled with its reputed contributors: judges subscribed for it: it lay on the tables of reverend Christians.

Towards the end of August 1821 there was a gross insult on Mr James Stuart of Dunearn, who, throughout the whole course of our emancipation was specially disliked for the activity of his public spirit. He caned the printer on the street; this, as he thought, being the correct form of dealing with such a person. Then came another of the many libels on Mr James Gibson [Sir James Gibson-Craig of Riccarton], who, having long suffered in silence, determined to discover his insulter, and set about it with his usual vigour. Having some ground for suspecting that the Lord Advocate* was more than the patron of the paper, he wrote to him and asked whether he was not a partner. His lordship denied all partnership; but, to the horror of his associates, blew them all up at once by admitting that he and some others, not named, had subscribed a bond, of which he enclosed a copy. This deed was found to bind certain persons, as sureties to a bank, for any debt that might be incurred in conducting

* The Right Hon. Sir William Rae, Bart. *See* also *Scotsman*, Sept. 22, 29 and Novr. 10, 1821.

The Beacon, to the amount of £100 each; the bank account to be operated upon by any party to be named by them. The practical result of which was that, whether partners in law or not, they having provided and kept the command of the funds had the control of the newspaper. The names of the other bondsmen soon transpired, and to the amazement of the public. Many of them were official men.

On finding such persons implicated, Stuart opened a communication, plainly of a hostile tendency, with the Lord Advocate, demanding a disavowal of the articles concerning him. After a short correspondence his Lordship's accession to the articles was disavowed. Mr Gibson then addressed another bondsman; and it is dreadful to think that a life like Scott's was for a moment in peril in such a cause. But it had actually gone the length of the accuser providing a second— an office which the Earl of Lauderdale insisted on undertaking. But at this stage some of Scott's friends came forward with a proposal that this and all similar calls should be abandoned on an assurance that Scott had no personal accession to any of the articles complained of, and that the paper should be discontinued. Mr Gibson, having only a public end in view, agreed to this arrangement. On this, the other obligants withdrew their names from the bond, and the mask that had been kept on to the last, of pretending that they had no command of the paper, fell off, and not another number appeared.*

* " A more pitiable mass of blunder and imbecility was never heaped together than the whole of this affair exhibited " (Lockhart's *Life of Scott,*

It is a relief to turn from such a subject. It was in October 1821 that an institution for the instruction of mechanics, since known as " The School of Arts," was opened in Edinburgh. If not the first, it was certainly the second establishment of the kind in Britain. The whole merit, both of its conception and of its first three or four years' management, is due exclusively to Leonard Horner. His good sense, mildness, and purity made it a favourite with the reasonable of all parties and classes. It has gone on prosperously ever since.*

chap. liv.). So, speaking of his own side, says Lockhart. " The fact is, it is a blasted business, and will long continue to have bad consequences" —says Scott, speaking of himself (Letter to Croker, *Lockhart's Life*, chap. liv.). The biographer admits their " long train of humiliating distresses and disgraces." He could scarcely be expected to acknowledge, in direct terms, that these judgments arose from an organised system of defamation, acted upon by the tools of the bondsmen; but he does the same thing in substance, when he says, that " the rude drollery of the young hot-bloods, to whom they had entrusted the editorship of their paper, produced its natural consequences." Yet it is strange that both he and Scott, instead of applauding a retreat from a criminal folly, seem to think that it would have been more manful to adhere to it, since it had been committed. Lockhart says that " the seniors shrunk from the dilemma as rashly as they had plunged into it ;" and Scott, in a letter to William Erskine, which is not published, declares, " I am terribly malcontent about *The Beacon*. I was dragged into the bond against all remonstrances I could make, and now they have allowed me no vote with regard to standing or flying. *Entre nous*, our friends went into the thing like fools, and have come out very like cowards. I was never so sick of a transaction in my life ; though I thank God I have very little to do with it." So, when it was exposed, they all said. No subscriber had ever read a paper that he paid for and got. Many never heard of what all Scotland was ringing with.—H. C.

* It was situated in the south-west corner of Adam Square, which disappeared when Chambers Street was opened up. Under the name of the Watt Institution and School of Arts it re-opened in Chambers Street and is now represented by the Heriot-Watt College there.

The Whig party in Scotland had some time before this gained a material accession of strength by Thomas Kennedy of Dunure getting into Parliament. With great judgment, high principle, and a love of work, he was thoroughly acquainted with Scotland, and had no ambition greater than that of doing it good. And his power was considerably increased by his marriage with Romilly's daughter, which introduced him to important English connections. He and I had often conferred on the absurdity, and the flagrant injustice, of the power still left to the presiding judge to select the jury in criminal cases; and it was settled that the correction of this evil should be his first parliamentary effort.* The history of this reform affords one of the most incredible examples of the indiscriminate obduracy with which the clearest abuses were then clung to. Letting the judge name the jury, especially in Scotch criminal prosecutions, which are almost all cases between the Crown and the subject, was a practice utterly abhorrent to the general principles of the constitution, and unknown in any other part of the British empire. Even when exercised with the utmost purity, it exposed the administration of the law to obloquy. And the example of ballot and challenge had been set, and operated well, in civil causes for some years. In these circumstances, one would have thought that the criminal judges would have been the keenest to get quit of so odious a power. Yet partly because it gave them power, and partly because its removal was a

* *See* "Letters chiefly connected with the Affairs of Scotland."

Whig measure, they fought in its defence on their very stumps.

In 1821 Kennedy moved for leave to bring in a bill for the introduction of ballot. On this, the Lord Advocate circulated an authoritative rescript to the lairds to oppose the democratic measure. He suggested the very grounds to them, which cannot now be read without amazement. The reform was no sooner effected, than it was almost unanimously applauded; and there is not a single sane man by whom the old system is now defended. Yet, under this contemptible influence, did the handfuls of landlords who represent our counties pass resolutions in nearly every shire, re-echoing the sentiments of his lordship's ukase; just as the provinces of Russia might have done, if the Autocrat had asked them whether he had not better increase the severity of the knout. This provoked me to write an explanation of the whole case in the *Edinburgh Review* [No. 71, Art. 9]. Kennedy persevered, and in the Commons was always successful. But he failed in the Lords. However, the existing system was seen to be indefensible, and in the session of 1822 Lord Melville [second Viscount], who was then Scotch manager, got a bill passed giving each prisoner a few peremptory challenges, but still leaving the judge to pick. This broke the crust. But, as I explained in another article [*Edinburgh Review*, No 75, Art. 11], it left a very odd inside. Because, though the ballot-box takes no offence, a judge, whose nomination gets a slap in the face by a challenge, does. The only ground on which the picking system could be defended was, that the judge who picked was wise and pure. But as soon as this wisdom and purity were liable to be laughed at by peremptory challenges it became ridiculous. Indeed it was a great indecorum, and might be practised merely to annoy the Court. But they brought it on themselves. At last, after submitting to be snubbed for about two years, their fingers, which they kept clutched on as much of their favourite privilege as they could, were torn away from it entirely by the existing statute, whereby the impartiality of the ballot-box is combined with the corrective process of the challenge. This is sometimes called Lord Melville's Act; and he is certainly entitled to the praise due to him who first opposes a good measure, and then adopts it. It was Mr Kennedy's Act in every true sense.

During these discussions an important communication was made by Government about the criminal practice of Scotland. It came here in the form of a letter, dated 20th October 1822, from Sir Robert Peel, addressed to the Lord Justice-Clerk,* who, before giving the information required, was directed to consult the other three heads—namely, Charles Hope, Lord President, William Adam, Lord Chief Commissioner of the Jury Court, and Sir Samuel Shepherd, Lord Chief Baron, and also David Hume, our criminal commentator. There were six questions put, which in substance were these:—1st. Whether the presiding judge should be allowed to select the jury? 2nd. What are the powers possessed by the Lord Advocate as

* The Right Hon. David Boyle of Shewalton.

public prosecutor? 3rd. What other powers has he? and might these be separated from his power as public prosecutor? 4th. Would it be expedient to introduce grand juries into Scotland? 5th. Should the Lord Advocate's power of deserting diets *pro loco et tempore* be limited? 6th. " Can you suggest any alterations in the criminal law of Scotland, or in the practice of its courts, which it would be expedient to make, for the purpose of securing a greater degree of protection for persons accused of crimes? "

I have *seen* no answer to any of these questions, except the answer given by Adam to the last one, which, however, shows what his answer to the first question must have been. This part of his opinion was very long. It recommended the abolition both of the picking custom and of transportation for sedition. But (as I read him) he was for introducing the ballot and the challenge in place of the judge's selection, only in *political* cases, and in what he calls " state misdemeanours," and for connecting this with much of the machinery of English law. These unfortunate limitations must, I suppose, have impaired the weight of his general opinion. The *particulars* of the answers by the others on these two points of transportation and picking, I do not know; but I have the best possible authority, short of actually seeing them, for stating that they were all against any change.

Fox's birthday was again celebrated on the 24th of January 1822—General Sir Ronald Ferguson in the chair. There being no particular occasion for it, no effort was made to secure a large attendance, but about 300 were present—an animated and useful meeting.

Every gleam of Art deserves notice. In the beginning of February 1822, Edinburgh had a beautiful exhibition, consisting entirely of the works of one of its own artists—Hugh W. Williams.* He had returned a few years before from a journey to Greece, and now collected and displayed his delightful water-colour drawings of Grecian scenery and ruins. Each picture was illustrated by a classical quotation, selected for the catalogue by Pillans, and translated chiefly by John Brown Patterson, a young man of great promise.† It was an instructive spectacle;—like being suddenly transported into Attica.

The spring of 1822 was excited by a civic struggle which, in its indirect effects, was of permanent importance. It was enveloped in details, but its substance is simple enough. By the Edinburgh Police Act the Commissioners were elected by inhabitants paying £10 of yearly rent within their respective wards, and the power of appointing and of dismissing the Superintendent was vested in the Lord President of the Court of Session, the Lord Provost, and the Sheriff, who were called " The Functionaries." The Commissioners charged the Superintendent with

* He was popularly known as " Grecian Williams."—H. C.
† He died some years after this, minister in the Established Church at Falkirk.—H. C.

accession to fraud. The Functionaries, moved chiefly by pity for the man, refused to dismiss him. If there had been nothing really at stake beyond his fate, few would have thought of the matter. But, like everything else in the trembling balance of parties, his case was soon taken up as a political contest, and on the old ground. The great majority of the people supported the Commissioners. This single fact glued the whole Tories together, by exciting their instinctive jealousy of the growth of popular power; and as neither the Commissioners nor the Functionaries would yield, an appeal to Parliament became unavoidable.

The Commissioners only desired that they should have the power of dismissal. But the proposal by the opposite party showed that they were thinking of something far beyond the matter of police. They insisted—1st, That the Functionaries should both appoint and dismiss. 2nd, That the qualification should be raised from £10 to £15, which would have disfranchised a very large part of the existing voters. 3rd, That the same property should be held to qualify for as many voters, or nearly so, as it was worth fifteens of pounds; that is, that each of the rich should have several votes. 4th, That the wards should be " grouped "; that is, that the poorer wards should be so connected with the richer ones, as that the latter, with their double and triple voters, and their power of concussion, should swamp the poorer. The general result was, that there should be an aristocracy of electors. A *Report* was published in defence of these views. It was a quarto volume, ill-written, and

worse reasoned. Horner excited me to the public
virtue of writing *A Letter to the Inhabitants* on the
other side. My object was to clear the case of useless
complication, and to make the people strong by
reasonable concession.

After a month's ferment, the parties met in Parliament; where the whole tumult was composed, at
least on the surface, in a moment. Lord Melville, more
candid than his followers, took charge of the case for
the Town-Council, which represented the Functionaries and the quarto volume; and James Abercromby
for the people. These two at once arranged that the
power of *both* appointing and dismissing should not
be lodged in the same party, which was the view
taken in the Letter; all the Quarto proposals were
rejected; and the existing Superintendent retired.
This victory, following so soon after the ignominious
defeat of *The Beacon*, was useful and well-timed. The
vanquished groaned, and abused Lord Melville. The
victors let off their joy by a public dinner of about
300, where due honour was done to Abercromby for
the spirit and prudence with which he had conducted
the first Scotch matter he had undertaken.

This affair was soon succeeded by another, which
forms a very painful history—the case of Mr James
Stuart of Dunearn and Sir Alexander Boswell. Stuart's
trial, the proceedings against Murray Borthwick, and
the parliamentary discussions, disclose the details.

Soon after *The Beacon* was put down in Edinburgh,
The Sentinel, another newspaper of the same kind,
and encouraged by the general countenance of the

same party, was set up in Glasgow.* Mr Stuart being defamed, as he thought, in this new publication, instituted an action of damages against its editors, two persons called Alexander and Borthwick. Soon after this, Borthwick intimated that if this action was abandoned, he would make all the reparation he could, by disclosing the authors of all the attacks that had been made in this newspaper against Stuart, and by giving up the original articles. Stuart acceded to this, and went to Glasgow for the documents, which he never doubted, nor had any reason to doubt, Borthwick's right to surrender. He dealt with him as any slandered gentleman would with a penitent editor, who was only doing what is common with persons in his situation. It was afterwards pretended that Stuart had no right to receive the papers, because Borthwick had no right to give them; and that he had no right to give them, because he had stolen them. He had stolen the company property from his partner! This pretence was aided by the Lord Advocate indicting Borthwick for the theft. The mere fact of the partnership was an answer to this charge. No doubt, there had been a conditional separation between the partners. But Alexander having violated one of the conditions by not paying

* After stating that on the extinction of *The Beacon*, " the then heads of Scotch Toryism did not escape in any consolatory plight," Mr Lockhart adds that " *The Beacon* bequeathed its rancour and rashness, though not its ability, to a Glasgow paper of similar form and pretensions, entitled *The Sentinel*" (*Life of Scott*, chap. liv.). Besides form and pretensions, it might have been added that its patronage was substantially the same.—H. C.

a sum of money, had been sued before the Burgh
Court of Glasgow by Borthwick for restitution of his
rights; and that court had pronounced an unchallenged
interlocutor, authorising Borthwick to resume possession. He resumed it, and thus got legal access to
the papers, in which his interest as a partner had
never been extinguished even by the separation. He
gave them—not in property but for his temporary
purpose, to Mr Stuart, who could not, without idiotcy,
have declined receiving them.

On examining them, he was astonished to find that
the worst articles against him had been written by Sir
Alexander Boswell of Auchinleck, a relation, with
whom he had long been on good terms. Sir Alexander
had been aware of their impropriety, for they were
written in a disguised hand. Mr Stuart having at last
detected a respectable libeller, returned to Edinburgh
and waited the arrival of Sir Alexander, who was in
London. As soon as Sir Alexander heard of the delivery of the papers, which contained insults on many
other gentlemen, his conscience seems to have told
him that he must be challenged by somebody; because, before any challenge was given, he wrote to a
friend asking him to act as his second,* and proposing
a trip to the Rhine " in the event of my being the
successful shot." He came to Edinburgh in a few
days; when he was waited upon by the Earl of

---

* " Boswell wrote a letter to Robert Maconochie saying that he had
consulted Meadowbank about a second and that his Lordship had assured
him he might depend upon the said Robert. . . . Here was a judge
making himself a party to a duel."—Lord Cockburn to T. F. Kennedy,
June 12, 1822, *Letters on the Affairs of Scotland.*

2A

Rosslyn on behalf of Mr Stuart. He avowed himself
responsible for the article selected as the ground of
the call—a song in which Stuart was called a coward;
and declining to apologise, a meeting was arranged.
The song was in his handwriting; and the idle doubt
attempted to be cast on this by the prosecutor at the
subsequent trial was never hinted at by Sir Alexander
himself.

They met near Auchtertool, in Fife, on the 22nd
March 1822. Stuart, an awkward lumbering rider,
had never fired a pistol but once or twice from the
back of a horse in a troop of yeomanry. He stopped
at his beautiful Hillside near Aberdour, and arranged
some papers, and subscribed a deed of settlement.
Boswell, who was an expert shot, told his second, Mr
Douglas [afterwards Marquis of Queensberry], that he
meant to fire in the air. He fell himself, however, at
the first fire. Stuart told me that he was never more
thunderstruck than when on the smoke clearing he
saw his adversary sinking gently down. Sir Alexander
died at Balmuto in two days. Stuart came to Edinburgh, and immediately withdrew to France.

The death of so valuable a partizan as Sir Alexander Boswell, though in fair duel, by the hand of
James Stuart, threw the Tory party into a flame, the
heat of which, I fear, reached even the department
of the public prosecutor. Nobody who knew Stuart's
temperament could believe that he did not mean to
stand his trial. But lest there should be any doubt of
it, Mr Gibson, on Stuart's behalf, gave distinct notice
to the Sheriff that he would appear. Nevertheless,

after the original irritation had had months to cool, a statement that he had absconded from justice, under a consciousness of guilt, was put into his indictment. This was of no real importance, but it showed the feeling. It was from jail that he fled, not from justice.

The proceedings taken against Borthwick, on the other hand, had the effect of giving to Stuart's possession of the papers a criminal character and appearance. Borthwick was accused of theft; and being apprehended in Dundee, was brought to Edinburgh and cast into prison, where for some time access was denied to his friends and legal advisers. He was placed at the bar of the Glasgow spring circuit 1822, but the trial was not then proceeded with; the diet was deserted *pro loco et tempore*, and thus the harshness of his treatment could not regularly be exposed. His partner Alexander also came forward as his private prosecutor on a nominal variation of the same charge. The result was, that he was kept under accusation until after Stuart's trial. And at that trial, the counsel for Alexander attended—though not engaged in the case; and by rising and announcing that this and that witness, as each retired from the witness box, would be required for Borthwick's trial on the following Monday, gave Stuart's duel an appearance of being connected with Borthwick's theft. This was repeated till the court put him to silence.

The trial of Mr Stuart took place on the 10th of June 1822. No Scotch trial in my time excited such interest. If the prosecutors were really anxious for a conviction, their hopes vanished long before their own case was closed. Beyond the admitted fact that Boswell had fallen by his hand, there was not a single circumstance that did not redound to Stuart's credit. His injuries, his gentleness, his firmness, his sensibility, and the necessity that he was under, according to the existing law of society, of acting as he did, were all brought out by irresistible evidence; while the excellence of his general character was proved by many witnesses, several of whom were purposely selected from his political opponents. No verdict except the acquittal that was almost instantly given, could have followed. To try was quite right; and duelling was then, as now, an absurd and shocking remedy for private insult. But considering what the tyranny of society required, and what courts of justice had sanctioned, the earnestness with which this prosecution was pressed does appear strange. The Justice-Clerk [The Right Hon. David Boyle], who presided at the trial, behaved admirably. Stuart was no sooner acquitted, than the pretence of accusing Borthwick of theft was dropped; and he was liberated without ever being brought to trial.*

* Lord Cockburn was counsel for Murray Borthwick. He was also one of the counsel for Mr Stuart ; and opened his defence in a speech, which was thus characterised by Sir James Mackintosh in the debate on the Scotch public press, in the House of Commons, on 25th June 1822 : —" He did not know whether the right honourable gentleman had read the authentic report of the trial of Mr Stuart ; but he would there see a specimen of the manner in which a counsel might discharge his duty to his client with the utmost vigour, and at the same time pay a due respect to the tribunals and laws of the country. He might truly say, that the admirable speech of Mr Cockburn, in the case of Mr Stuart, had not been surpassed by any effort in the whole range of ancient or

Mr Stuart was singularly fortunate in both the seconds. Rosslyn, the model of an old military gentleman, combined the polite gallantry of that profession with activity and talent in the conduct of civil affairs, and was one of the most public-spirited and useful noblemen in Scotland. Mr Douglas, though of moderate ability, was worthy and honest. His candour in this affair, and the scorn with which, after the fatal issue, he refused to join the cry of his party against Stuart, made all gentlemen think of the jeopardy in which the survivor and truth might have stood, if Boswell had been otherwise attended.

Boswell was able and literary; and when in the humour of being quiet, he was agreeable and kind. But in general he was boisterous and overbearing, and addicted to coarse personal ridicule. With many respectable friends, his natural place was at the head of a jovial board, where every one laughed at his exhaustless spirits, but each trembled lest he should be the subject of the next story or song. The fact of a person of his rank writing anonymous libels, for a blackguard newspaper, against an acquaintance, in a disguised hand, affords a humiliating example of

modern forensic eloquence. It was a speech characterised by calm and forcible reasoning, by chaste and classical diction, by the utmost skill, delicacy, and address in the management of the most difficult topics, and by a rare combination of zeal and ability in the cause of his client, with respect to the feelings of all the parties concerned, and a reverence for the rules of law and the austere decorum of a court of justice. It was a speech, in short, which, as a specimen of forensic eloquence, considered with reference to the peculiar difficulties with which the advocate had to contend, was unrivalled by any similar effort in ancient or modern times."—Note by Editors of First Edition of *Memorials*.

the extent to which faction and bad taste may corrupt men even of bold temperament, and accustomed to the society of gentlemen. He was a short time in parliament; and it is curious that it was he who introduced, or at least took charge of, and carried the act [59th George III. c. 70], which abolishes our two old Scotch statutes against fighting a duel, or sending a challenge—by the former of which the mere fighting, without any result, was punishable by death. This was his solitary piece of legislation, I believe.

Abercromby had given notice of a motion respecting the conduct of the Lord Advocate with relation to the Scotch public press, but from aversion to interfere with a depending prosecution, had put it off. This obstacle being now removed, the motion was discussed on the 25th of June 1822. The motion was for a committee; from which there was a shabby escape by a majority of only twenty-five. Another motion for papers in Borthwick's case was successful; and these papers being obtained the following session, Abercromby moved, on the 3rd of June 1823, that the conduct and proceedings of the Lord Advocate had been " unjust and oppressive." This fatal charge was negatived by only 102 against 96. On the 9th of December 1822 Mr Gibson got a verdict, with £500 of damages, against Mr Stevenson, the printer of *The Beacon*, for libel. In the preceding June Lord Archibald Hamilton had also got a verdict against the same defender, but, by a blunder of the Lord Chief Commissioner in trying the case, the jury only gave a shilling of damages, thinking that nothing more was asked. But the defender, or his constituents, had to pay about £300 of costs in each case, besides his own expenses. And soon after the paper stopped, it was found to be considerably in debt. So that, upon the whole, what with thrashing, and shooting, and parliamentary exposure, and damages, and expenses, and detection, and disgrace, I don't believe that they found libelling a good trade.

These judicial and parliamentary proceedings abated the political cannibalism by which our comfort had been torn. For the crisis—in which not merely opinions, but interests, were at stake, some violence, and finally even acrimony, was perhaps unavoidable. But a very little of the oil of charity would have levelled and softened the surf. The irritation, however, instead of being soothed by anything of this kind, was exasperated by the unfortunate rise of a few young men who happened to be skilful in the art of personal ridicule, and whose test of its excellence seemed to consist solely in the pain it inflicted. Even they could have been very easily kept in order by their leaders, who, however, unfortunately encouraged them in the course they were following. In particular, Scott's conduct cannot be thought of without the deepest sorrow. The happiness of the city was disturbed, persons he had long professed and truly felt friendship for were vilified, private feelings were lacerated; and all this he could have prevented by a word or a look. But instead of preventing it, he gave it his countenance. Yet there could not be a better natured, or a better hearted, man. It was neither malice nor selfishness that made him go wrong; but the inconsiderate weakness of yielding to those of his party whose talents he admired, and who worshipped him as their star. When they clustered round him, and read him their verses, and represented their measures as essential to the common cause, and appeared to be bowing before him whom in truth they were misleading, they supplied him with feelings quite sufficient to account for his tolerance of their iniquities, without any necessity for our supposing that he was aware of the full extent of their guilt or its mischief. His was the fault of unreflecting acquiescence.

It is very painful to remember these things. But truth must not be sacrificed utterly. The annalist restrains himself to the full extent of all reasonable charity, if he abstains from the statement of every personal defect which is not necessary for the right comprehension of an important public character, or of guilt or folly which was felt and spoken of, by candid men, as publicly dangerous at the time. No one can have lived and acted in Edinburgh in my day without finding much in its public characters and transactions to be loved and admired, a great deal to be overlooked, and something to be unsparingly condemned. My error is in being too gentle with the last.

It was about this time that the Earl of Moray's ground to the north of Charlotte Square began to be broken up for being built on. It was then an open field of as green turf as Scotland could boast of, with a few respectable trees on the flat, and thickly wooded on the bank along the Water of Leith. Moray Place and Ainslie Place stand there now. It was the beginning of a sad change, as we then felt. That well-kept and almost evergreen field was the most beautiful piece of ground in immediate connection with the town, and led the eye agreeably over to our distant northern scenery. How glorious the prospect, on a summer evening, from Queen Street! We had got into the habit of believing that the mere charm of the ground to us would keep it sacred, and were inclined to cling to our conviction even after we saw the foundations digging. We then thought with despair of our lost verdure, our banished peacefulness, our gorgeous sunsets. But it was unavoidable. We would never have got beyond the North Loch, if these feelings had been conclusive. But how can I forget the glory of that scene! on the still nights on which, with Rutherfurd and Richardson and Jeffrey, I have stood in Queen Street, or the opening at the north-west corner of Charlotte Square, and listened to the ceaseless rural corn-craiks, nestling happily in the dewy grass. It would be some consolation if the buildings were worthy of the situation; but the northern houses are turned the wrong way, and everything is sacrificed to the multiplication of feuing feet.

The year 1823 opened with the annual Fox dinner. Sir James Mackintosh, fresh from his installation as Jeffrey's Rectorial successor at Glasgow, presided;

Cranstoun was croupier. Sir James, though didactic, was good; Cranstoun in his best style of finished precision. Abercromby, who was now known as the representative of the citizens, though not of the city, calm and sensible, inspired the 400 who were present with hope. A very successful convocation.

It was thought that the time had now arrived when a decided move might be made for a reform of our parliamentary representation; and it was resolved, that, instead of weakening the particular claim of Edinburgh by sinking it in the general question, we should put forward our own case by itself. The reasons for this were, that Edinburgh being the only city in Scotland that elected a member for itself, no arrangement with other places was necessary, and our claim was the strongest and simplest that could be exhibited. In order to prepare the way, I was induced to write "Considerations submitted to the Householders of Edinburgh, on the State of their Representation in Parliament," explaining the material facts and views. On the 8th of March 1823 the Pantheon was again filled. Mr John Craig, a merchant, and the biographer of his relative, Professor John Millar, presided, and a petition to Parliament, written by Jeffrey, was adopted. Nobody was allowed to sign it but householders. Of these, old enough to sign, there were about 10,000 in the city, of whom, in a few days, about 7000 subscribed the petition— a fact which compelled certain eyes to see. Abercromby presented this petition on the 5th of May. On the 2nd of June Lord Archibald Hamilton moved for a reform of the Scotch county representation generally, and was supported by 117 against 152— a cheering vote.

CHAPTER VII

MATTHEW ROSS, a very distinguished person, and Dean of the Faculty of Advocates, died in October 1823. As it is not the custom for our Deans to die, it having never happened before (as was said), we ran little risk from the precedent of an official funeral, with which, therefore, he was honoured. He was a most curious creature. A worthy innocent man, and a very great chamber counsel, but with not a particle of worldly knowledge except what he got from law cases and from novels, of which he was a great devourer. He had very extensive practice with the pen and the head, which brought him a respectable fortune. His tongue never produced a guinea, for he equalled his blushing brother Rolland in bashfulness. Learned in every department of the law, a clear and rather elegant legal writer, and of the deepest and most inventive ingenuity, our judicial records contain no arguments more deserving of study by anyone who is anxious to instruct his understanding or to improve his taste, from the fountains of a great master. He was one of the Pundits who cannot be pushed forward. Office, even on the bench, had no attractions for a legal monk, who dined in solitude at least 360 times a-year, and who could not be looked at without his face becoming pink. He was so dis-

tressingly shy and awkward that, when George the
Fourth was here, he had to be deposed for the nonce
from the Deanship in favour of Lord Lauderdale,
because the attempt to deliver an address from the
Faculty must have killed him. The rough and changing world got tired of his timidity, and his practice
left him while his powers were still entire. His glory
and his luxury was in a legal doubt. Sir Harry
Moncreiff once made him give two opposite opinions
in one day on the same case, by changing the names,
and hinting a difficulty. Matthew instantly followed
the false scent, and without seeing that the cases were
identical, hunted himself down. How often have I
seen the little short body, with his thin powdered
hair, his silk-clad bits of legs and silver-buckled toes,
sitting in his evening chair, in his little room in Queen
Street, with his blushing cheeks and cunning eyes,
reasoning himself into no result except that the
matter on which he was consulted was all doubts, on
each of which he would have a still finer and deeper
doubt, till at last he would good-naturedly acquiesce
in some practical man's proposal that we should all
keep our thumbs on these doubts, and that neither
the Court nor the opposite party would dream of
them—which they very rarely did.

In 1823 Lord Bannatyne resigned his seat on the
bench, and John Clerk was announced as his successor.* With his crotchets, and his tendency to

* " When Clerk became a judge of the Court of Session in 1823 he
took from the paternal estate the title of Lord Eldin, saying that the
difference between him and the Chancellor (Eldon) ' was all in my i.' "
—Brougham's *Life and Times*.

torpidity, when not excited, Clerk could not perhaps have made a safe judge at any time; but it was a severe trial to be promoted in his sixty-fifth year, and when his vigour had begun to ebb. He had drawn more money than any man had ever done at the Scotch bar, probably not under £100,000 in the last twenty years of his energy. But pictures, books, hospitality, charity, and general bad management left him a poor man after all. People could not believe their ears when they heard that John Clerk was to go, or was to get upon the bench. They could not think of him except as a man who was born to tear and snarl at judges. In the wiry uncombed locks, breaking out from below the wig, and the shrewd sensible face, the contracted limb, and the strong arms, they saw the traces of a thousand tough battles; and could not believe that these were all over, and that John was henceforth only to be seen seated decorously on a high place. The Court was unusually crowded when he took his seat. As he was limping from the floor to the bench, an old agent, who remembered other days, was overheard ejaculating to himself—" Eh! is he gaain' up amang them! " He expected a worry the instant that the wolf got among the lambs. Clerk was a warning to all counsel to beware of leaning on violent energy as their permanent staff. It is attractive to clients, and therefore does vulgarly well for a certain time. But, among other misfortunes, it is necessarily temporary. It does not become grey hairs; and though it did, old blood can't keep it up. Clerk did not increase, as

Blair did, in awfulness and weight with age. This is the ripening of wisdom. He let himself settle into the habit of having little intellect except under excitement; and this age must always chill. Energy of thought may last as long as the lamp burns, but fierce vehemence dies out, and the lamp is quenched before its time.

The Court of Session was now doomed to stand its trial again, for the third or fourth time within twenty years. The object in view in 1807, and effected, was to cut the old court into two divisions. The introduction of civil juries was the problem of 1815. And now came the examination of its forms of proceeding. Each of these was a natural and necessary step in the process of fitting the tribunal to modern circumstances. This last inquiry was by sixteen Royal Commissioners; including our four heads—namely Hope Lord President, Boyle Justice-Clerk, Shepherd Chief Baron, and Adam Chief Commissioner, with the Dean, the Lord Advocate, and the Solicitor-General, Baron Hume, the Depute-Keeper of the Signet, and four English lawyers. These four were Tindal, afterwards Chief Justice of the Common Pleas, William Alexander, afterwards Chief Baron of England, Littledale afterwards a judge, and Courtenay afterwards Earl of Devon. They began work in 1823, and the invaluable statute of 1825 was the result of their labours. These were two years of as great excitement, and as keen discussion, as legal reform ever produces. The great points considered and resolved upon in the

Commission were—1. The introduction of a system of pleading, particularly by records; 2. The diminution of writing, and the consequent extension of oral debate; 3. The earlier finality of judgments; 4. The maintenance of civil juries.

What was called *the country*, that is, the country as represented by town-councils and lairds, was nearly unanimous against this reform. These persons never exhibited themselves more discreditably. They knew nothing, and indeed were incapable of being made to know anything, of the subject; but being at all times saturated with aversion to innovation, they gave their voices to certain professional persons who misled them. These persons had the usual professional addiction to the things they had lived by; and their zeal was most extraordinary. Thus instructed, resolutions against trial by jury, and in favour of the system under which all evidence was taken on commission, records were unknown, no single judgment, however solemn, was final, and all statements and arguments were in writing, were passed by almost every burgh and every county in Scotland! All this ignorant hubbub was met, on the part of Government, by the single fact, that every Commissioner had set his hand to the report. Of all the flights of pamphlets with which the air, throughout these two years, was darkened, there were only two, or rather only one, now worth being looked at. This was an " Explanation " addressed by George Joseph Bell to the Lords' Committee—an admirable sketch containing a clear exposition of our old forms, and a powerful defence of the proposed new ones. The other consisted of two letters, published anonymously but understood to be written by Lord Rosslyn. These judicial shakes remind one of James the Fifth's letter to the judges about a fortnight after the institution of the Court, ending, " And we'll be at ye, peradventure, sum day whan ye nocht think." *

It was in 1823, I think, that the last fragment of our Royal Botanical Garden was removed from its situation on the west side of Leith Walk, and that the transplantation of the whole to its present site at Inverleith was completed. No garden could be made to walk a mile with less injury to its health. Scarcely a single plant or tree was lost, and after recovering from their first sickness, they looked fresher and prouder than ever. Dr Graham, the Professor, was a respectable botanist, and a good teacher, and in his first lieutenant, Macnab, he had a most admirable practical man. That chair is one of the best botanical prizes in Britain. Few things of the kind are more enviable than a taste for that science, with such a garden, such funds, and such a class.† It was

* I dare say these English lawyers thought our system very strange, and had no misgiving about touching it. But did any of them think of their own ? Their day had not come then. But since that, reforming Peers and Commoners, Committees, Law-improving Societies, and Parliaments, have been all toiling to prove that " the perfection of right reason " is the accumulated imperfection of the greatest folly. They would have been infinitely the better of having a few Scotch lawyers among their native reformers. For in point of simplicity and common sense we are far before them. While they were changing some of our forms, it is a mercy they had no authority to meddle with our law.—H. C.

† On the publication of Art. 2 of No. 115 of the *Edinburgh Review* (April 1833), the Town-Council of Edinburgh, who are the chief patrons

2 B

nearly about the same time that " The Horticultural Society," which had been set up in 1809, opened its kindred and adjoining " Experimental Garden." Conducted, as it was at first, by such men as Ellis and Neill, it could scarcely fail, and has always done as well as low funds allow. But Flora and poverty make but a bad match.

Recent events provoked me to write an article in the *Edinburgh Review* [No. 78, Art. 5] on the nature of the office of Lord Advocate; and this, in about a year, forced me in self defence to answer a plausible pamphlet ascribed to one of the Lord Advocate's deputes [No. 82, Art. 8]. The institution of a public prosecutor is certainly a very valuable part of our system, and the duties of the office cannot be better performed than they have long been in Scotland, in ordinary cases. But this is surely quite consistent with its being a dangerous office; when its holder is employed as a political agent. My object was to explain the causes and temptations which may make his position injurious to his purely accusative virtues. Yet I now see that, under the feelings of the period, I stated the expediency of keeping the Lord Advocate to the public prosecutor's desk far too strongly. His being in Parliament, and considered as a high public

of this chair, were much blamed for having preferred Graham to Sir Edward Smith. And if they had done so, they would have deserved all the censure that could be given them. But the fact is, that Graham was appointed before Smith's willingness to take the chair was known, and the folly of the patrons consisted in their making any appointment so hurriedly.—H. C.

officer, and intrusted with a liberal direction of all matters connected with our legal polity, is essential both to the dignity and to the practical usefulness of his place. I am also wrong—grossly wrong, in saying a word in favour of grand juries.* The disclosure of an inclination to tolerate such an incumbrance in a country with a public accuser, shows the desperate remedies that the misconduct of these days had driven us in quest of.

The Fox dinner was held on the 26th of January 1824, under the presidency of Lord Archibald Hamilton and Mr Ferguson of Raith, with about 300 present. Jeffrey made one of his noblest bursts in admiration of the good parts of the constitution of America.

In the following month, Abercromby moved for leave to introduce a bill for reforming the representation of Edinburgh. He was defeated, of course; but only by 99 against 75. The amount of the minority, and the admission of the majority that, *taken by itself*, the Scotch representation was indefensible, but that we were under the shelter of the representation

* When writing his *Edinburgh Review* articles in 1821 on the office of Lord Advocate, Lord Cockburn conceded his doubts on the advantages arising from the introduction of Grand Juries into Scotland to the pressure of outside opinion. In a letter to Mr T. F. Kennedy, 25th March 1821, he says: "I shall leave out the doubt about the use of grand juries; but I am clearly of opinion that the introduction of them should not be rashly broached. I agree with you about the extravagant powers of the Lord Advocate, but I doubt if grand juries *by themselves* would tend at all to abridge his authority."—Letters in the *Affairs of Scotland.*

of England, confirmed us in our resolution to per-
severe. He renewed his motion on 13th April 1826.
It was then supported by 97, but opposed by 122.
The increase on the vote was good: but the admission
by Canning that, if any change had been expedient,
the idea that articles of Union could be held up as an
insuperable obstacle, as had been urged, ought to be
" scouted " was still better.*

Leonard Horner and I had often discussed the
causes and the remedies of the decline of classical
education in Scotland; and we were at last satisfied
that no adequate improvement could be effected so
long as there was only one great classical school in
Edinburgh, and this one placed under the Town-
Council, and lowered, perhaps necessarily, so as to
suit the wants of a class of boys to more than two-
thirds of whom classical accomplishment is foreseen
to be useless. So one day on the top of one of the
Pentlands—emblematic of the solidity of our foundation and of the extent of our prospects—we two resolved to set about the establishment of a new school.

---

* Sir Walter's account of the state of the burghal classes about this
time is very candid, and very correct. In a letter to Sir Robert Dundas,
written in March 1826 (Lockhart's *Life of Scott*, chap. lxix.) he says,—
" The whole burgher class of Scotland are gradually preparing for
radical reform—I mean the middling and respectable classes ; and when
a burgh reform comes, which perhaps cannot long be delayed, *ministers
will not return a member for Scotland from the towns.* The gentry will
abide longer by sound principles ; *for they are needy, and desire advancement for their sons, and appointments, and so on.* But this is a
very hollow dependence." This is the defence of existing things, by
their most intelligent defender ; who calls men " scamps " for being
in favour of these reforms.—H. C.

On taking others into council we found that the conviction of the inadequacy of the High School was far
more general than we supposed. Scott took it up
eagerly. The sum of £10,000 was subscribed immediately; and soon afterwards about £2000 more. We
were fiercely opposed, as we expected, by the Town-
Council; and, but not fiercely, by a few of the friends
of the institution we were going to encroach upon.
But, after due discussion and plotting, our contributors finally resolved to proceed, and in 1823 the
building was begun. It was opened under the title of
" The Edinburgh Academy," on the 1st of October
1824, amidst a great assemblage of proprietors,
pupils, and the public. We had a good prayer by Sir
Harry Moncreiff, and speeches by Scott and old
Henry Mackenzie, and an important day for education in Scotland, in reference to the middle and upper
classes. Mackenzie's vigour was delightful. Though
about eighty he made an animated address, exulting
in the rise of a new school upon a reformed system.
About a month before this he one day appeared at
Bonaly to breakfast, played bowls most part of the
forenoon, had a party at dinner in his own house,
where Richardson and I left him predominating in
full talk to a larger party at eleven. He almost admitted that a report of his being under temptation
by a bookseller to write a volume of his personal
reminiscences was correct. I hoped the temptation
would prevail; for he has seen all the curious men of
a bye-gone age. Yet it is nearly impossible for an old
good man to remember truly. Whatever it is ami-

able to soften or to forget, is forgotten or softened, the angularities of nature are smoothed down, and everything is coloured by the haze of tenderness. He told us many interesting anecdotes that day; but on our hoping to see them in the book, we got a shake of the head. I suspect there was a good deal of prosaic truth in the account which a Highland gentleman, who had marched all the way to Derby with the Pretender, gave him of that romantic adventure. Mackenzie asked him whether he did not always think the idea of dethroning the House of Hanover absurd? " Na, Sir! I ne'er thocht aboot it. I just ay' thocht hoo pleesant it wad be to see Donald riflin' Lon'on."

Another luminary, which for several years had been attracting notice, was now fixed in our Scottish sky —I mean Thomas Chalmers. I have known him long and pretty well. There can scarcely be a more curious man. When I first became acquainted with him, he used to leave his parish of Kilmany twice or thrice a week to lecture in St Andrews on chemistry. And not confining himself to physical science, he stored his mind during this first stage of his course by a general study of the principles of moral and political philosophy. In this position, of an indifferent minister, and a lecturer rather ardent than exact, he produced a strong impression of his energy and ability on all who were within his range. But it was only on being elevated by the deep religious feelings which afterwards took possession of him that his powers were

developed in their full force. From that moment he
was a new creature; and devoted himself, as if with
new faculties, to the moral and religious improvement of his countrymen. The high station which he
soon attained wakened his ambition, and has dignified
his powers. Of the result, in so far as it is contained in
a constant and copious stream of published composition and of public exertion, any one can judge.
But eloquence records its character feebly. He is
awkward and has a low rough husky voice, a guttural
articulation, a whitish eye, and a large dingy countenance. In point of mere feature, it would not be
difficult to think him ugly. But he is saved from this,
and made interesting and lovable, by singular
modesty, kindness, and simplicity of manner, a strong
expression of calm thought and benevolence, a forehead so broad that it seems to proclaim itself the seat
of a great intellect, a love of humour, and an inde-
scribable look of drollery when anything ludicrous
comes over him.

In spite of the external disadvantages of a bad
figure, voice, gesture, and look, and an unusual plainness of Scotch accent, he is a great orator; for *effect*
indeed, at the moment of speaking, unapproached in
our day. Yet he seldom utters an extemporaneous
word. His habit is to have every thing written, to the
very letter. The success of the very few attempts at
unprepared speaking which he has ever been obliged
to make removes all doubt of his power, if he had
chosen to practise it. But it is not his way. He feels
stronger in building up before hand, and giving the

public the mere recitation. But then he premeditates and composes with an exact anticipation of his speaking position; and, neither in recollecting nor in reading, could any one unacquainted with his system discover that his memory or his eye were particularly engaged; and he does truly glow with the warmth of present conception. Still, the habit impairs his power of reply. But it does not impair his general impressiveness. On the contrary, by withdrawing him from the temptations of personality, and the little tricks and idle flashes of what is commonly called debate, it leaves him freer for his own loftier range, into which he rarely fails to put views and statements which, in truth though not in form, are answers to all that can be said on the opposite side. But neither devotional fervour, nor enlightened philosophy, nor vivid language, nor luminous exposition could produce the effect he does, without the aid of his manner. I have often hung upon his words with a beating heart and a tearful eye, without being brought to my senses till I read, next day, the very syllables that had moved me to such admiration, but which then seemed cold. The magic lies in the concentrated intensity which agitates every fibre of the man, and brings out his meaning by words and emphasis of significant force, and rolls his magnificent periods clearly and irresistibly along, and kindles the whole composition with living fire. He no sooner approaches the edge of his high region, than his animation makes the commencing awkwardness be forgotten, and then converts his external defects into positive advantages, by showing the intellectual power that overcomes them; and getting us at last within the flames of his enthusiasm, Jeffrey's description, that " he buried his adversaries under the fragments of burning mountains," is the only image that suggests an idea of his eloquent imagination and terrible energy. Personally, he appears to me to be simple, affectionate, and true, devoted to useful objects, and utterly unspoiled by applause. I was so much struck with the wisdom and energy of his system for the management of the poor, that I wrote an article in explanation and defence of it [*Edinburgh Review*, No. 81, Art. 11].

In June 1824 a noble range of houses, forming the upper end of the south side of the High Street, and the north-eastern corner of the Parliament Close, was burnt to the ground. This was talked of at the time as the most extensive conflagration remembered in this stony city. But it was soon eclipsed by what have ever since been referred to as " The Great Fires."

These fires broke out on the evening of Monday the 15th of November 1824, on the south side of the High Street about half-way between the Tron Church and St Giles Cathedral; and before morning a range of houses six or seven storeys high, with fifteen windows in front, and extending back almost to the Cowgate— as dense a mass of buildings as was perhaps in the world, was a burnt shell. People thought this bad enough; especially as the adjoining ruins of the June fire were still untouched. But about noon next day an alarm was given that the Tron Church was on fire.

We ran out from the Court, gowned and wigged, and saw that it was the steeple, an old Dutch thing, composed of wood, iron, and lead, and edged all the way up with bits of ornament. Some of the sparks of the preceding night had nestled in it, and had at last blown its dry bones into flame. There could not be a more beautiful firework; only it was wasted on the day-light. It was one hour's brilliant blaze. The spire was too high and too combustible to admit of any attempt to save it, so that we had nothing to do but to admire. And it was certainly beautiful. The fire seized on every projecting point, and played with the fretwork, as if it had been all an exhibition. The outer covering boards were soon consumed, and the lead dissolved. This made the strong upright and cross-beams visible; and these stood, with the flame lessened, but with the red fire increased, as if it had been a great burning toy. The conflagration was long presided over by a calm and triumphant gilded cock on the top of the spire, which seemed to look on the people, and to listen to the crackling, in disdain. But it was undermined at last, and dived down into the burning gulf, followed by the upper half of the steeple. The lower half held out a little longer, till the very bell being melted, this half came down also, with a world of sparks. There was one occurrence which made the gazers start. It was at a quarter before twelve, when the minute hand of the clock stood horizontally. The internal heat—for the clock was untouched outwardly—cracked the machinery, and the hand dropped suddenly and silently down to the

perpendicular. When the old time-keeper's function
was done, there was an audible sigh over the spectators.
When it was all over, and we were beginning to move
back to our clients, Scott, whose father's pew had
been in the Tron Church, lingered a moment, and
said, with a profound heave, "Eh, Sirs! mony a weary,
weary sermon hae I heard beneath that steeple!"

About nine that evening I went over to the old
town to see what was going on. There were a good
many people on the street, but no appearance of any
new danger. I had not been home again above half-
an-hour, when it was supposed that the sky was unnaturally red. In spite of Hermand's remonstrances,
whose first tumbler was nearly ready, I hurried back,
and found the south-east angle of the Parliament
Close burning violently. This was in the centre of the
same thick-set population and buildings, but the
property was far more valuable. It was almost touching Sir William Forbes's bank, the Libraries of the
Advocates and of the Writers to the Signet, the
Cathedral, and the Courts. Of course the alarm was
very great; but this seemed only to increase the confusion. No fire ever got fairer play. Judges, magistrates,
officers of state, dragoons, librarians, people described
as *heads of bodies*, were all mixed with the mob, all
giving peremptory and inconsistent directions, and
all, with angry and provoking folly, claiming para-
mount authority. It was said to have been mooted,
and rather sternly discussed, on the street—whether
the Lord Provost could order the Justice-Clerk to
prison, or the Justice the Provost, and whether

George Cranstoun, the Dean of the Faculty, was bound to work at an engine, when commanded by John Hope, the Solicitor-General, to do so, or *vice versa*. Then the firemen were few and awkward, and the engines out of order; so that while torrents of water were running down the street, nobody could use it. Amidst this confusion, inefficiency, and squabble for dignity, the fire held on till next morning; by which time the whole private buildings in the Parliament Close, including the whole east side, and about half of the south side, were consumed.

On going to Court that morning, I found that an adjournment had taken place; and that the College, Arthur Seat, and all the southern and eastern objects which had been screened for ages were now seen over the fallen ruins. The only remaining danger was from two walls, standing alone, which it was thought a breeze might make smother everything near them. Both were brought down on the Saturday (20th Nov. 1824), one by ropes, and one by powder. The one that was subdued by ropes was near the east end of the south side of the square. It was part of the tallest house in Edinburgh, and was then probably the tallest self-standing wall in Europe—being, from the Cowgate, about 130 feet high. It was pulled down by a party of sailors from a frigate in Leith Roads, who required two days to get it within their toils.

The dissolution of the other was a grand thing. It had formed nearly the whole east side of the square, and was steadied by a piece of wall standing at a right angle to it, which acted like a buttress. Five holes, or mines, were sunk in this buttress, into each of which a pound of powder was put. Two of these failed to explode, and two exploded too late, so that one shot did the business. In going off this made a dull noise like a thump—as if to warn the spectators on the house tops, that the time was come. In a second or two, during which hardly a breath was drawn, the buttress fell across the main wall, which stood alone, staring with its windows. But seeing its old associate down, it bent slowly and slightly forward, as if turned on a hinge at the ground, bringing with it its windows and grates and other vestiges of recent order and comfort, without the least noise, or any visible fracture, but with awful steadiness and tenacity. This scarcely lasted above a second or two when every stone dropped from its place, and falling straight down, the whole mass disappeared in a shower of fragments, which, after dashing themselves on the ground, sent up a thick fog of lime dust, that powdered every coat on the top of the Outer House, where I stood; while the shout of the people was heard through the white gloom. It was sublime. I can never forget the emotion when the large scorched screen, beholding all its old companions gone, and not another stone in its place on that side of the square, bent forward, and laid itself in chaos on the ground.

Jeffrey presided at the Fox dinner on the 24th of January 1825; Moncreiff was croupier. It was a new position for Jeffrey; but he adorned it by great thought, and great beauty of diction. This, I think, was the last of these festivals. They were never meant to be perpetual; but were only resorted to for political union and excitement during the stage that we had now passed through. Public meetings of all kinds soon became so common that, as substantive events, they are not worth recording. These Fox dinners did incalculable good. They animated, and instructed, and consolidated the Whig party with less trouble and more effect than anything else that could have been devised. A kindred gathering upon a larger scale was held on the 5th of April 1825, when a public dinner was given to Brougham upon his first return to Edinburgh. About 850 were present; being more, I believe, than had ever attended a public political dinner in Scotland. Of these about fifty were known, and other fifty understood, to dissent from the political creed of the meeting, and to have been attracted by curiosity, or by personal regard to Brougham. But there certainly were 750 persons there openly professing Whiggism. I had the misfortune to be in the chair. When the waiters were clearing the tables, and the talking time was approaching, Brougham told me that he thought the most alarming moment of life was, when the Speaker, after settling himself into his chair for an important debate, paused for an instant before calling up the mover; but that he would rather endure that a hundred times than rise and address the audience before him, which, he said, was the largest he had ever spoken to under a roof. If this was the feeling of that practised orator, I need not be ashamed to confess that I felt very uneasy. However, it was on the whole a successful and impressive meeting.

We were now in a pretty keen conflict about the *Edinburgh Improvements*, a subject which blazed for a good many years after this. It all related to the creation of the new southern access by George the Fourth's Bridge, and of the new western access by the west approach along the Castle Hill. There were three parties—1st. Those who would be taxed for nothing. 2nd. Those who, being personally interested, insisted to have themselves and everybody else taxed to any extent. 3rd. Those (of whom I took the lead) who were willing to be taxed, provided new statutory securities were given for the perpetual openness of Princes Street and the Mound. This last party finally prevailed; and had it not been for its efforts, Edinburgh would have been destroyed. These statutory precautions may possibly be all disregarded hereafter. This will be the loss and the disgrace of the people themselves, of whom, from their ordinary apathy about the beauty of their city, I certainly forebode no good. But meanwhile we did our duty, by both giving them the means of new improvement, and of saving what excellence they already have.* Some people let their picturesque taste get so sickly that they sigh over the destruction of every old nuisance

* Scott's Monument has since been erected on Princes Street; and the Art Galleries are rising on the Mound; and a railway pollutes the valley. But the last of these perfidies was irresistible; and the other two abatements of the strict exemption that was obtained were consented to, and were quite right.—H. C.

or incumbrance. But they never try to live among
these fragments, nor think of the human animals who
burrow there. Everything that has an old history, or
an old ornament, or an old peculiarity, if it *can* be
preserved, ought to be preserved in spite of all living
inconvenience. In these matters mere antiquity is
better entitled to be respected than existing comfort.
It is not once in a thousand times that the two are
really incompatible. But it does not follow that present necessities and tastes are to be sacrificed for the
preservation of every tottering gable that would look
well in one of Weirrotter's etchings. That the new
approaches are immense improvements cannot be
doubted. That the assessment was too high, and that
there was jobbing, and mismanagement, and trick,
and ill humour, and folly, is true. But this bad was
temporary, and the good is permanent. And it is also
true that the south approach might have been joined
to the New Town at a better level, and in a far more
handsome manner. But still what we got was better
than nothing.

There was at this period, and for some years both
before and after, a very pretty quarrel between the
people of Leith and the Town-Council of Edinburgh.
The Council was the proprietor of the harbour and
superior of the town of Leith; and, as such, had the
entire mismanagement of that place. The result consequently was that the docks were bankrupt, and that
though Leith was then even baser in its politics than
its masters, the masters had scarcely a friend in that

town. At last, after a long, and now incomprehensible, but most rancorous jumble which, whatever its details, was in principle a struggle for liberation on the one side, and for power on the other, Edinburgh fell into a pit dug by itself. It proposed to sell the harbour and the docks to a joint-stock company, which was to pay the debt, and to make money by imposing higher rates. The shares were speedily sold, and a bill to legalise the transaction was brought into Parliament. But the opposition to it was made irresistible by the discovery that several of the Town-Council were shareholders; that is, that the public trustees had sold the subject of the trust to themselves for individual profit. After this truth had transpired, Abercromby had little difficulty in getting this municipal job quashed. The merchant company of Leith, a strongly Tory body, thanked him and their other parliamentary supporters—almost all Whigs, for " defending the rights of an *unrepresented* trading port against the influence of a great city having powerful parliamentary friends." The expression of this truth, that Leith had suffered *from want of representation*, was worth the whole struggle. The conflict raged for a long time: but its result was that, bit by bit, Leith was successful; till at last, though not a royal burgh, it, like some other places, was included in the general measures that were adopted in a few years after this for the cleansing of those chartered abominations. Throughout the course of the dispute, the parties were fairly enough matched in point of intemperance and unreasonableness; and if Leith had

2 C

the advantage in coarse violence, Edinburgh was compensated by its superiority in disdainful insolence. In the eyes of quiet observers, the true value of the affair lay in its aiding the growth of independence in Leith. The Town-Council actually succeeded in creating a public spirit in that prostrate place.

The opening of the year 1826 will ever be sad to those who remember the thunderbolt which then fell on Edinburgh in the utterly unexpected bankruptcy of Scott, implying the ruin of Constable the bookseller, and of Ballantyne the printer. If an earthquake had swallowed half the town, it would not have produced greater astonishment, sorrow, and dismay. Ballantyne and Constable were merchants, and their fall, had it reached no further, might have been lamented merely as the casualty of commerce. But Sir Walter! The idea that his practical sense had so far left him as to have permitted him to dabble in trade, had never crossed our imagination. How humbled we felt when we saw him—the pride of us all, dashed from his lofty and honourable station, and all the fruits of his well-worked talents gone. He had not then even a political enemy. There was not one of those whom his thoughtlessness had so sorely provoked, who would not have given every spare farthing he possessed to retrieve Sir Walter. Well do I remember his first appearance after this calamity was divulged, when he walked into Court one day in January 1826. There was no affectation, and no reality, of *facing it;* no look of indifference or defiance;

but the manly and modest air of a gentleman conscious of some folly, but of perfect rectitude, and of
most heroic and honourable resolutions.* It was on
that very day, I believe, that he said a very fine
thing. Some of his friends offered him, or rather proposed to offer him, enough of money, as was supposed
to enable him to arrange with his creditors. He
paused for a moment; and then, recollecting his
powers, said proudly—" No! this right hand shall
work it all off! " His friend William Clerk supped
with him one night after his ruin was declared. They
discussed the whole affair, its causes and probable
consequences, openly and playfully; till at last they
laughed over their noggins at the change, and Sir
Walter observed that he felt " something like Lambert
and the other Regicides, who, Pepys says when he
saw them going to be hanged and quartered, were as
cheerful and comfortable as any gentlemen could be
in that situation."

In spite of great mercantile depression, this was
the period of the most violent Joint-Stock mania that
ever seized this kingdom. I could not have conceived
that madness could be so universal. There was no
peculiar temptation, from high profits, for men not
regular merchants to adventure in trade; nor were
purses too heavy with unemployed guineas; nor was
any new field suddenly discovered. It was a mere

---

* Scott says in his Diary, 17th January 1826, "I felt rather sneaking
as I came home from the Parliament House—felt as if I were liable
monstrari digito in no very pleasant way," etc. (Lockhart's *Life*, chap.
lxvi.) Very natural for him to feel so; but it was the feeling of nobody
else.—H. C.

joint-stock epidemic. Wofully were those who relied on the prudence of the Scotch deceived. Neither the Parisians during the Mississippi insanity, nor the English under the South Sea delusion, exceeded the folly, or the knavery, of the cautious and moral Scot under his excitement of 1825 and 1826. The newspapers of the day contain little else than advertisements and recommendations of joint-stock associations, in not one out of five hundred of which was there either plausibility or honesty. Everything unattainable, or useless if attained, was to be made easy and valuable, provided people would only take shares, which the ignorant, the excited, and the deceived by gambling directors or by paid secretaries and agents, took—to no other effect than enabling fraudulent speculators to make gain in the market by crazy prices, paid by fools, for what did not exist. The schemes were so numerous, that after exhausting every subject to which they could be applied, there was actually a joint-stock company instituted for the purpose of projecting and organising joint-stock companies. The fever lasted about a year. Not one honest penny was made out of all this villainy and folly. The loss was enormous.

Among other remedies for the prevailing commercial distress, Government proposed to check the unlimited circulation of small notes by the Scotch banks. Whether this was wise or not, there can be no doubt that the matter was taken up by the ministry in a narrow, ignorant, and exclusively English spirit. This country was instantly in a blaze from one end to

the other. I never saw Scotland unanimous before. It
was really refreshing to see the spirit with which the
whole land rose as one man. Even the Tories were for
a season reconciled to resistance and public meetings.
The Lord Provost of Edinburgh presided at an
assemblage of the lieges, where there was more
violence, though the meeting was composed solely of
what are technically called *respectable persons*, than
in all the past gatherings of the Whigs put together.
Scott, tempted by the bankers, came forward, under
the name of Malachi Malagrowther, in the new
character of a political pamphleteer. Poets may be
excused for being bad political economists. If a nice
question of monetary or commercial policy could
be settled by jokes, Malachi would be a better
economist than Adam Smith. His lamentations over
the loss of Scotch sinecures was very injudicious, and
did neither him nor such of these things as remained
any good. He was mentioned in Parliament by his
own friends with less respect than one would ever
wish to be shown him.

The opening in 1826 of an establishment called the
New Town Markets at Stockbridge recalled some
curious, though not distant, recollections of Edinburgh. It was only about fifteen or twenty years
before that our only fish market was in the Fish
Market Close, a steep, narrow, stinking ravine. The
fish were generally thrown out on the street at the
head of the close, whence they were dragged down by
dirty boys or dirtier women; and then sold unwashed

—for there was not a drop of water in the place—
from old, rickety, scaly, wooden tables, exposed to
all the rain, dust, and filth; an abomination the recollection of which greatly impaired the pleasantness
of the fish at a later hour of the day. Yet when the
market was removed to its present situation below
the North Bridge, there was an outcry as if hereditary
nastiness, like other abuses, had been made, by time,
necessary for comfort. I doubt if there was a single
fish shop in Edinburgh so early as the year 1822. Our
vegetables had to pass through as bad a process.
They were entirely in the hands of a college of old gin-
drinking women, who congregated with stools and
tables round the Tron Church. A few of the aristocracy
of these ladies—the burgo-mistresses, who had
established a superior business—the heads of old
booths—marked their dignity by an awning of dirty
canvas or tattered carpet; and every table had its
tallow candle and paper lantern at night. There was
no water here either, except what flowed down the
gutter, which, however, was plentifully used. Fruit
had a place on the table, but kitchen vegetables lay
bruised on the ground. I doubt if there was a fruit
shop in Edinburgh in 1815. All shops indeed meant
for the sale of any article, on which there was a local
tax or market-custom, were discouraged by the
magistrates or their taxman as interfering with the
collection of the dues. The growth of shops of all
kinds in the New Town is remarkable. I believe there
were not half-a-dozen of them in the whole New
Town, west of St Andrew Street, in 1810. The dislike

to them was so great, that any proprietor who allowed one was abused as an unneighbourly fellow.

At the east end of what was formerly " The Physic Garden "—the low flat ground between the North Bridge and Leith Wynd, stand two venerable relics—Trinity Church, the best, and almost the only, ancient Gothic edifice in Edinburgh; * and Trinity Hospital, a very curious place.

More than fifty years ago, this Garden was the favourite open-day haunt of the literature and polite flirtation of Edinburgh. But in those days the Assembly Room was in a close (still called the Assembly Close) in the High Street; St Cecilia's Hall was in the Cowgate; the Canongate was occupied by the nobility and gentry; the ploughed fields now covered by the New Town were no more thought of than the fields of Fife. Ever since the Physic Garden was removed to Leith Walk—where it was called the Botanical, and from whence it has made another move to its present situation at Inverleith, the old place has been gradually falling every year into a more neglected and squalid condition. Although probably the North Loch, with its bad drainage and burghal sediments, was seldom an inoffensive neighbour, yet in spite of its lowness this must have been rather a good site originally, when there were no buildings to the north or east. The Calton Hill, with its rockiest face, stood right in front on the north; the sea must have been visible on the east; the

* It was taken down in 1848 to make room for the North British Railway.

Castle rose on the west; and the ridge of the Old Town bristled up to the south. Holyrood had not a better position.

The hospital is for the benefit, not of common paupers, but of old men and women once in the prospect of a better fate. A few of them are presented by the heirs of donors. All the rest must be burgesses of Edinburgh, or of burgesses' families; and they are selected by the Town-Council. There are generally about thirty-five or forty in the house, and many more out of it. The institution was founded in 1462 by Mary of Gueldres; but the building underwent considerable alteration about 1587. It would not be easy to produce anything meaner than its outside. It consists merely of a respectable commonplace house, at right angles to which there runs a long, thin, two-storeyed building like a long granary—all cased in dingy rough-cast, without any attempt at ornament or proportion. There is a bit of garden about a hundred feet square; but it is only turf, surrounded by a gravel walk. An old thorn and an old elm, destined never to be in leaf again, tell of old springs and of old care. And there is a wooden summer-house, which has heard many an old man's crack, and seen the sun soften many an old man's wrinkles.

But the door is no sooner opened, than antiquity is seen standing within it. Narrow stone stairs, helped out by awkward bits of wooden ones; oak tables of immovable massiveness; high-backed carved chairs with faded tapestry on their seats and elbows; a few strong heavy cabinets; drawers, and leaves, and bolts, and locks, and hinges, once the pride of their inventors, and now exciting a smile at ancient carpentry; passages on miscalculated levels; long narrow halls, and little inaccessible odd-shaped rooms; these and other vestiges of the primary formation arrest and delight the visitor. All the apartments except four are very small.

Of these four, one seems to be their academic grove. It is a long place, apparently for mere lounging; for it contains nothing except a large shelved press, which is the library. This library consists, so far as I can guess by the eye, of about 500 or 600 volumes. Many of them are suitable for the readers; many not. There are several beautiful books of the sixteenth and seventeenth centuries. These, some think, it would be no disrespect to the ancient donors to sell for the purchase of more useful works. The chaplain, however, with a just pride in his antiquities, is shocked at the proposal; and he is right. There is sometimes a good deal of reading among these aged students; at present very little. It comes in fits like other fashions. A second of these long apartments is used as a chapel and banqueting room. There are two long tables, with chairs, and a passage between the tables. The pensioner's position is the same, whether he is at dinner or at sermon. An old low pulpit stands at the end of the room; and before the pulpit there is a black article, said to be positively " John Knox's sacramental table." The third of these rooms seems to extend the whole length of the building. It is about ninety or a hundred feet long, and was originally about thirty or thirty-five feet wide. But its width has been contracted by operations, which have converted it into a city for human beavers. Along one side a range of ten wooden cabins projects into the room. It is just a range of wooden boxes, placed on the floor, along one side of the wall. Each box is about seven feet square, detached from its neighbour, and with its own door and window—all the windows looking into the room. These cabins, each of which houses a pensioner, narrow the room to the extent of their own depth, on the one side. On the opposite side it is narrowed by a partition reaching from the floor to the ceiling. Between this partition and the outer wall there are two rows of cabins, one above the other. The lower row is entered by doors opening into the long room. The upper row is reached by neat wooden stairs. There are five of these stairs, and most picturesque they are. They project into the room, all to the same extent—probably three feet, and all with the same curve to the left, not unlike outer stairs to hay-lofts. Each of the five leads to a small landing place, off which are two cabins.

There are thus thirty cabins in that room; ten in the form of boxes, on the floor, on one side; and twenty within the partition on the opposite side, ten of which are below and ten above; these last ten reached by the five outside wooden stairs. And between these lines of pigmy palaces there is a space of about fifteen or eighteen feet left free, along the whole length of the room. These human pigeon-holes have immemorially been termed " arks "—a name which, holding ark to mean chest, describes them very correctly. Each ark contains the bed, chair, table, and little mirror, of its single inhabitant, and any other article of comfort or decoration that the occupier may happen to have. They are all neat and comfortable. Several contain chests of drawers; and some are gay with ornament. One duenna had her cupboard, with her own books, and her umbrella hanging from a brass hook, and every " coigne of vantage " graced by shells, and human figures, and trees, and animals—all cut by herself, out of pasteboard, and gloriously painted. Several others have carried with them into these sad though kindly retreats similar articles; plainly once the pride of their better days.

The fourth long apartment is lined on one side by another row of cabins; and there is space for an opposite row if required. Besides these roosts, which being both the parlour and the bed-chamber are truly the ark of each occupant, there are common rooms, with fires and carpets, where the inmates repair when they want talk, heat, or a social doze. The walls of the chapel are entirely covered with wooden tablets, containing inscriptions in gilt letters on black grounds immortalising the memories of the various donors of merks or pounds Scots. The name of many a citizen, illustrious in his day, is there; the title of many a family, once green bay-trees, now dead roots. I observe one donation in 1632; and no doubt there are some still older.

The community is presided over by a chaplain and a governess. The chaplain spends most of his day there, and may reside constantly if he pleases. However, he can never be long absent; for, besides worship twice a day, he has to ask a blessing on all their meals. His drawing-room is scarcely ten feet square. But it is dignified by old chairs, an old table, an old desk, an old mirror, besides books and prints. The little cheerful round incumbent talks so happily of his own position, and so affectionately of every individual pensioner, that a bishopric, nay, even a Scotch kirk, could scarcely increase his delight. The elysium of the queen is fully as tiny, and as old, and as nice. Besides being graced by various achievements of her own needle, it is enlivened by a blue parrot, on a bright perch, and a canary in a brass wire cage, with doors and windows like a cathedral. On my last visit she insisted on my entering her bedroom—smaller than even the parlour; but what a coverlet of patch work! Cheerfulness beamed from her face, and pride elated her heart. How cruel that, with such a pair, celibacy is the law of the place.

The subjects of these two sovereigns seem to be as happy as age, when combined with final destitution and with the recollection of more hopeful days, can probably ever be. They are decent in their apparel, clean in their domicile, and, so far as a stranger can discover, are kindly used and kindly thought of. That they are followed into the last asylum that can ever shelter them by grateful recollections, and even by some friendships, as well as by discontent, jealousy, quarrels, and all other passions that cling to the still beating heart, is certain. They are human. They doubtless have their magnates, their disputed principles, their wrongs, intrigues, and factions. The dulness of their day is, no doubt, relieved by occasional dissension and ingratitude. But there is as little of this, I understand, as generally enlivens hospitals. And certainly their bodies are not ill cared for. Every one seems proud of his own ark. They sit in these retreats, and come out and go in—opening and shutting their own front doors, as if each felt that it was he who had got the state-room.*

One of the present female pensioners is ninety-six. She was sitting beside her own fire. The chaplain shook her kindly by the hand, and asked her how she was. " Very weel—just in my creeping ordinary." There is one Catholic there—a little merry woman, obviously with some gentle blood in her veins, and delighted to allude to it. This book she had got from Sir John Something; her great friend had been a Lady Something Cuningham; and her spinet was the oldest that had ever been made; to convince me of which she opened it, and pointed exultingly to the year 1776. Neither she nor the ninety-six years old was in an ark, but in an ordinary small room. On overhearing my name, she said that she was once at Miss Brandon's boarding school in Bristo Street with a Miss Matilda Cockburn, a " little pretty girl." I

* Arnot (*History of Edinburgh*, p. 563) gives a bad account of their conduct in his day. He states that in 1778 their mutinies, dishonesty, and dirt had "aroused the attention" of the governors. I understand that this is all quite inapplicable to their present state. If the attention of governors was quietly *kept up*, instead of requiring to be *aroused* by great excesses, things would generally go on better.—H. C.

told her that I remembered that school quite well, and that that girl was my sister; and then I added, as a joke, that all the girls at that school were said to have been pretty, but all light-headed, and much given to flirtation. The tumult revived in the vestal's veins. Delighted with the imputation, she rubbed her hands together, and giggled till she wept, and exclaimed, and protested, and giggled more, and appeared to force back recollections that made her blush. She said she liked her fellow pensioners, " but no' their religion; an' they dinna like mine." Of the last fact I had a tolerable proof, on going into a room where several of the women were. One of them asked me if I could tell them the name of a bird they had just got, and which was in a cage there. I told them it was a cardinal. On which the Presbyterian sybils burst out into a jocular, but not ill-natured roar—" A caardinal! hear that! a caardinal! od, ou' maun send it doon to the Caatholic! " This is Trinity Hospital. Time, in its course over Edinburgh, has left no other such picturesque deposit.*

* In a short time, the place shall know it no more ! But the public will be gratified by a railway station. Trinity College Church, too—the last and finest Gothic fragment in Edinburgh, though implored for by about four centuries, will disappear for the accommodation of a railway ! An outrage by sordid traders, virtually consented to by a tasteless city, and sanctioned by an insensible parliament. I scarcely know a more curious instance of ignorant insensibility than the apology that is made for this piece of desecration. It is said that the edifice is to be replaced *exactly as it is*, in some better situation.* And it is really thought that the Pyramids would remain the Pyramids, or Jerusalem Jerusalem, pro-

* The church was rebuilt in Jeffrey Street in 1872, the old stones which had been marked and preserved, being used in the recon-struction to a considerable extent.

Lord Hermand having retired, Cranstoun succeeded him, and took his seat on the bench in November 1826. His removal was a great loss to the bar, which he had long adorned, and where he had the entire confidence of the public. And though his judicial qualities, at least the most difficult ones, were of the highest order, it was seen that a long apprenticeship in the obscurity of the Outer House might prevent his real eminence from being soon felt. One of the great obstacles with which a Scotch judge has to contend is, that so little is done publicly, in open court, and on expositions of fact or of argument which the whole audience may understand. Everything, even talent and learning, is buried under perplexed incomprehensible written statements, through which the highest legal luminousness may often struggle in vain to shine with any splendour visible except to the few who know the case.

Moncreiff was appointed Dean in place of Cranstoun; and at his election made a characteristic address, warm in heart, and solid in honesty. Cranstoun's name had been placed after that of Hope,* the Solicitor-General, in the Commission for the visitation of the Universities of Scotland issued in 1826. This induced Cranstoun to put a protest on the proceedings of the Commission, claiming precedence for the Dean of Faculty over the Solicitor-

vided only their materials were replaced in London. Oxford would be Oxford, though in Manchester, if its stones were preserved. These people would remove Pompeii for a railway, and tell us they had applied it to a better purpose in Dundee.—H. C.

* John Hope.

General. As soon as Moncreiff's address was done, therefore, the Solicitor, to make all sure, rose and stated that though, *from courtesy*, he intended to yield the professional precedency to the present, as he had done to the last, Dean, he still claimed it as the *right* of his office, and meant to put his claim by protest on the Faculty records. This was irresistible to the combativeness of Moncreiff; who sprung on the point like a tiger, and said firmly—"And gentlemen, I shall *certainly* answer that protest. For I do solemnly aver and assert that your Dean *has* precedence over his Majesty's Solicitor-General." It was all a very gratifying scene; marked by much kindness and liberality on all sides. Everybody felt the justice of Moncreiff's triumph; a man who had fought his way, every inch, purely by his own exertions. I thought of the feelings of Sir Harry.

It was in April 1827 that the hearts of those who had long been labouring for the liberation of Scotland and had watched and directed the course of improved public opinion, and had been sometimes encouraged by its progress to hope that their country might see better days, were at last cheered by the advance of the liberal party, under the administration of Canning. The retirement of Lord Melville from the government of Scotland was not an event for which, *in itself*, any candid Scotch Whig could rejoice; because no man, individually, could have conducted the affairs of the country with greater good sense and fairness, or with less of party prejudice or bitterness. But, his ceasing

to be in power was the mark of a change absolutely
necessary for the elevation of this part of the kingdom; and accordingly it was viewed first with stupid
dismay, and then with abuse of his want of skill, by
those to whom the idea of this elevation was unbearable. Abercromby opened his mind fully to Canning
on the state of Scotland; particularly on the necessity
of letting it be governed by the ministry, or by some
known and responsible part of it, specially assigned
to the duty by constitutional office, instead of hand-
ing us over as a province to some proconsul, and
taking no more thought of us. Previous to this
communication, Canning had, in his ignorance, proceeded on the notion that this was the established
system for the government of Scotland, and had
consented " to let Lord Binning *have* Scotland."
But the remonstrances of Abercromby, Kennedy,
and other Scotch members, put an end to this, and
the reign of the new vicegerent, which began upon
Saturday, ended by a formal abdication on the following Tuesday.

But Canning's death, which took place in the
autumn of 1827, greatly alarmed us; the more so,
from the undisguised expectation of those whom
aversion to the liberality of his principles had half
excluded from power, that they would be restored
again to their ordinary omnipotence. But after a few
weeks of fearful doubt, they were disappointed; and,
in so far as regarded Scotland, matters were rather
worse for them than before; because Lord Lansdowne,
a steady Whig, and in the confidence of the leaders

2 D

of that party in Scotland, became Home Secretary, with Abercromby and Kennedy as his chief Scotch advisers. The extent to which, so long as there was any doubt which party was to prevail, both seemed inclined to coalesce, afforded an example of the meaning of the policy, by which kings are said sometimes to play one faction off against another, by giving none any ground for despair. The Whigs, thankful for every approach towards a better system, and wisely considering that each step facilitated the next one, gave their aid, honestly, to the improved Government. The Tories, thankful for not being altogether excluded, but alarmed at every infusion of Whiggism, concurred, though with a deep inward grudge, in that apparent approbation which could not safely be withheld. And so for a season both were amiable and reasonable; but always with the material difference that the one was gay and hopeful, the other gloomy and desponding. The result over the community, on the whole, was a very great rise of confidence in the ultimate, and not very distant, triumph of the principles, which it had for so long been nearly the sole object of the Tory party to resist; and a consequent increase of the boldness and openness with which those principles were pushed, not merely by their known and established friends, but by many who had never come forward on such matters.

There could scarcely have been a better example of this than in a little bit of rebellion which broke out even in the peaceful and loyal Society of Writers to his Majesty's Signet. Mr Colin Mackenzie, the Deputy Keeper, having resigned, William Dundas, the Principal Keeper, wished to appoint a son of the Lord President. It is said that the President objected to this on the ground of his son's youth; he being, if major, not much more, and not yet a member of the Society. It was then resolved to associate him with my schoolfellow Richard Mackenzie of Dolphinton, a sensible and honourable man; and a commission was issued in favour of them both. The Writers took this to be a mere veil, and not a thick one, for putting a boy over them, and got into a blaze, and expectorated in resolutions and protests; after which, obtaining no redress, they resolved (18th January 1828) not to allow the offensive deputies to preside at their meetings. This brought the matter into Court, where, I believe, it was afterwards found that the Keeper, and in his absence the Deputy Keeper, was *ex officio* chairman of all meetings of the Society. This outbreak was after only a few months of an improved government. A similar impatience of domination was evinced in every town-council, every corporation, every court of freeholders, and in general in all meetings over the country. The Faculty of Advocates would not have behaved with such vigour. But we have no pure corporation spirit; and the writers are full of it. Our merit is personal, and we care little for the body. Their professional glory arises from that of their order, and it is the idol. And I doubt if the Writers, indignant as they were, would have been seized with so unusual a fit of virtue, if they had suspected what happened within one single week; which was, that the political scene was suddenly changed, and the old hands restored to their old work. Huskisson and the other friends of Canning who, on his death, had joined the Whigs to exclude the Tories, found it convenient to prove false to their dead master, and now joined the Tories to exclude the Whigs. Lansdowne and his party withdrew from the Government. The restored seemed to be perfectly aware of the increased strength given to any party by its return to power after a short and abortive exclusion. Our fears were not much less than our hopes. Neither of us saw with sufficient certainty how strongly the course of public opinion was setting in towards reform.

When the repeal of the Test and Corporation Acts was under discussion this spring, we had an excellent public meeting [17th March 1828] in aid of the first great modern triumph. Sir John Dalrymple was in the chair; Sir James Moncreiff, Dean of Faculty, and the Rev. Dr M'Crie were the principal speakers. Moncreiff's speech was most excellent; nervous, well informed, and breathing in every word his deep and pious honesty. The Assembly Room was crowded by people of the middle ranks of all sects and parties —except one. I did not observe a single adherent of Government. Their absence said little for their discretion; the crowd little for the security of their power.

On the 11th of June 1828 Dugald Stewart died,

at the age of about seventy-five. He was the last of his illustrious class. Though enfeebled for some years, the decline of his life, down almost to the very last day, was personally comfortable, and in reference to his philosophy splendid. His intellect continued so entirely unbroken, that the period between his first attack of palsy in 1821, and his last on the day before his death, was employed in the revision and improvement of his works, which he could not touch without having the favourite occupations of his earlier days recalled to him in their original freshness. His two last volumes, of which he even corrected the press himself within a very few months of his death, are so tinged with his lectures, that I cannot read them without thinking I hear his pleasing voice. He was buried in the north-west angle of the Canongate churchyard. The magistrates and professors attended but there was no attempt to make it a public funeral. I could not resist going to the Calton Hill, and contemplating a ceremony which awakened so many associations. The very Canongate has a sort of sacredness in it. Independently of more distant historical recollections, such as its once containing the residences of many of the nobility of Scotland, by whose titles its principal places are still marked, and its being the avenue to our Palace, Parliament House, and Castle, what an interest is imparted to its old ridgy back and smoky chimneys by the still unchanged houses of Smith, Kames, Monboddo, and of him whose ashes were that day committed to its soil!

A meeting of his friends was held on the 9th of July, when it was resolved to erect a monument to his memory. The Lord Chief Commissioner (Adam), who was in the chair, stated that he himself was then the only person alive who had heard Stewart first read his essay " On Dreaming." This was at a literary society when the author was under twenty.* The prevailing, though not the unanimous, feeling was that the monument should be architectural, and placed on the Calton Hill; which was this very summer (1828) relieved of a horrid old rubble dike which used to surround the Observatory, and was adorned by a handsome wall, protecting, yet disclosing, the astronomical building and the monument of John Playfair. There has always been an opinion with some that nothing should have been built on the Calton Hill, and that it should have been left to what is called nature—that is, as a piece of waste ground for blackguards and washerwomen. Those who think so must, of course, have objected to the Temple of Minerva on the Acropolis of Athens. So as the prospects are preserved, it cannot be too much ornamented by handsome stairs, broad level walks, sculptured stone benches, and above all, monumental buildings. The silent beauty of architecture, if consecrated to great names, would make that eminence the noblest cemetery of immortals in Europe. But no edifice connected with common habitation ought to be permitted. The nearest tolerated approach to

* The essay " On Dreaming" was read before the Speculative Society in 1773.

the living ought to be the Observatory, holding communion with the heavens, and the Parthenon, used as a receptacle of art. And no building, not even a monument, ought to be tolerated, except at a price implying a high order of merit, and probably expressing the contributions of public gratitude. If anything under £2000 be admitted, we shall have the tombs of Provosts. The air of the place ought to be kept pure, and its associations inspiring.

In September 1828 Richardson and I visited Scott for a few days at Abbotsford, and had the rare good fortune to find him nearly alone; and nothing could be more delightful.* His simplicity and naturalness after all his fame are absolutely incredible. I remember him when he was famous for almost nothing except imitating Eskgrove (a power which fortunately he has never lost), and his manners are the same now that they were then. No bad idea will be formed of Scott's conversation by supposing one of his Scotch novels to be cut into talk. It is not so much conversation as a joyous flow of anecdote, story, character and scene, mostly humorous, always graphic, and never personal or ill-natured. His habits at this time were these. He rose about six; wrote from about half-past six till nine—the second series of the *Tales of a*

* "I do not know why it is that when I am with a party of my Opposition friends the day is often merrier than when with our own set. Is it because they are cleverer? Jeffrey and Harry Cockburn are, to be sure, very extraordinary men, yet it is not owing to that entirely. I believe both parties meet with a feeling of novelty."—Sir Walter Scott's *Journal*, December 9, 1826.

Grandfather being then the work; breakfasted and
lounged from nine to eleven; wrote from eleven till
about two; walked till about four; dined at five,
partaking freely, but far from immoderately, of
various wines; and then, as soon as the ladies withdrew, taking to cigars and hot whisky-toddy; went
to the drawing-room soon, where he inspired everybody with his passion for Scotch music, and, if
anxiously asked, never refused to recite any old
ballad or tell any old tale. The house was asleep by
eleven. When fitted up for dinner, he was like any
other comfortably ill-dressed gentleman. But in the
morning, with the large coarse jacket, great stick,
and leathern cap, he was Dandy Dinmont, or Dick
Hattrick—a smuggler or a poacher. Would that his
money and his care had been given to a better subject
than Abbotsford.

I was much amused by his account of an early
anticipation of Cranstoun's professional success.
Within a few weeks after he, Scott, and William
Erskine had put on the gown, being in Selkirkshire,
they were all invited to dinner by an old drunken
Selkirk writer, who had—what was worth three
young Advocates' attention—a great deal of bad
business. Cranstoun, who was never anything at a
debauch, was driven off the field, with a squeamish
stomach and a woeful countenance, shamefully early.
Erskine, always ambitious, adhered to the bowl
somewhat longer; but Scott who, as he told us, " was
at home with the hills and the whisky punch," not
only triumphed over these two, but very nearly over

the landlord. As they were mounting their horses to ride home, the entertainer let the other two go without speaking to them; but he embraced Scott, assuring him that he would rise high, " And I'll tell ye what, Maister Walter—that lad Cranstoun may get to the tap o' the bar if he can; but tak ma word for't—it's no be by drinking."

A deep sensation of horror was excited at the end of the year by the exposure of what are called " The West Port Murders." It was only for a single murder that Burke and Macdougal were tried; but it was nearly certain that, within a year or two, Burke and Hare had murdered about sixteen people, for the sale of their bodies to anatomists; and after his conviction Burke confessed this. Moncreiff and I were drawn into the case by the junior counsel. The evidence against Burke was far too clear to be shaken by even Moncreiff's energy and talent; but the woman, who had been assigned to my care, escaped, because there were some material doubts in her favour.* We carried two important points, after a battle with the Court, which would probably have been decided otherwise, if

---

* It is stated in vol. xliv., p. 101, of the *Quarterly Review*, that at the moment I was addressing the jury, I whispered " Infernal hag !"— "the gudgeons swallow it !" and I suppose that a credulous Quaker, whose work (on the principles of morality) was reviewed in that article, believes this, and, as I understand, comments upon it as a piece of professional fraud. It is utterly untrue. No one could be more honestly convinced of anything than I was, and am, that there was not sufficient legal evidence to warrant a conviction of Helen Macdougal. Therefore, no such expressions or sentiment *could be* uttered. At any rate none such, and none of that tendency, were uttered.—H. C.

the leaning of their lordships had been feebly resisted. These were—our right to have each murder tried separately, and to impeach the credit of the accomplices by questioning them about their accession to other murders or crimes. No case ever struck the public heart or imagination with greater horror. And no wonder. For the regular demand for anatomical subjects, and the high prices given, held out a constant premium to murder; and when it was shown to what danger this exposed the unprotected, everyone felt himself living in the midst of persons to whom murder was a trade. All our anatomists incurred a most unjust, and a very alarming, though not an unnatural odium; Dr Knox, in particular,* against whom not only the anger of the populace, but the condemnation of more intelligent persons, was specially directed. But tried in reference to the invariable, and the necessary practice of the profession, our anatomists

* With reference to Lord Cockburn's opinion, from the legal point of view, of Dr Knox's association with the West Port murders it is interesting to compare other two now available—Sir Robert Christison's from the medical, and Sir Walter Scott's from the general public standpoint.   Sir Robert—then Dr—Christison was appointed along with Mr Newbigging to conduct the medico-legal examination of the body found in the dissecting-room. He says : " My own opinion at the time was that Dr Knox, then the most popular lecturer on anatomy in Edinburgh . . . had rather wilfully shut his eyes to incidents which ought to have excited the grave suspicions of a man of his intelligence."— *Christison's Autobiography.* Sir Walter Scott writes : "Called on Mr Robison and instructed him to call a meeting of the Council of the Royal Society as Mr Knox proposes to read an essay on some dissections. A bold proposal, truly, from one who has had so lately the boldness of trading so deep in human flesh ! I shall oppose his reading in the present circumstances if I should stand alone."—*Journal,* January 14, 1829.

were spotlessly correct, and Knox the most correct of them all. Had it not been for the evidence exhibited in Burke's case of the necessity of providing a cheap, safe, and legal mode of supplying anatomical subjects, it is more than probable that the Anatomy Act would not have passed so soon, if ever.

Except that he murdered, Burke was a sensible, and what might be called a respectable, man; not at all ferocious in his general manner, sober, correct in all his other habits, and kind to his relations. Though not regularly married, Helen Macdougal was his wife; and when the jury came in with the verdict convicting him, but acquitting her, his remark was—" Well, thank God you're safe! "

In March 1829 we had a magnificent meeting in the Assembly Room to assist Wellington and Peel in their tardy and now awkward Emancipation necessity, by a petition in favour of the Catholics. A shilling a head was taken at the door, and about 1700 shillings were got. As from the confusion several passed untaxed, there must have been about 2000 present; and there were at the least double that number outside, who could not get in. It was a union of both the ordinary political parties. Sir William Arbuthnot, a strong Tory, and who had been Provost when George the Fourth was here, was in the chair. The speakers were Moncreiff, Dr Maclagan, Jeffrey, Murray, the Solicitor General (Hope), Chalmers, and myself. No meeting could be more successful; and the combination of persons in general so repugnant, gave it great weight

over the country. It must have suggested a striking
contrast to those who remembered that it was in this
very city that, only about forty years ago, the law
had not strength to save the houses and chapels of the
Catholics from popular conflagrations. There were, as
there still are, some who, if they could have done it,
would have thought the repetition of that violence a
duty; and there were many even at this meeting who
had no better reason for their support of emancipation than that it implied the support of ministry.
Those, whose religious horror of Catholicism made
them think the application of the principles of
civil toleration to that faith a sin, did not appear; but
procured signatures to an opposite petition by harangues and placards borrowed from Lord George
Gordon. The petitions exhibited a striking proof of
the strong Anti-Popish taste of the people of Scotland.
The one in favour of toleration, notwithstanding
every fair exertion, was only signed by about 8000
persons; while the one to the Commons against it was
signed by about 13,000, and the one to the Lords
(which lay a little longer for signature) by about
18,000.   The 8000 were a higher and more varied
class than ever concurred in any political measure in
Edinburgh.

Government had for some years been lopping our
two Scotch Revenue Boards of Customs and Excise,
and preparing for their final eradication; and all being
ready, in 1829 the last vestige of them was obliterated. This was the first of a series of reductions, some

of which more reasonable men than Malagrowther lament as hurtful and degrading to Scotland. No doubt, in point of respectability, we were much the better of all our ancient establishments—had there been any decent pretence of their still being of use. But simple uselessness was not their only defect. Very useful for corruption, they were systematically employed for that purpose. Considering how far beyond the successful applicant the influence of patronage reaches, the offices in these two Boards alone, skilfully distributed among our few freeholders, were sufficient to purchase a shamefully large extent of servility. Their being abolished notwithstanding this quality, was the strongest possible proof of their indefensibleness; and the preference of economy to such power of corruption was the true merit of Government.

The death of David Cathcart, Lord Alloway, in 1829, made two important changes in the local leaders of the Whig party, by the promotion of Moncreiff and Jeffrey.

Alloway was an excellent and most useful man; kind in private life, and honest in the discharge of his public duties. Without learning or talent, and awkward in expressing himself either orally or in writing, he was a good practical lawyer, and remarkably knowing in the management of the common business of life; and having more sense and modesty than to aim at objects he could not reach, experience and industry gave him no competitor within this not very high, but most useful, range. He was one of the many examples, indeed, of the moderate degree in which ability, learning, or accomplishments are necessary in the composition of a good practical puisne judge. Devotion to duty, zeal to be and to do right, blandness, industry and practical skill, made his want of the higher qualities of talent and general knowledge perfectly immaterial, and indeed scarcely observed. He was deeply involved in all the affairs of the Whig party during his whole life, till he became a judge; after this, his sole object was to justify his appointment.

Moncreiff succeeded Alloway, and Jeffrey became Dean of Faculty instead of Moncreiff. This was not the first time that Peel had raised one of his opponents to the bench. No doubt Cranstoun, Fullerton, and Moncreiff could not have been passed over without flagrant injustice, and an obvious sacrifice of the public interest. But these considerations are not always conclusive on such occasions; and at any rate it is the highest praise of a minister that he prefers justice and the public to his party. There is no other person whose government of Scotland can be expounded by so honourable a fact as these four promotions. The advancement of Moncreiff and Jeffrey— the Preses of the Pantheon meeting, and the Editor of the *Edinburgh Review*—made those whose memories went back a few years feel as if they had got into a new world. Jeffrey expressed a wish that I should second his nomination as Dean; which I did. What a crowd of recollections and feelings did that scene awaken. In deference to others who might think that

the Dean of Faculty should not conduct a party publication, he gracefully gave up the editorship of the
Review, the ninety-eighth number of which was his
last.*

The Arts suffered their severest loss, in the summer
of 1829, in the death of my friend Hugh Williams; by
far the most beautiful painter in water colours that
Scotland has yet produced. But, warm-hearted and
honourable, of singular modesty, and almost feminine
gentleness, our affection for the man exceeded even
our admiration of the artist. The heroic and gentle
cheerfulness with which he endured several months of
pain and weakness, under a certainly fatal disease, was
a striking example of the power of a brave and gay
spirit over the greatest bodily suffering. Speaking to
me, within three days of his death, of the coming
event, he lamented his separation from his living
friends, but said it would be temporary, " and in the
mean while, I shall see Gordon." Delighted with the
splendid prospects of art which he thought he saw
opening to Scotland, he urged me, nearly to the very
last, never to relax till I had completed the reformation of the Academy, which was then in progress; and
which was effected shortly after his death.

The formation of the " Scottish Academy of Painting, Sculpture, and Architecture," lately completed,
was one of the most important occurrences in the
progress of Scotland. There is an advanced state of art
at which probably all artificial associations of artists

* *See* Cockburn s *Life of Jeffrey.*

are useless, if not hurtful. But in an infant stage, during which the public taste requires to be excited and educated, and artists need importance and protection by formal brotherhood, such unions are nearly indispensable. The only thing of the kind that existed in this country was the " Institution for the encouragement of the fine Arts," which had done little good. It excluded all artists from its management, without substituting more reasonable men in their room; and this produced jealousies and dissensions; which induced the artists to swarm off, and begin the Academy.

When it was first formed it consisted merely of the artists who were particularly displeased with the Institution for the Promotion of the Fine Arts; the majority, and the best, of their brethren still adhering to that body. After about two years' more experience of the system of management in the Institution, it was found by the adherents that there could be no cordial union between them and it, and not even a comfortable endurance of each other. Each, as usual, blamed the other; and I, who know the whole facts, think that though there was unreasonableness on both sides the artists had the least of it. It was plain, however, that they must part; but the original members of the Academy objected to be swamped by a gush of so many acceders all at once. This for a while threatened to be insuperable; till the one party referred it all to the Solicitor-General (Hope), and the other party to me; and we married them in a week. This left the Institution without an artist, and united

all the considerable ones, to the number of forty-two,
in the Scottish Academy,* which, if not distracted by
the jealousies of the profession itself, may render
Scotland as illustrious in art as in other walks of
genius.

Amidst many of the improvements under which
Edinburgh was still growing in beauty, there was a
scheme by my country neighbour Alexander Trotter of
Dreghorn, to which there was only one objection—that
it was too magnificent for execution. Its object was to
join the New Town to the Old, worthily. And this was
to be done by sinking the upper end of the Mound
to the level of Princes Street; and, avoiding Bank
Street, to carry that end of the Mound eastward along
the north of the Bank of Scotland, and then south to
the High Street, by an opening right upon St Giles
Cathedral. He illustrated the general effect, and all
the details, in captivating views, and working plans;
and combined, as it was to be, with much subordinate
decoration, it would have been a very handsome
terrace.   But we have no Pericles.   The next best
project—the object being to get from the one town to

* The new building at the north end of the Mound was opened in
1826, under the title of "The Royal Institution." The building,
though pleasing, is not what it ought to have been. It should have
been set on a higher table.   But this was not allowed ; and thus controlled, the architect, William Playfair, did all that taste and the funds
admitted of.   Strictly, it ought to have been named after the old
historical *Board of Trustees* for the improvement of manufactures ;
because it was by their money, and for their accommodation chiefly
that it was made ; and " *The Trustees' Hall* " had been the title, ever
since the Union, of the place in the old town where they had met.—H. C.
2 E

the other without rising to the summit of the High Street or Lawnmarket—was Sir Thomas Lauder's. He proposed to bring down the south end of the Mound to the level of Princes Street, and then to cut a Roman arch through the Lawnmarket, and under the houses, and so to pass on a level to George Square. This was both practical and easy; but it was not expounded till too late.

In January 1830 Sir Samuel Shepherd resigned his Chief Baronship; and James Abercromby, to his amazement, was sent for by the Duke of Wellington, and offered the place; which, after great hesitation, he accepted. Nobody could dream of making judicial work out of our Exchequer sufficient to give occupation even to a single judge; and therefore all the good that Abercromby's friends look for is the pleasure of his society. Publicly he is thrown away here. Soon after this the Lord Advocate explained to Parliament the measures which Government had extracted out of the report of the last Committee on the Scotch Courts. They all resolved into economy; and their result was to be a saving of about £23,000 yearly by the abolition of nineteen offices, including the Lord Chief Commissioner and the two jury judges—that Court ceasing; two judges of the Court of Session; two Barons; the Judge Admiral; the four Consistorial judges; the Justice-General (at least his salary); and two Clerks of Session. Vigorous pruning; resorted to by Government from mere economy; and submitted to by our judges, undoubtedly, in order to strengthen the claim for a rise of salary. But it was all right in itself; though if it had been suggested by any one a few years ago, he would have been treated as a lunatic or a rebel.*

George the Fourth died in summer. The first important public occurrence in Edinburgh under his successor was a meeting (20th August 1830) of congratulation to the French on their revolution of " The Three Days," which drove Charles the Tenth from his throne, and confirmed the principles of their constitutional charter. Whatever was afterwards thought of this successful outbreak, no similar event was ever so generally hailed in this country. Many even of the most sensitive Tories found it impossible to withhold their cheer from an act of popular resistance that was just, gallant, as bloodless as was possible, and completely effective. Their fright at the former revolution revived, and they were grateful to the Parisians for not repeating its horrors. The requisition for our meeting contained about a hundred names, of which about twenty were those of persons to whom not merely revolutions, but popular assemblies, were abhorrent. Even Sir Walter Scott said to John Richardson,

---

* I took this occasion to write another legal review (*Edinburgh Review*, art. 5, No. 101—April 1830). I wished I could have given some instances of English ignorance of Scotch law, and contempt of it, in that part of the article which relates to our appeals to the House of Lords. For example, when Tindal, afterwards head of the Common Pleas, was here on the Law Commission of 1823, he asked—gravely, and solely for information, whether Mr Andrew Skene, advocate, to whom he had just been introduced, was the author of the work " *De Verborum Significatione*."—H. C.

" Confound these French Ministers! I can't forgive them for making a Jacobin of an old Tory like me." And the Lord Provost was so far seduced from the usual habit of his place and his party as to preside, though it was known that Joseph Hume was to be present. Similar assemblages took place over all the country—assemblages, in Scotland, where a revolution, which had just dethroned a monarch, was applauded openly, and with no opposition or disapprobation! Who could fail to see the indication of our own state which this fact implied!

On the 8th of October there was another public meeting about slaves. The Lord Provost was again in the chair. Jeffrey made a speech and moved certain resolutions. The Rev. Dr Andrew Thomson, very imprudently, opposed them, because they pointed at gradual, and not at immediate, emancipation. This produced an unexpected and awkward discussion, in the course of which a decent looking man, who agreed with Thomson, said " Fiat justitia, ruat cœlum."* On this the chairman, anxious perhaps to repair the error of presiding at the " Three Days " meeting, started up and declared—" as Provost of this city I cannot sit and hear such sentiments." He then walked off; and nobody having sense to take the chair, the meeting broke up in disorder; being the first accident of the kind in Edinburgh. On the 19th Thomson and his

* Dr Thomson is reported to have concluded his argument with these words, and it was his using them which gave offence to Lord Provost Allan.

friends met again, and after a powerful speech from him, carried everything their own way. And after all, the whole difference was verbal; for *immediate*, as explained, meant only *with all practicable speed*, which was exactly what the cautious meant by gradual.

I this autumn wrote an article on the Parliamentary Representation of Scotland (*Edinburgh Review*, No. 103, art. 10). This was preparatory to a renewal of the subject in Parliament. I certainly did not imagine that we were within a few weeks of a great change. But innumerable and conclusive circumstances showed that the public mind was advancing rapidly towards some important result. It was the certainty that, in reference to the state of public feeling, the discussion was well timed that induced me to revive it.

And now the year 1830 is just closing in the midst of events which will perhaps affect all the future course of my life, and will certainly be deeply marked in the page of history. In the beginning of December the Whigs came into power, avowedly on the great principle, and for the great object, of Parliamentary Reform. Their return has as yet been hailed with very general joy. The Tories seem struck by a thunderbolt. They can ascribe what is going on to no political trick, court intrigue, or temporary accident; but reflect with alarm, that this is the third time within these two years that Whiggism has been recognised in the Cabinet; and that its triumph now is the natural result of deep-seated causes.

I close this page by saying that Jeffrey has been made Lord Advocate, and I Solicitor-General, under the ministry of Earl Grey. We have come upon the public stage in a splendid, but perilous scene. I trust that we shall do our duty. If we do, we cannot fail to do some good to Scotland. In the abuses of our representative and municipal systems alone, our predecessors have left us fields in which patriotism may exhaust itself.

Index

Impressment in Edinburgh, 89
Inglis, Rev. Dr., 190, 218
Institution, Royal, for promotion of
Fine Arts, 337

Jacobinism in Scotland, 75
Jeffrey, Lord, xviii, xix, xx–xxi, 9,
69, 86, 158, 282, 351, 430, 438.
See also *Life of Lord Jeffrey*.
Johnston, Sophia, 54
Joint-Stock mania of 1825, 403
Journal, xii, xviii–xix, xx
Judges taking wine on the bench,
326
Jury Court opened, 283
Jury trial in Scotland, 283

Kennedy, Thomas F. (of Dunure),
xxn, 38n, 361
Kinedder, Lord, 214
King's Birthday, 62, 63n
Krames, The, 100

Ladies, old Scottish, 52
Laing, James (clerk of the Town
Council), 89
Laing, Malcolm (historian), 253,
330
Laing, William (bookseller), 162
Lancastrian School, 261, 262
Lauder, Sir Thomas, 60
Lauderdale, Earl of, 199, 359
Law, English and Scottish, 385n
Leith, and Edinburgh Town Coun-
cil, 400
Leslie, Professor Sir John, 186
Leyden, John, 172
Life of Lord Jeffrey, xx
Literary position of Edinburgh in
early nineteenth century, 161
Lord Advocate: and Scottish press,
374; office of, xiii, 386
Lords Spiritual, Presbyterian objec-
tions to designation, 272

Loyalty exhibited in dress, 62
Lyceum, 231

MacCulloch, John Ramsay, 297
Macfarlan, John (advocate), 246
Mackenzie, Henry, 256, 328, 336,
389
M'Kinlay, Andrew, trial of, 315
Mackintosh, Sir James, xv, 348,
377
Macknight, Rev. Dr., 48, 187
Maclaren, Charles, 297
Maclaren tried for sedition, 310
Maconochie, Allan. *See* Meadow-
bank, Lord
Maconochie, Alexander, 214
Macrae, Lieutenant, 8
Magazines: *Blackwood's*, 300 *Edin-
burgh*, 168; *Scots*, 72, 300
Markets in Edinburgh, 405
Meadowbank, Lord, 129, 287
Meadows, the Edinburgh, 2, 11
Medwyn, Lord, 261
Melville, first Viscount, xiii, 1, 79,
201, 242
Melville, second Viscount, 215,
362, 367
Mercantile classes of Edinburgh in
early nineteenth century, 164
Merchant Company of Edinburgh,
332
Middleton Inn, scene at, 13
Midlothian Volunteers, The, 180
Midlothian Yeomanry Cavalry, 181,
343
Miller, Hugh, 339n
"Modern Athens," first applied to
Edinburgh, 277
Monboddo, Lord, 38, 102
Moncreiff, Rev. Sir Harry, 38, 188,
190, 219, 241, 262, 271, 345,
389
Moncreiff, Sir James, Lord Mon-
creiff, 69, 249, 353, 415, 430
Montgomery, Sir James, 176
Montrose, magistracy revived by